For Tony

Just do it

Love

GO!

Work, Travel & People
in the Third World

by
Janice R. Stevens M.D.

Bloomington, IN Milton Keynes, UK

authorHOUSE

AuthorHouse™
1663 Liberty Drive, Suite 200
Bloomington, IN 47403
www.authorhouse.com
Phone: 1-800-839-8640

AuthorHouse™ UK Ltd.
500 Avebury Boulevard
Central Milton Keynes, MK9 2BE
www.authorhouse.co.uk
Phone: 08001974150

This book is a work of non-fiction. Unless otherwise noted, the author and the publisher make no explicit guarantees as to the accuracy of the information contained in this book and in some cases, names of people and places have been altered to protect their privacy.

First published by AuthorHouse 2/14/2006

ISBN: 1-4208-7137-4 (e)
ISBN: 1-4208-7136-6 (sc)

Library of Congress Control Number: 2005906650

Printed in the United States of America
Bloomington, Indiana

This book is printed on acid-free paper.

Janice Robinson Stevens, MD
Emeritus Professor of Neurology and Psychiatry
Oregon Health & Sciences University
Portland, Oregon 97239 USA

Mailing Address: PO Box 422, Wilsonville , OR 97070

Map Drawings by Kaj Wyn Berry

FORWARD:

Whatever you do, you must do it as if it was a matter of life and death ...knowing that it is only a play in which you appear briefly.

-Nitya Chaitanya Yati

INTRODUCTION

Dr. Janice Stevens is an eminent neuroscientist who, addition to her groundbreaking research, has volunteered part of her time each year in Third World nations. "Go" is a fascinating account of her observations,and vividly illustrates the common roots of humanity. Dr. Stevens is especially perceptive regarding the difficult role of women, and this book will be of special interest to those with a similar interest. But "Go" is an imperative to all of us who hope to better understand our own role, and the role of America in the wider world. If you cannot experience it first-hand, you cannot do better than experiencing it through Dr. Stevens' eyes.

Dr. E.Fuller Torrey
Stanley Foundation

Dedicated to the women of the third world:
the bravest I have ever known.

PREFACE

When I was l6, our high school civics class visited the state mental hospital. It was a snakepit of a place where women with wild unkempt hair and mad faces crawled up and down the barred cages or smeared excrement on the walls and floor. Men, in another part of the building sat in rows on long benches, mute, grim and blank faced.

"This is schizophrenia," said our hefty nurse guide, who wore a heavy bunch of keys tied to her waist.

"What causes this?"

"No one knows."

That was a turning point for me.

I completed medical school, years of postgraduate training, practice and teaching in neurology and psychiatry, and published more than 150 articles on epilepsy or schizophrenia in scientific journals and books. However, nothing in undergraduate schools, medical school or my subsequent years as a professor of neurology and of psychiatry helped me do much about the most serious problems in our society, inequality and poverty.

I have spent weeks or months every year for more than 30 years in poor countries in Africa and Asia, where I started family planning programs for poor women and free schools without uniforms for children in India and Africa for children too poor to pay the school fees or buy the uniforms required by government schools. Many others have done the same. But our efforts are only a drop in a very large, very empty bucket. In India, where government schools are supposedly free, teachers were too few or often absent. Families able to do so paid extra sums so their children could receive outside of class tuition. In 2003, Nigeria abolished fees and uniforms in government schools, leading to overcrowded classes of several hundred students. Predictably, although rich in petroleum and fertile land, the government allegedly had no money to hire new teachers even though thousands of trained teachers were waiting for jobs.

This is the world we can change together.

AUTHOR'S NOTE

Studies of brain function by many neuroscientists, including myself, demonstrate the aggressive, self-aggrandizing, self-preserving dominance of certain parts of our brains called the limbic system. By education and experience limbic brain areas can be brought under control of the cerebral cortex, a brain area that can curb avarice. I hope these true stories may interest and even inspire others to undertake similar journeys and make them count for others as well as themselves.

Janice Robinson Stevens
Aurora, Oregon, USA
January 2005

Note: Author's revenue from this book will be given to Zambia Open Community Schools

CONTENTS

FORWARD: v

INTRODUCTION   vi

PREFACE   ix

AUTHOR'S NOTE   xi

Chapter I
McLEOD GANJ: HOME OF THE DALAI LAMA   1

*Home of the Dalai Lama and a center for study of Tibetan
religion and medicine. Why some of the people I met there
were there.*

Chapter II
WOMENS LIB   23

*Life, especially of women, in Buddhist monasteries in the far
north of India.*

Chapter III
MALANA: WHERE I WAS AN UNTOUCHABLE   47

A remote village in India.

Chapter IV
AN ASHRAM IN KULU   83

*An ashram in the Himalayan foothills is led by a wise guru
who attracts many acolytes from North America and why they
are there.*

Chapter V
MUSTANG! UP THE KALI GANDAKI VALLEY TOWARD TIBET   111

*How the Buddhist monks dealt with locusts in the wheat
fields in a remote area of Nepal.*

Chapter VI
"OM," A DISCIPLE OF SAI BABA   131

*First word of the Buddhist prayer, Om Mani Padme Hum (Indeed
the soul is in the heart of the lotus) and the name taken by an
American woman who became a Sannyasi (enlightened one)
in Sai Baba's famed ashram in South India. There I met many
westerners seeking happiness and enlightenment through the
guru.*

Chapter VII
MAN'S FATE MAN'S HOPE   151
Shanghai and Beijing 1980. Lives of some of the unforgettable
ordinary people I met there.

Chapter VIII
PARADISE FOUND   185
True stories from the islands of the south Caribbean, where I
worked as a psychiatrist for 6 months.

Chapter IX
PARADISE LOST   193
Paradise for tourists can be hell for the native population in
the idyllic islands of the south Caribbean Sea.

Chapter X
UHURU! (FREEDOM!)   205
Means freedom in Swahili, but not for women in East Africa.

Chapter XI
EIGHT WOMEN OF AFRICA   217
East African women must work to support themselves and
their children, while their husbands are free to wander.

Chapter XII
LIFE AND DEATH IN THE COUNTRY LIFE AND DEATH IN TOWN   241
Lives of women and the AIDS scourge in contemporary
Zambia.

Chapter XIII
PEACE CORPS   257
An idealistic young American is disillusioned after serving a
year in a village in West Africa.

Schools started for poor children in India

Immunization day in Ammenpettai S. India

Hay to market in Thanjur S. India

Zambia Open Community Schools

Chawcwa boys
& Sr. Agnes (supervisor)
a teacher at school (ZOCS)

This school has now been replaced by generous donations to ZOCS

1999

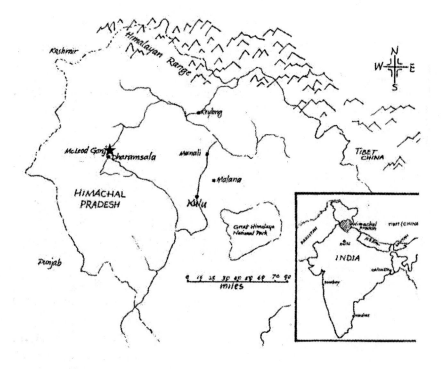

Chapter 1

McLEOD GANJ: HOME OF
THE DALAI LAMA

Om Mani Padme Hum: Indeed the jewel is in the heart of the lotus.

(The most sacred prayer in Buddhism)

"When mind enjoys pleasure and satisfaction, mere material hardships are easy to bear."

"It was I who had to find the answer and make the decision. But with my inexperience in the affairs of the world, it was not easy. I have no fear of death. I was not afraid of being one of the victims of the Chinese attack. I honestly believe that my strict religious training has given me enough strength to face the prospect of leaving my present body without apprehension."

Dalai Lama 1959

In April 1978, I traveled eight hours by bus from New Delhi, capital of India, 300 kilometers to Dharmsala in north India. Then another hour by an older bus up a winding climbing road to McLeod Ganj, home of the Dalai Lama since the Chinese Army invaded Tibet in 1959. The Dalai Lama, 14th incarnation of Chenrisi, the Buddha of Mercy, was only 24 years old in 1959 when the army of the Peoples Republic of China invaded his country. Faced with surrender or flight, this inexperienced young leader took the agonizing decision to leave his homeland to escape across the deep snows of the Himalayas to India. I had come to visit the home in exile of this remarkable man and to learn about his mission and his religion. Even more, as a physician, I wanted to learn something about the practice of Tibetan medicine, an ancient profession totally different from western practice.

McLeod Ganj is, or was then, a small village set against a background of high snow covered peaks of the Himalayas.

After renting a room in a local hostelry, I set out to explore the town. In the market, small shops sold old jewelry, new and second-hand clothing and newly manufactured tourist trappings - shirts, rugs, prayer wheels and striped woolen shoulder bags. The agreeable jolly Tibetans seemed to be born traders. They carried on a brisk business selling their wares to visiting Indian tourists, local people and to the few touring Westerners, whose pale color and huge well-filled backpacks distinguished them everywhere in Asia. Further down the street, more practical fare was for sale - chilis, carrots, mounds of grains and spices, plastic shoes and cheap, ready-made western-style trousers and shirts, both new and second-hand. The streets were rutted and unpaved, but swept clean morning and evening by the energetic Tibetan women.

Unlike their secluded sisters in Muslim Pakistan or the only slightly less cloistered Hindu women in rural India, Tibetan women were vigorously selling and bartering. Busy in the shops and streets, they were part in every facet of village industry and commerce. Slim, strong, ruddy cheeked and self-assured, their proud carriage and clear steady gaze immediately distinguished them from the shy, sari-clad, head-scarfed Indian ladies who were visiting the town.

Tibetan women did not cover their shining black hair with either veil or head scarf. They wore black, ankle-length, sleeveless, jumper-like long gowns (*chubas*) over brightly colored blouses. A length of wool with narrow yellow, green, and red stripes was wrapped around the waist so that the corner hung to a point at knee level back and front.

Coming to this place after weeks in Afghanistan and Pakistan was a delightful surprise. In those Islamic lands, women were literally absent from the streets in all but large cities. Even in the cities, most looked like ghosts in their black or white all-enveloping gowns (*burqua, chaddar*).

In contrast to small town and rural India, where women wore the graceful sari or chemise *shalwar* (long blouse and wide trousers) and men wore *dhotis* (a sort of a wraparound sheet over the lower half of the body), Tibetan men wore cotton shirts and slacks of western cut. Their sleek black hair was fashionably long. Often quite handsome, they resembled American Indians except for their flat noses and eyes narrowed by an overhanging upper eyelid (epicanthal fold). Old women, leather-brown faces patterned with wrinkles, were generally dressed in black but glowing turquoise stones hung from their ears by bits of soiled string. Heavy strands of smooth red coralline, roughly cut turquoise or striped stones called "tiger's eyes" circled their necks. Some old men or women wore peaked triangular felt caps I remembered having seen in old *National Geographic* photos of Tibet when I was in primary school.

Early in the morning and again at sunset, the townsfolk walked along the wooded path toward the temple, fingering prayer beads, murmuring mantras, or twirling the wooden handles of small metal prayer wheels that enclosed sacred mantras printed on parchment paper.

The trail between the village and the temple was a natural cloister. On the right the forest dropped off steeply to the valley below. To the left the green hillside rose to a crown of great snow-capped peaks that touched the clear blue sky. In the nearby pine forest, Tibetan men and boys were busy clearing brush and trees to make way for new houses.

Back in the town there was a constant sense of bustling activity. In every doorway of the close adjoining houses, women of all ages stood knitting and talking. On one stoop, two young women were drying and combing their long black hair. On another, women nursed babies or swept the area with brooms made of coarse sticks. Children were everywhere; so were dogs -- mostly feisty little snub-nosed Lhasa Apsos. Cows, goats, and sheep meandered by, nosing piles of litter.

Maroon-robed lamas and nuns, their close-shaved heads bare, strolled past, talking and laughing. A dozen monks, orange robes flashing in the sunlight, shouted with fun at their mass badminton game behind the Buddhist School of Dialectics. Other monks sat drinking tea in the local cafes or shopped in pairs at stalls of vegetables or sweets. In front of the *gompa*, orange-clad old lamas with faces of mellow gold walked together in the garden between the temple and the green-roofed dwelling of His Holiness, the Dalai Lama.

In addition to the large school and library established by the Dalai Lama and his followers, several well-known practitioners of Tibetan medicine lived and worked there.

After exploring the town, I visited the local government health clinic where I met Dr. Nowergee, the government physician for the village. We quickly became great friends. At dinner in one of the small Tibetan cafes that evening, I asked him about Tibetan medicine. "Does it rely only on meditation and herbs?"

Dr. Nowergee smiled. There are two very respected doctors of Tibetan medicine here in McLeod Ganj," he replied. "Dr. Dolmo is a special friend of mine. Why don't you meet her tomorrow and judge for yourself?"

I agreed with pleasure.

By ten next morning, Dr. Nowergee was through with the few patients who came to the government clinic. But the two Tibetan doctors in town were seeing more than a hundred patients a day, often at considerable personal cost to the patients in time, travel and rupees.

Dr. Dolmo's waiting room had been full since early morning. This was surprising, since the now empty, generally poorly attended government clinic was free and the Tibetan doctors charged handsomely for the herbs and powders unfailingly prescribed for every patient and disorder.

After a brief walk from the government clinic, we climbed down steep stairs and entered a wooden building that housed Dr. Dolmo's clinic. In the large entry area, the walls were lined with several hundred small hand-labeled wooden drawers containing herbs and other components of the Tibetan pharmacopoeia. Although it was nearly noon, half a dozen patients were still seated on wooden benches waiting to consult Dr. Dolmo. Seeing no one to announce us, we entered the spacious consulting room.

Dr. Dolmo, a Tibetan woman of 40 or so, dressed in the traditional Tibetan long, black cotton jumper-like *chuba* over a vivid orange cotton shirt, welcomed us. Her flat round face had an unusually sweet and intelligent expression as she sat with her legs folded beneath her on a mat by the window. Although she had never seen me before, she knew Dr. Nowergee, the town's only government doctor. Smiling warmly, she folded her hands together in *namaste* (the traditional greeting of India-- Tibetans stick out their tongues). Then she held out her right hand in Western fashion to shake mine. After introducing me, Dr. Nowergee asked if we might observe her at work. Dr. Dolmo seemed pleased. She motioned for us to sit on the mats near her. We sat down by the cluttered table that served as her desk.

On the other side of the table was her patient, a young Caucasian woman with long blond hair, dressed in a filmy cotton shirt. Her companion, a bearded westerner of about twenty, waited anxiously on the bench next to her.

Behind them, a middle-aged, western-looking woman wrapped in a dark woolen shawl and a thin, pale thirtyish man wearing a lama's maroon robe sat on mats on the floor. The woman was Dr. Lubinka, a Russian oncologist and member of the prestigious Academy of Sciences of the Byelo-Russian Republic. This lady was sent by her institute in the (then) Soviet Union to study Tibetan medicine for a year with Dr. Dolmo. The young man in the lama robe was Dr. Pinay, a physician from France who came to McLeod Ganj two years earlier, also to study Tibetan medicine. Over his long robe, his curly, flaxen hair flowed to his shoulders from a receding hairline above a pink, acne-scarred face. Both doctors greeted us cordially.

Dr. Dolmo called for an assistant to bring tea. Then she turned back to her western patients and continued the consultation.

"Tibetan birth control pills have special properties and special requirements," she explained in Hindi. Dr. Pinay translated into French, which the patients appeared to only partly understand. "You take them for only ten days and then you will not conceive for a year. But this will only happen if you follow the special instructions carefully. During those ten days you must not only refrain from all sexual contact, but even from *thinking* about sex."

The boyfriend, a pleasant-looking young man, looked concerned. "And after that?" he inquired in strongly accented British English.

"Zen you can carry on as usual," smiled Dr. Pinay in heavily French accented English. Everyone looked relieved.

"I have a problem too," said the young man. He rolled up the sleeves of his long white Indian shirt to display his arms. White lumps the size of large grapes stood out over the course of the median nerve on both forearms. Dr. Dolmo now reached for his wrist. Palpating the pulse thoughtfully for several minutes, first on the right and then on the left, she finally turned to us and said,

"This is *sandoot*."

Dr. Lubinka wrote busily in her large notebook. Dr. Pinay looked worried. Dr. Nowergee lit a cigarette and looked over his shoulder, hoping for tea.

I asked, "What is the cause of *sandoot*?"

"It is a question of energy in the blood channels," explained Dr. Dolmo in liltingly accented English. "When the energy is blocked in certain places, these lumps appear." She scribbled a few Tibetan characters on a scrap of paper and handed it to the young man.

"No medicine will make these go away permanently," she explained. But this will prevent new ones." She pointed to her assistant who rose to fill the prescription.

Both patients seemed satisfied and rose to leave. I was sure the young man would get another opinion when he got back to England, but I was worried about the girl putting much faith in these birth control pills. Turning to Dr. Pinay, I asked him if they really worked for a year.

"*Certainment*," he replied. "*Si on suive les instructions particulier.* And," he added in Gallic accented English, "uff course, eet weel not work so well if zee girl has taken Western birth control peels een zee past!"

Next, an old Tibetan man, bent and wearing worn sandals on tough brown feet, walked in, bent and bowing repeatedly. I noticed with admiration how Dr. Dolmo's splendid eyes, full of concern and interest, now gave all their attention to him. She gazed sympathetically into his face and lifted his wrist to palpate his pulse. Continuing to look at him searchingly for a long minute, she then moved her fingers gently over his wrist. She did not consult a watch – indeed, she hadn't one. She noted down some particulars in Tibetan script on a little sheet of paper. Then she lifted his other hand and again her fingers searched, palpated, and finally rested gently and thoughtfully over his pulse. She sat silently for another full minute or two, apparently intent upon what she was sensing through her fingers.

While this rather unusual consultation was in progress I looked around the room. A picture of the Buddha, his right hand touching the ground in the position of Enlightenment and a faded photograph of the bespectacled Dalai Lama hung on the far wall. A Tibetan calendar, bright with monsters and multi-figured wheels of life, was pasted high on the wall behind Dr. Dolmo.

Sitting near the only window in the rather dark room, Dr. Dolmo was clearly at ease and in command of what she was doing. Dr. Pinay, the French doctor, an ardent student of Tibetan medicine, watched attentively. Later, he told me that he hoped to translate Tibetan medical teachings for the enlightenment of Western medical practitioners. In melodious cadences of Parisian French, somehow incongruous in this simple room, Dr. Pinay told us about the patient who was being examined.

Luckily, I had studied French during high school, college, and my graduate psychiatry training in Geneva. I could understand reasonably well and translate into English for Dr. Nowergee and the Russian lady. "This case is one of liver disease," I translated. "Here it is considered a disorder of 'wind,' which means of the flow of energy in the body." I raised my eyebrows in surprise,

But Dr. Pinay was quite serious. Dr. Lubinka leaned forward eagerly to listen, and wrote something rapidly in Russian in her large, cloth-bound notebook. Dr. Dolmo completed her instructions to the patient in Tibetan, explaining the case to Dr. Nowergee in Hindi. Dr. Nowergee translated Hindi into English for Dr. Lubinka and me. I relayed the essentials on to Dr. Pinay in my savage French.

Then Dr. Dolmo spoke in heavily accented English. "The *vayu* (wind, energy) moves in the body like the *vayu* of the universe moves the clouds in the sky."

"Zees ees ze same energy zat keeps planets in ze sky," explained the monk-robed Dr. Pinay.

Earnestly, the Russian oncologist made more notes. I asked if I could take photographs. Dr. Dolmo agreed.

She prescribed a certain compound (of thirty-five ingredients, according to Dr. Pinay). The patient, somewhat overcome but visibly pleased at this multi-national consortium of consultants, stood up, smiled broadly, and trotted from the room, muttering, "*tukche, tukche,*" ('Thank you, thank you' in Tibetan).

The other two foreign doctors and I asked questions and made notes about the treatment. Dr. Nowergee looked hopefully around for tea. When it finally arrived, Dr. Dolmo gracefully served each of us. I asked Dr. Dolmo for a few of her birth control pills (I thought I'd have them analyzed back home but never did). She reached into her desk drawer and presented me with a packet of ten tablets.

"This is a year's supply," Dr. Dolmo explained. "Seven rupees" (approximately one dollar then), she said with a smile. Large, tan, and organic looking, the pills came in a plain brown wrapper without a label. I asked what they were.

"They are made from more than one hundred ingredients," Dr. Dolmo explained. "Some are available during only a few weeks a year on certain hillsides in the Himalayas."

Several weeks later, Dr. Khanna of Dharmsala Civil Hospital told me that, in addition to various rare herbs, one of the ingredients was yak semen. Unfortunately, tests by the Indian Council of Medical Research in Delhi had found the compound altogether ineffective for contraception.

Dr. Dolmo was most cooperative. There we sat, five physicians from five countries, with five different languages. Four of us were trained in modern Western medicine, including Dr. Nowergee, a graduate of one of India's most distinguished medical colleges. Yet, all of us were listening very seriously to this little woman from Lhasa, who continued to instruct us with both modesty and assurance.

"Tibetan medicine is based entirely on palpation of the pulse," she explained. "It is a science that has been practiced in Tibet for many centuries, but is little known elsewhere. From the character of the pulse, its strength, its compressibility, its fullness, we can diagnose many ailments and know their cause."

Dr. Dolmo trained for fourteen years in Tibet and was a master of all the specialties of Tibetan medicine. Here in Dharmsala, more than a hundred patients visited her clinic every day, seven days a week. I wanted to think about that before visiing the other practitioner and the Tibetan Hospital.

The morning after my visit to Dr.Dolmo's clinic, I explored the upper village and visited the *gompa* (temple). A tall kind-faced monk smiled and made a little bow to me as he circumambulated the temple's yellow walls. Then I followed a sturdy old lama, his sparse pigtail tied with a red ribbon at the end as he walked before me, twirling a silver prayer wheel in his left hand and counting off the beads of his *malla* (a rosary-like necklace) with his right.

Although I frequently visited the Indian subcontinent and thought I was beginning to know much of its fantastic variety, this wholly Tibetan town took me by surprise. The vigorous central Asian feel of the local Tibetan culture sharply contrasted with the ambling pace of most of rural India.

The self-assurance of the Tibetan women, like the Sherpa women of Nepal (who share the same origin and religion), seemed to spring from the philosophy of Buddhism itself - a feeling of people at home in their world. In contrast to Islam, Hinduism, or orthodox Judeo-Christian religions, Buddhism is less preoccupied with subordination of women. Buddhists teach non-attachment to material things and compassion for all beings. Buddhism insists we are all of us one and the same substance - thus equals.

Quite a difference from the Bible's record of woman being created from man's rib to be his faithful servant, shadow, or mistress. If, as Buddhists believe, all are one, there can be no real basis for hostility and envy between sexes.

But sexism was not absent. A year earlier in Nepal, a Buddhist nun came to me for birth control tablets during my stay in a Buddhist village. She explained that monks sometimes forced her and other Sisters into unwanted sexual liaisons. So much for the idyllic equality of the sexes. Tibetan Buddhists worshipped a galaxy of gods and idols. And far from being detached, many valued material wealth immensely and were traders for whom buying and selling seemed the very breath of life.

Several days after my morning with Dr. Dolmo, I visited the hospital run by Tibetan doctors. I was welcomed by Dr. Goma, a young woman of around 25 years. The hospital was a small, reasonably clean building of sixteen or eighteen rooms without laboratories, x-rays, nurses' stations, or any of the other paraphernalia of western hospitals. Through the doors of several rooms I saw patients lying in bed, surrounded by their families. I asked Dr. Goma about treatment.

Unlike Dr. Dolmo, who was born and trained for a number of years in Lhasa, Dr. Goma came to McLeod Ganj from Tibet with her parents as refugees when she was still a child. After secondary school, she was trained in Tibetan medicine by Dr. Dolmo and other practitioners from the Tibetan school in Dharmsala.

The principles of practice in the hospital were the same we had observed the day before with Dr. Dolmo - diagnosis by pulse palpation and treatment with various herbs. This included the treatment of tuberculosis, a scourge in these parts.

Explaining that I was a neurologist, I asked her about Tibetan medicine treatment of epilepsy, my own specialty. Dr. Goma took me to the ward to introduce me to two teen-age girls sent to this clinic for treatment of epilepsy. Marcia, from Italy, had failed to respond to medications prescribed by her doctor in Rome. He referred her to Dharmsala for cure. The other, Vita, from New Delhi, had also failed treatment for epilepsy there and was brought here by her family.

Dr. Goma explained that usually epilepsy was due to a disturbance in planetary relationships, but occasionally resulted from an infestation of "white worms." Special diets and activities designed to avoid the consequences of both problems were prescribed. Astonished but polite, I made no reply. Since both patients spoke quite passable English, I talked with them. Both were bright and cheerful, lying happily in side by side beds in the room they shared. Both assured me they had not had any spells at all since receiving treatments in this hospital.

Treatments consisted of special concoctions containing dozens of herbs and other less palatable ingredients. *Moxas*, rituals during which hot gold needles or burning potions were placed on special areas of the skin, were used by both doctors and lamas. No stethoscopes, thermometers, electroencephalograms, xrays or blood pressure measurements complicated the diagnostic process. There was no laboratory and no surgery. The only diagnostic instruments used by the Tibetan medical practitioners were small wooden sticks they used to stir urine to a froth. The color of the froth was of great significance for diagnosis.

Next day, I visited Dr. Dolmo's clinic again to ask more questions. I asked about treatment for cancer and prevention of neonatal tetanus, a scourge here that was directly related to the local custom of applying cow dung to the umbilical stump of newborn infants. I asked about hemorrhage following childbirth, which, along with other complications of childbearing, was the cause here as in many other third world countries of a shorter average life span for women than for men. (In contrast to the West, where women live five to fifteen years longer than men, here and elsewhere in Asia as in Africa, it is men who outlive women by a similar margin.) When her clinic was over, a young man in white shirt and baggy trousers brought tea.

Dr. Dolmo answered all my questions confidently.

"For cancer we prescribe medicine and massage. To prevent infection of the navel after childbirth we use pure cow's butter, not buffalo. We use special herbs for bleeding and other complications of childbirth. For the mother, we have one mixture for retained placenta and another for post-partum hemorrhage."

I didn't know whether to laugh, protest, or cry. I asked for more tea.

Every evening during my stay in McLeod Ganj, I had dinner with Dr. Nowergee. We always dined in one or another of the four little Tibetan restaurants in the town. On more than one occasion we were joined by a young monk, Dawa, who spoke hesitant but passable English. Dawa was a *trepa* (student) in the School of Dialectical Buddhism, behind the temple. One evening as we three sat together sharing a bowl of noodles and spicy meat sauce, I asked Dawa to explain what was behind the extraordinary equanimity and poise of Tibetan women here.

Dawa, his orange robe and serene countenance a striking contrast to the disreputable group of stoned westerners at the next table, replied in hesitant English, "We say that when the stream reaches the stone it should not try to go over it, but should go around."

I thought about that. Are we trying to push against stone walls when there might be an easier way?

Dr. Nowergee, the Hindu doctor, smiled and quoted Tagore, "Liberation is not necessarily renunciation, but it is the state of completeness free from the bondage of Karma."

"But Karma is a Hindu, not a Buddhist notion, and means deeds and action. Does freedom from Karma imply an end of all doing, all action?" I asked. Both Buddhist *trepa* and Hindu doctor smiled indulgently. This bit of Western logic made no impression on them at all.

"It is being able *not to act*, not action, that is important," explained Dawa, his expression puzzled at my lack of understanding.

Turning to more familiar ground, I asked them to explain about Tibetan medicine. "Does it also rely on psychological liberation or is it mostly a matter of these exotic herbs and ceremonies?" I asked.

"You should next visit Dr. Yoshi Donden, personal physician to the Dalai Lama," suggested Dr. Nowergee. "He may be able to answer your questions."

Several days later, after obtaining permission from one of his students, I spent a morning in Dr. Donden's consulting room. A renowned practitioner and teacher of Tibetan medicine, Dr. Donden's patients came from wide areas of India.

Before my visit to this distinguished man's clinic, Dr. Nowergee lent me a copy of Dr. Donden's *"The Ambrosia Heart Tantra: Secret Oral Teachings on the Eight Branches of the Science of Healing; Revealed Truths from the Aquamarine Buddha."* Translated into English by Jhampa Kitsay, this volume summarized many of the principles of Tibetan medicine. I wanted to read it before visiting Dr. Donden's clinic. I prepared myself by climbing high above the village to the snow line, where I lay down on a carpet of new grass and tiny white and yellow flowers. There, I read his book from cover to cover.

"The doctor should instruct his patient as follows," wrote Dr. Donden:

"1. To think of himself as ill. 2. To think of teaching as medicine. 3. To think of his teacher as a doctor. 4. To regard Awakened Ones as supreme. 5. To have the intention to overcome faults. Awakened ones are those who have overcome the four maras: Attachment, Hatred, Bewilderment and Jealousy."

Treatment addressed these causes through medications such as the use of hot and cool substances and fragrant plants. The methods should be taught with *Compassion*.

Foods for disorders of wind are *"horse meat, donkey meat, human or marmot flesh, aged meat, dark sugar, aged butter, garlic and onions.* Various moxa (hot needles, oil, cumin seeds, and salt dipped in hot butter) may be applied to the skin over ailing parts. For treatment of disorders of bile, blood letting or standing naked under a cold waterfall are recommended."

In Tibetan medicine, diseases are considered to be due to imbalances between humors of wind, phlegm, and bile, beliefs similar to those held in the West in medieval times. But the reasons for imbalance were different: *"Attachment, Hatred, and Bewilderment."*

Finally, *"There is but one cause of illness: ignorance, due to not understanding the meaning of identitylessness."*

Hmmm. I wondered what my students would think of that.

Next morning, I dressed carefully in a clean, pressed cotton shirt and trousers before my appointment to visit the renowned physician. After breakfast of Tibetan pancake and hot coffee at my favorite cafe, I prepared myself to meet the day by visiting the *gompa*. There I watched devout monks and young women murmur their daily prayers. Rosy-cheeked Tibetan women prostrated themselves repeatedly full length on the temple veranda, facing the Buddha within. Then they gained further merit by making several dozen ritual circumambulations of the gompa. After making a couple of circles around the temple myself, but omitting the prostrations, I walked slowly back to town behind a gentle looking nun who twirled a prayer wheel and hummed Om Mani Padme Hums steadily.

In an alley below the crowded street, a stairway led down to the ground floor of Dr. Donden's two-story house to his clinic. The doctor, plump and impressive in his sleeveless maroon lama robe, was standing outside near a well stirring a white china cup of urine with a small wooden stick. His patient, a distinguished-looking Tibetan gentleman of around fifty-five years of age, watched anxiously. Finally the urine developed a head of froth that seemed to satisfy Dr. Donden. He beckoned to the patient and to me to follow him inside. Twenty or more patients sat in rows on wooden benches in the small waiting room. With surprise, I saw a middle-aged German nurse who was also lodging in the same guest house where I stayed, sitting in the queue.

Dr. Donden nodded to the waiting patients and hurried into his small consulting room. This office was furnished humbly, containing only five wooden chairs and a desk. Several long, narrow maroon covered Tibetan texts lay on the desk. He motioned to the patient and then to me to be seated. After settling behind the desk, he reached for the patient's pulse and palpated it carefully, first the right and then the left, each for at least a minute.

Was this the mainstay of diagnosis?

A young Tibetan apprentice came in quietly and sat down on a chair on the opposite side of the desk, where he watched the master closely. Dr. Donden muttered something to him and then turned back to his patient. After pulling down the lower lid of each eye, he scrutinized the patient's eyeballs intently. Then he drew one of the narrow, cloth-covered Tibetan tomes toward him and read silently for a few minutes. Apparently these volumes were the local equivalent of the *Physicians Desk Reference*, which American physicians often consulted for dosage or side effects of various drugs when in doubt regarding treatment (before availability of Palm Pilots). Finally satisfied, Dr. Donden scribbled some Tibetan characters on a scrap of paper.

Then he stood and put his arm around the patient, explaining what was to be done. His manner was concerned and utterly convincing. He nodded to the apprentice to explain the problem and treatment to me. This young man, who had already completed more than ten years of training in Tibetan medicine, turned to me and translated briefly, "liver."

"And the treatment?" I inquired soberly.

"Liver pills." The morning went on like that, the parade of patients never ceasing. Rarely did Dr. Donden do more than take a moment's history and a long feel of both pulses. If the Buddhist philosophy of non-attachment and the end of ignorance entered into the treatment process, I missed it. But the doctor, who is also a distinguished lama, was extremely impressive in his long maroon robe and sober, attentive manner. His intelligent round face was full of interest and compassion. Unhurried, unfailingly courteous, comforting, and kind, I thought of my own students and how much they could learn about bedside manner from such a teacher. As for the treatments prescribed, it was like stepping back 2000 years in the history of medicine.

After seeing several patients, Dr. Donden took a moment to explain his methods to me through his young apprentice.

"The cause of illness may be attributed to three things: 1. Humors and their imbalance; 2. Actions committed in former lives; 3. Combinations of the above."

On the day before, I had read recommendations for treatment in Dr. Donden's book, *The Ambrosia Heart Tantra*.

"If one is sleeping too much, take medicine to induce vomiting, fast, and enjoy the company of women. For insomnia, drink milk, curd, alcohol and meat broth. Anoint the head and body with sesame oil and pour a drop of oil into each ear. Refrain from sexual intercourse with non-humans, another's spouse, a person unpleasing to oneself, a pregnant woman, or one who is weak, ill, or menstruating." Finally, *"Refrain from sex more than every two weeks during monsoon."*

For hours I sat in the clinic, listening to and observing the stream of patients who filed in from the waiting room to this office. The apprentice, who spoke quite good English, graciously translated and answered my many questions. After half a dozen Tibetans with alleged "liver problems" (they do like to drink), an intelligent looking Indian of around forty, wearing a white shirt and pressed gray slacks entered. He carried a Fanta bottle containing "the urine of a friend."

Once again, Dr. Donden stepped outside, where he poured the clear yellow liquid into the white china cup, stirred vigorously, and contemplated the result for a few minutes. Then he returned to his office and scribbled a prescription on a scrap of gray paper that he handed to the man. The patient departed contentedly for the compounding room next door. There the prescription was filled from the thousands of remedies filed in the racks of small wooden drawers that extended from floor to ceiling.

"Impotence," explained the apprentice Indian doctor to me. "The man was given a local remedy for sexually transmitted disease which cost ten rupees."

"Does it work for the impotence too?" I asked.

"Not for long," he replied gravely.

The next patient was a lovely young Indian girl whose face was half covered with a filmy scarf. She carried a baby with large brown eyes and a bulging abdomen. The girl wore a brilliant gold jewel in her nose, and her ears were decorated with small gold rings from top to bottom. More rings adorned all but the small toes of each bare foot. She leaned forward earnestly and launched into a tale of pain and weakness. Dr. Donden listened attentively, not once interrupting. When she paused for breath, he took her wrist gently and palpated the pulse - first the right and then the left.

"Kidney and womb," he intoned firmly in Hindi. Medicine was prescribed. The woman stood uneasily. Her husband, a neat looking man of around forty, stepped out of the shadows by the door. Dr. Donden pressed his hands warmly and explained further the nature of the trouble and how it should be treated. Then all three nodded in satisfaction.

"And the baby with the bulging belly?" I whispered to the apprentice.

"He was not the problem," the apprentice replied.

Next, the wife of the young apprentice doctor entered. A handsome Tibetan girl of twenty-five, she had been suffering from severe abdominal pains for more than a month. Medicated by Dr. Donden, the pain had subsided a little, but now she was complaining of swollen ankles. Again, the pulse ritual. Listening sympathetically while gazing intently into her eyes, but ignoring the rest of her body, hidden under her long Tibetan dress, Dr. Donden now prescribed a new medicine.

Her husband explained to me that his diagnosis was "gas" and that the cause was "too much thick tea." Diet and special herbs to induce "cold" were prescribed. The girl stood to leave. I caught my breath as I glimpsed her ankles - they were as broad as an elephant's! Later in the day I saw her on the street and suggested she also visit Dr. Nowergee at the government clinic.

Dr. Donden sat down and shuffled his bare feet against the dusty crossbars of his desk. Through the apprentice interpreter I asked him how the Buddhist trinity of *"non-attachment, compassion,* and *meditation* entered into any of these pulse takings and herbal cures. He chuckled, flashing a single gold tooth in a patient smile.

"Our medicine is based on wisdom and method," his assistant translated. "Renunciation and meditation are not possible for everyone. We have a saying that may help you understand. 'Pain exists to measure pleasure by.' With that I had to be satisfied.

"How successful are these unusual practices?" I asked Dr. Nowergee at dinner that evening. "All physicians can cure some patients by a combination of good luck, non-intervention, and the powerful forces for health that exist in most people."

"True," he replied, "but the impressive urine stirring and warm reassurance given by Doctors Donden and Dolmo no doubt add to the natural likelihood of recovery."

The enormous difference not only in medicine but also in education, perception, and logic of Tibetan Buddhism from the monotheistic religions of Europe, the Americas and the Middle East was brought home to me the next afternoon. I walked to the Tibetan Library and Archives located in a beautiful temple-like structure on a forested hillside between McLeod Ganj and Dharmsala. When I introduced myself to the young woman seated at the desk near the entrance, she gave me a temporary permit to use the collections. She then summoned an aged lama who showed me about and tried to help me understand.

First we visited a museum filled with silk and satin robed statues of the multitude of saints and gods of the Tibetan Buddhist pantheon. As I examined the gorgeously garbed and painted, many headed, multi-armed figures, the lama explained. "All religions teach moral principles to mold the functions of the mind. Buddhists strive through a series of lives toward the perfection of Buddha-hood. We know that there are past lives, because some adults and even some children can remember them."

We paused before an exquisite Buddha, his bland benign countenance shining with perfect serenity. The old lama continued, "Suffering is *samsara*, the round of earthly existence. *Sutra*, the teaching of the Buddha, teaches that liberation from *samsara* comes through meditation and a moral life. The *tantras* are the methods by which one achieves liberation."

I shook my head, still not understanding.

"The Four Noble Truths: know the suffering, give up their causes, relinquish attachment, and be earnest in cessation. This is the way to Enlightenment."

"But what about these *tantras?*" I asked, hoping for an explanation of those exotic rites of sex, reverse ejaculation and consumption of human flesh I had heard rumors about but never witnessed or understood.

"*Tantrayana* is the yogic method to stop the flow of evil thought and the wanderings of the projecting mind through concentrating on the physical makeup of one's body and the psychological quality of one's mind. These are the wisdom and the method."

I had to be content with this ambiguous reply. Later, as I walked from the building out under the archway bright with carved dragons and gods, two Western looking girls with long hair, long skirts and white blouses hurried across the courtyard. Students in the Tibetan school, they ran up the stairs to the library, their arms loaded with books. An eagle soared far overhead, silhouetted against the snow peaks. Far below us, streams sparkled in the narrow valley.

"Why are so many Westerners being attracted to this strange and incomprehensible philosophy?" I wondered that evening at dinner. "There must be something here that I'm missing."

Dr. Nowergee, an open-minded Hindu, thought it was a result of over indulged but often lonely western society - they were searching for the secret of happiness.

After dinner, Dr. Lubinka, the Byelo-Russian oncologist and I walked toward the *gompa* in the moonlight. She was also puzzled by the philosophy of Tibetan medicine. But her mind was either more open than mine - or, she may have been under orders to continue her studies until she understood what was going on. As we came to a dark part of the path a gnome like old man darted out of the bushes and ran toward us, grunting loudly. He rushed toward me and clapped one hand over and firmly squeezed my left breast.

I was so startled I didn't know whether to scream or to run. Dr. Lubinka had no such problems. She hurried to the side of the path, picked up a large stone, and started chasing after the little fellow, who ran off at top speed. I burst out laughing and thought that this Russian lady academician was better suited for life in Detroit or Chicago than I was.

No story of Dharmsala would be complete without describing the Tibetan refugee children's village. Dr. Nowergee and I walked the mile or so over there one Sunday afternoon. We found the doctor in charge in the dispensary. A tall, tanned, handsome young Canadian volunteer, he seemed happy to take time to show us around.

"The buildings of the children's village previously belonged to the Indian army," he explained. "The hospital and schools were built with donations from many Western countries. More than 800 children orphaned or abandoned in the Tibetan holocaust and diaspora live in the Childrens' Village in an atmosphere dedicated to preserving Tibetan culture."

As we wandered about, I was struck by the quiet courtesy of the children of all ages. It was quite a contrast to my recent experiences in rural Afghanistan, where children shouted *"foringee"* (foreigner!) or *"Baksheesh baksheesh"* (give me money) as they chased me down the streets. Sometimes they threw stones at me.

These Tibetan children, whether on the playground or out for strolls into the surrounding countryside with their counselors were invariably polite. Folding their hands together, they greeted us with soft *namaste*s. When I sat down in the village square a small child snuggled in my lap. Snub-nosed little folk dressed in bright western shorts and shirts, the children seemed happy and well-cared for in this way station between traditional Tibetan and modern Indian life.

Did the Buddhist eight fold path: *right action, right concentration, right effort, right intention, right livelihood, right mindfulness, right speech, right views* - lead to a better world? Could this ancient religion be a guide for a workable fruitful life? For me? For my patients? As a doctor, I wanted to understand this Tibetan way of life and whether it might offer relief from the anxiety and depression suffered by so many of my patients in far-off America.

Every morning I sat in the doorway of the temple for an hour or more listening to the chanting of prayers by the monks. What was I seeking? To see, hear, and experience the peace and satisfaction I saw in the faces of the priests and acolytes of the Himalayan temples I had visited. Could I learn enough to take it home to my patients in America?

A year before my visit to McLeod Ganj, a nun who came to me for birth control tablets during my stay in a Buddhist village in Nepal explained that monks sometimes forced them into unwanted sexual liaisons. So much for the idyllic equality of the sexes. Furthermore, Tibetan Buddhists worshipped a galaxy of gods and idols. And far from being detached, many valued material wealth immensely and were professional traders for whom buying and selling seemed the very breath of life. It's hard to beat the greediness of the human brain.

Tibetan Buddhism is a religion that attracts many new followers from the West. Ironically, as is often the case in the violent history of our world, dispersion of a people by invading armies brought an isolated creed to the attention of the outside world. In addition to the discovery of Tantrism and the Tibetan *Book of the Dead* by hippies, Tibetan Buddhism attracts a number of serious scholars and followers who would never have been allowed inside the old cloistered Tibet. These Westerners, mostly young and restless, are often themselves dissatisfied refugees from their own society. A few come to India to study Buddhism, Tibetan medicine, language and dialectics. Back in the U.S. and Europe, many more are learning from monks and lamas who fled Tibet to cities in the West.

There were other lessons and examples to ponder. Tibetan babies were held close and nursed before they had a chance to cry. No one was ever alone. Even the few homeless souls who slept each night in tattered bundles under the prayer wheels in the village square seemed part of the ceaseless street action and were greeted politely by townsfolk each morning. The village whore, a blowzy Tibetan woman with red-rimmed alcoholic eyes, lounged on a *charpoi* in the middle of the street greeting each passerby with coarse shouts or obscene songs in a husky whiskey voice. Seldom ignored, she earned good-humored laughter from her neighbors.

Motorcycles, goats, buffalo, sheep, dogs and the constant blare of music were drowned out intermittently by the sound of the straining motors of the big old Tata buses bursting with arriving and departing passengers.

Although superficially Indian and Tibetan society seemed to have merged amicably enough, their personal relationships in the town were few. Tibetans traveled the entire subcontinent buying and selling. They made more money than most of the Indians in town who tended to stay put all their lives.

Tibetans also drank alcoholic brews with gusto and enjoyment. They had little to do with the Indian population. Tibetan men, away working on roads, participated less and less in family life. Tibetan mothers, instead of staying at home like Indian mothers, worked in the local handcraft centers making rugs, or ran hotels, shops, or restaurants. The tiny apartments in their adopted country were poor settings for joint family life. Most disruptive of all to their traditional close family and religious bonds was the free secular education of children. This sign of progress for us and for the Indians now largely replaced their religious schools. As in the West, public schools also weakened the firm bonding of children to their parents and to their religion. The inevitable changes in habits and aspirations that follow public education may soon extinguish the traditional ties described by the Dalai Lama:

"Whole families are linked together by the strongest bonds of love and kindness."

There were other signs that all was not serene here. Placards around the town and on my hotel wall read "End genocide in Tibet" or "Chinese go back to China." There were no powerful organizations like the Palestine Liberation Organization to agitate for the twelve million displaced or subjugated Tibetans still in Tibet. Like Palestine, there was no oil or mineral wealth here to interest the Western world in opposing Chinese rule. Businessmen in America were more interested in tapping into China's huge population of potential consumers of western products.

The Tibetan medieval way of life did not promote "progress" as we in the West define it. Before the Chinese invasion, automobiles, electricity, literacy, sanitation and modern medicine were unknown to the vast majority of the population. But so were concentration camps, gas chambers, hydrogen bombs, AK47s, rockets, deserted children, broken families and elderly persons abandoned in nursing homes. Personal and social security lay in ties of family and religion, which bound each member of the society from cradle to grave.

On my last evening in McLeod Ganj I walked the path from village to temple. In front of me were two old lamas walking toward the gold-spired *gompa* where the haunting chant of prayers rose in the still air. Laughter and music drifted up from three young monks practicing on long ceremonial Tibetan trumpets in the wooded glen below. Two women and an aged, shaven-headed nun prostrated themselves on the temple veranda. My favorite monk, who always invited me to watch from the back of the temple at prayer time, was circumambulating the yellow walls in quiet meditation. Back in the village, people crowded every doorstep in their endless togetherness.

"Know the meaning of suffering and relinquish the causes of misery," taught the Buddha. *"Be earnest in cessation of passion, desire, anger, pride, and hatred. As much as you are able, be of service to those who are filled with misery. Turn away from bad action even if others advise it. In time of need, give freely. Acknowledge failure, and if you have success, be satisfied. If you are learned, subdue your pride. Do not look down upon the lowly and avoid jealousy toward those above you."*

Or will we, and our society, prevail?

1979   USSR invades Afghanistan to save Communist government

Shah of Iran deposed by fundamentalist Islamic Government

Civil war in Nicaragua between Sandanistas and U.S. backed Contras

Mother Theresa, born of humble origins in Albania, received Nobel peace prize for her work with the poor in the slums of Calcutta

Pol Pot, Chinese-backed communist Khmer Rouge leader in Cambodia, overthrown by invasion from Vietnam

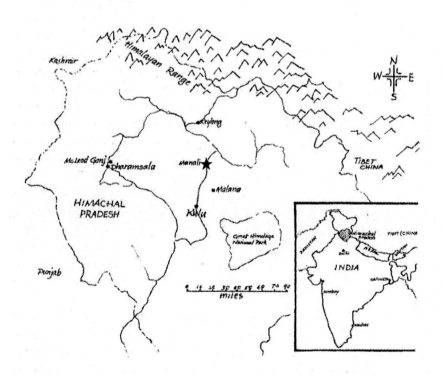

Chapter II

WOMENS LIB

"Before enlightenment, chop wood, haul water"

Kulanthapitha means "the end of the habitable world." explained my guide book. "It is the ancient name of the famous valley of the upper River Beas as it escapes from the western Himalayan snows in north India, and was one of the main caravan routes between China and India." These seemed like good reasons for me to go there. I would also escape from the heat on the Indian plains. It was mid-April of 1979, six months before the then unanticipated Russian invasion of Afghanistan. I had just completed a six-week tour of duty there as a volunteer for CARE as a "visiting specialist" in Jamhuriat hospital in Kabul, watching with dread the big Russian cargo planes landing at the Kabul airport. Now I had two weeks to enjoy the mountains between Afghanistan and a scheduled lecture at the Institute of Technology in Bangalore in south central India.

En route, I stopped at Manali, a good starting point for a journey to the Buddhist monasteries of the Keylong valley. Being interested in Buddhism as a religion promoting tranquility and requiring no belief in god or gods, I had long tried to know and understand more about Buddhist beliefs and practices.

Manali is a town where the River Beas races from the Himalayan foothills into the Kulu valley. One of the loveliest spots on earth, this valley is a place of forests, green meadows, and spectacular waterfalls. Tiny villages perch on slopes descending from Himalayan peaks that pierce the sky. Every year, like a giant magnet, these mountains drew me back and back again to stand in their awesome shadow.

Snow still covered the roads and trails a few miles north of Manali when I set out to cross the Rothang pass separating Manali from the Keylong valley. This 13,000 foot pass was still feared in winter by travelers familiar with its toll of men and beasts since ancient times. Although I hadn't much gear and the footpath was well traveled, I hired two local men, a guide and a porter, to make the journey with me. When traveling alone in these mountains, I preferred hiring two companions rather than one. Then no one is too heavily laden. I can skip along with a free conscience, burdened by little more than my canteen.

We started our trip from Manali by bus. Although dawn was just breaking, the old vehicle was packed with Kulu and Nepali people and their voluminous and varied baggage. Kulu women were wrapped in long homespun blanket-like gowns of heavy brown wool, held together over each shoulder with a large brass or silver safety pin. They wore bright head kerchiefs or pillbox hats and their ears were decorated with a dozen or more small gold rings around the edges. A single pink coralline jewel pierced their short noses above one nostril.

Nepal people, coming from farther east, had broader faces and narrower eyes than the Kulus. Their half folded upper lids gave them a faintly Oriental appearance. Nepali women were warmly bundled in bulky shawls, wore their sleek black hair in a single long braid hanging down their backs to the waist and decorated their ears with a single brilliant blue turquoise stone held in place by a bit of string. Necklaces of pink coralline alternating with large chunks of turquoise circled their sturdy brown necks.

As in the west, men were much less colorfully dressed than women. Most men wore homespun gray breeches and worn, western style dark jackets, doubtless obtained from the huge shipments of second-hand clothing from Europe and the U.S. sold by traders in every town. Despite the chilly weather and the hike ahead of us over deep snow, many of the Nepalis wore worn sneakers or rubber thongs, evidently not owning leather shoes or boots. In the total absence of parkas or warm jackets common in the West, men wrapped a brown or gray blanket over their clothes. Children, and there were many, were small, well-behaved replicas of their parents. Wide-eyed, they sat silently gazing out of the bus windows, apparently oblivious to the laughter and chatter in a variety of tongues around them.

Great bundles of blankets and cooking utensils were stacked in the aisles. Conical baskets, bulging at the top beneath cloth covers, were propped against each row of seats. When everything possible was crammed into or on top of the bus, we chugged off noisily just as the sun rose above the eastern slopes of the valley.

Six miles north of Manali we reached the snow line at the tiny village of Kothi. On a steep hairpin turn, the bus shuddered to a stop. It could go no further. Everyone rushed from their seats and gathered their numerous bundles and children. Men shoved the doors open. We all hurried out into the cold morning. More baggage, including mine, was tossed down by small bundled men who scurried over the roof of the old bus. Then we all pushed from behind as the motor labored to turn the vehicle around on the snow-covered road. Finally, with a loud cough, the now empty bus rattled down the road back to Manali.

We were left, the whole busload, standing alone between white snow and white sky. The high pass we were to traverse was invisible above. After a moment of gazing about this deserted place, we shouldered our various loads and set out, or rather up. We were more than fifty, not counting babies and children on backs. At once, the trail left the road and led straight up the mountainside over snow, rock and heather.

After two hours of steady climbing, we reached the snowbound little village of Myrrhi at about 9000 feet. In summer, Myrrhi is a hostel stop on the Kulu-Keylong road. Now both road and town were still buried in snow with only a few rooftops visible. Tossing our packs on a big wooden table outside in the snow, we descended low steps down into the local hostelry. Rice, *dahl* and tea were simmering over the fire on the floor in the center of the room.

"Today, we stay here," announced my guide. I was perplexed. It was only ten in the morning. Why not get on with it? We had walked for barely two hours since leaving the bus. As we joined other travelers for tea, rice and *dahl*, my guide assured me it was now too late to set out as the snow would be too soft to climb over the pass. So I learned one of the most valuable lessons of traveling in a so-called backward country: Relax. I spent the day exploring the snow covered hills around Myrrhi while my guide and porter slept contentedly by the fire. The hostel provided more rice and *dahl* for dinner.

Before dawn the next morning, we set off up a broad snowfield toward the summit of the Rothang pass which separated us from the Lahoul and Spiti valleys to the north. Our trek led over the old caravan route to Ladakh, formerly used by traders who traveled west from north India to exchange rice, tea and spices for salt and wool from Tibet. Many of our companions from the bus must also have slept in Myrrhi the night before. Now they accompanied us on the climb. There were also several dozen Indian Army soldiers carrying billowing packs of sleeping and cooking gear. As we climbed higher over the broad snow slope, now well above the tree line, the famous wind from the south grew stronger behind us. The Indian officer, a bearded Sikh, regaled me with tales of past disasters.

"Madam," he told me cheerfully in excellent English, "whole parties of traders and porters have been blown off the top of this pass and dashed to death on the rocks below!"

We were resting in the warm sun, sitting on a huge outcropping of stone. The officer smoked a cigarette while I gazed mesmerized at the snowfields stretching to the horizon. His troops lay about on the rocks, some sleeping, some staring unmoved at the vast vista below.

I propped my back against one of their packs and extracted sunburn lotion and zinc oxide from my rucksack. After applying these substances generously to my face and mouth, I passed them around. The Indian soldiers shook their heads with amusement. The irrepressible Nepalis, however, were soon gaily smearing and daubing the white cream on their chins and noses and admiring the effect on each other's dark faces.

We pushed on and up. The wind grew stronger. So did my admiration for the game Nepali women, each with an infant strapped on her back over a load of household gear. Laughing and chattering, uncomplaining, they strode through the deep, now softening snow in soaked felt boots or sneakers.

When we reached the top of the pass, it was nearly noon. The sun was blazing hot. The wind suddenly stopped. Sitting in our shirtsleeves on huge warm rocks, we ate our lunch of cold rice. Beside us, tattered prayer flags on a wooden frame fluttered gently in the clear air. After lunch, Tikomoran, my guide, and Tikomoran, also the name of my porter, stretched out contentedly to nap on the snow. Both were now clad in tan army parkas purchased during lunch from the soldiers. They paid with fifty-rupee notes, (about seven U.S. dollars) an advance on their salaries requested from "Memsahib," as they called me.

While the Tikomarans closed their eyes and slept, I watched the procession of our fellow travelers troop past. Single file, each placed a foot carefully in the footsteps of the last to avoid the deep soft snow. The husky Nepali women in their long skirts, bright aprons and woolen shawls still packed their conical straw baskets of household goods on their backs. Many baskets were topped by a sleeping infant. Men were bent under heavier loads supported by a leather tumpline across the forehead. Lahouli woman, in their long brown woolen gowns and plastic shoes, carried less but led more children. Scattered in small groups in this parade trudged the heavily laden soldiers in uniforms of pale green. Despite the heat, all but two still wore their quilted parkas. All were shod in high black rubber boots.

I was surprised that the soldiers could bear the intense sunlight, for unlike Nepalis and Lahoulis, Indian eyes are not protected by an epicanthal fold of the upper eyelid. During our lunch break, I asked the Sikh lieutenant who sat beside me polishing his sun goggles why all his men were not also provided with glasses to protect their eyes against the sun and snow.

"Madam," he replied, shaking his head, "the men have all lost their army issue sunglasses or sold them. They refuse to wear them. It's no use to provide." On the following morning I was to learn the unhappy consequences.

The view from the top of the pass was spectacular. To the north, we looked down steep white slopes of the northwest face where we would soon descend into the snow-filled valley of the River Chandra 3000 feet below. Beyond the frozen river, a wall of snow-capped peaks filled the horizon from west to east. Behind us, the wide plateau of unbroken snow at the summit fell away gently toward the south. On either side, steep cliffs of rock and ice rose above the prayer flags stirring beside us.

Intensely satisfied, as I always am by high mountains abetted by the intoxication of thin air, I reluctantly roused my companions to continue our journey. We began the scramble down a fall of rocks that ended in the smooth snow slope of the north face of the mountain. Gazing down the unbroken snow field that stretched to the river far below, I couldn't resist trying to glissade down. I borrowed a walking stick from one of the Tikomorans to serve as a brake and rudder.

Soon I was joyously careening down the steep slope just as I do on the familiar shoulders of my own mountains in far off Oregon. I landed in a flurry of snow behind a crowd of Nepalis.

The irrepressible ladies of this little troop also wanted to try the same technique. Like a giant bobsled we sat on our behinds, each hugging the woman ahead. With baggage and draperies flying, we shot down the mountainside, a long train of girls and women, shouting with laughter. A thousand feet below we picked ourselves up where the rocks began. In high spirits, we brushed off our wet bottoms and continued our descent on foot.

Now the narrow trail turned westward over ice and rock away from the Kunzan Pass guarding the Spiti valley to the east. Dropping more gradually now, we soon reached Kokhsar, the first of the Lahouli villages. While our companions trudged on, we stopped at the government rest house near a small cluster of one-story wooden dwellings. The river, gray with glacial debris, separated us here from the main part of the hamlet's twenty-odd houses on the opposite bank.

At the beginning of winter, the plank floor had been removed from the bridge crossing the torrent to prevent collapse from the heavy snow. Although the next morning we picked our way across the narrow steel girders, I felt a silent panic when I looked down from our slender footholds at the deep churning rapids below. The bridge was to prove a nasty stumbling block the next day for the train of pack mules accompanying a group of English mountain climbers who joined us at the rest house that evening.

As the sun dropped behind the great peaks, the Tikomorans and I dined on tea and mountains of rice and *dahl* in a *chaikhana* (tea stall) near the government rest house. Then I stretched out happily on the veranda to watch the glow of brilliant orange warm the snow peaks on the far side of the river.

The next morning, I awakened to the shouts of an Indian soldier rattling the window of the rest house. Half the army that trooped across with us were now snow blind. The poor fellows were being led about the little clearing in front of the rest house by those who could still see.

Certain that my small supply of cortisone eyedrops would not be enough for so large a crowd, I trotted over to the one-room government medical dispensary near the rest house. An amiable young man, the local paramedic, lounged on a wooden bench outside. After introducing myself, I asked what he was dispensing for snow blindness. Smiling and proud, he led me inside. The dingy room was fitted out with the collection of dusty bottles and packets of pills and powders usually found in rural dispensaries. Taking a round squat jar from the shelf, he unscrewed the lid revealing a dark tarry goo inside.

"Ayurvedic," he explained, scooping up a fingerful and extending it for my approval. Although odorless, it otherwise resembled the solid dark grease I used to lubricate my bicycle wheel axles when I was a kid. A quick tour of his other supplies indicated that, although this was a government health clinic, it was only for "ayurvedic" (traditional) Indian remedies. There were no antibiotics or modern ophthalmics. I thanked him and departed to squeeze out my limited supply of cortisone eye drops under the fiery red lids of the dozen or so soldiers suffering most severely.

By the time I finished, the Tikomorans had water boiling over a brisk fire in the yard. Already fortified by cocoa brewed over kerosene stoves offered by the generous English climbers, I joined my guide and porter for tea and rice. We packed up our gear and wished good luck to the climbers. Tight-lipped, they were busy using their short-handled ice axes to dig out the planks for the bridge from beneath a twenty-foot snowbank. Then they would have to put them over the girders so their pack animals could cross.

Whistling Colonel Dolbie's march from *The Bridge over the River Kwai*, I set off behind the Tikomorans. A snow-packed trail followed along the far bank of the Chandra. Although it was already May, the river was still bridged by snow at narrow places. After nearly two hours of gradual descent, the snow cover grew thinner and gave way to melted ice, mud and rock. Suddenly, we were on the wide dirt road to Keylong. If it weren't for deep snow, we could have followed the same road north over the l7000-foot Baraclava pass that barred our way to Ladakh and Leh. It was not until many years later that approaching from the west, I visited these famed Buddhist centers.

The road hugged the river bank, winding gently beneath a splendid series of snow-capped peaks rising vertically from the opposite shore. We passed small farms, their naked brown fields newly exposed by the receding snows. Bundled Lahoulis emerged from small, snug houses. Woolly yaks and *dzos* (half yak, half cow) pulled wooden plows across the thawing fields. At mid-afternoon, we reached our first village, Ghondla.

Located high on the riverbank where the narrow valley widens briefly to enclose sloping brown fields, Ghondla was a town of several hundred low wooden houses. There was also a school, a hospital and a high wooden tower, which I was told once housed the local noble family. The people of the village were sturdy, almond-eyed, with straight black hair and light brown skin. Flocks of sheep, their heavy wool dyed bright pink, poured over the trail down to the village ahead of us.

In a clearing at the center of the village, horses and goats were gathered near a well surrounded by a low stone wall. Clear-eyed village women, wearing long brown homespun dresses stood talking and laughing with several men on horseback. The men wore long belted cloaks and Tibetan-style triangular hats. Children, too shy at first to approach, were soon popping out of doorways of the mud-brick houses to pose happily for photos. A bent old shepherd directed us toward the government rest house. As we walked toward it up the hillside, villagers looked up in friendly surprise, dogs barked but never chased us or snarled. Cows and dzos gazed at us mildly.

The government rest house, a single-story long narrow structure, was stunningly situated on a small plateau overlooking the churning river. Directly across the stream, a glacier hung on the wall of an ice fluted mountain rising 20,000 feet into the clear air.

Next door stood the village hospital. In the yard, a class was in progress. Twenty or more young men were seated cross-legged on the ground. They were listening attentively to a slightly older man dressed in white cotton trousers and shirt, seated on a straight-back wooden chair. The class stopped abruptly as we passed. Everyone stared at us curiously. I stepped diffidently into the outer rim of the class near the riverbank. After greeting the teacher in Hindi, I explained in English that I was a doctor from America. The Indian teacher, Doctor Sessu, gave me a beaming smile. As always, our common work, medicine, forged an instant link. In excellent English, he insisted that I take his chair and join the group. He called into the hospital for another chair and tea, then seated himself beside me. Hot, dirty and embarrassed before the curious eyes of his students, I suggested he go on with the class and I would return later.

"No, no, the class is now finished!" he replied gallantly. "And I hope you will take tea with me." Famished, not having eaten since the luke-warm rice of early morning, I readily agreed. The class was dismissed. As they dispersed, Dr. Sessu and I got acquainted. Not yet thirty, he was stationed at this outpost serving the five-year bond exacted by the Indian government in exchange for his medical education. Dr. Sessu was a graduate of the Government Medical College a Chandrigarh, a first rate institution. Like most Indian physicians I encountered in rural centers, he nourished high hopes that at the end of his period of service he could go the U.S. for "advanced training."

"Why not train here in India?" I asked as our tea arrived and Dr. Sessu sent the servant racing off for biscuits. "So many of your best doctors come to the U.S. for training and never want to go home again."

"Well," he replied, "things are not working out very well for me here. I want to do surgery but here in Ghondla there are no facilities for surgery at all. I spend my days treating scabies, tuberculosis and gastrointestinal problems. For nine months each year, I'm totally cut off from the world by snow, except for the radio." He sighed. "If only the government had assigned me to Keylong - only twelve miles away. There they have a surgical facility but no surgeon!"

Welcome to India, I thought to myself. *This is why your best young docs come to the U.S.*

Looking out over the peaceful fields and silent majesty of the mountains, I asked Dr. Sessu about his life in this magical place.

"I was born in this valley, only twenty kilometers from here," he replied. "There's a very neighborly feeling among the people here. I think it comes from being shut up together the whole long winter."

"What about mental illness, my specialty, in such a confined community?" I asked.

Dr. Sessu laughed aloud at my question. "None of that at all!" he replied. "People here work too hard. We do see a lot of peptic ulcers though - but only in men. Probably from the home-made brandy. It almost never occurs in women."

"But I suppose women have their own problems," I suggested, watching a man in the brown fields below. He was shoveling dirt from a huge pile of fresh earth into the conical baskets on the backs of three women who squatted down in front of him. "There must be many problems and complications of childbirth." I reached for a biscuit.

"No," he replied. "Women who survive here are so healthy that I've never even been called to a birth. We have two midwives, but nearly all babies are born at home with only the family or neighbors to help. These women rarely complain of anything."

Below us a man in a field loaded a compost filled basket on each of the women's bent backs. Slowly, they stood up and trudged off to dump their loads in a nearby field.

"But these women are working like donkeys," I objected. Another of the long-skirted ladies below stood between two dzos. She was being harnessed to a plow by the man who loaded the baskets. Then she bent her shoulders to the pulling. Dr. Sessu followed my gaze and smiled.

"These women are very strong," he continued. "Even if they get beaten by their husbands, they take it philosophically. If they don't like it, they can leave and go back to their families. But that is very unusual!"

"They must get rather depressed with all the heavy work, plus beatings, cooking and the children to look after," I objected. "I understand many of them are also at the beck and call of several husbands!"

"Yes, you are right," he agreed. "People in Lahoul, like Kulu and much of northern Nepal all practice polyandry. This allows all the younger brothers of the husband to marry the oldest brother's bride. Polyandry prevents division of scarce property that each inherits from his father. But the women never complain. And depression is unknown in this place."

"Well, having many husbands, unlike many wives, is also an excellent means of birth control," I commented. "But what about jealousy between these husbands, and depression in the over-worked, over-used wife?"

"In all the time I've lived here - nearly three years now - I've rarely seen anyone with depression. No suicides have occurred. Even stealing and fighting are rare. Perhaps it's partly due to lack of jealousy. Even when they are drunk, the men here are rarely aggressive. Confrontations are always avoided. When a woman marries, she is wife to all the brothers. It avoids a lot of trouble."

I found this incredible. "How about loneliness - the biggest psychiatric problem in the West. How do they fare here in the long winter when everyone is confined to their houses?"

"No loneliness," replied Dr. Sessu. "This is probably the most important of all, no one is ever lonely. All winter long people get together, drink *chang*, have festivals, care for their animals and children."

"No one is ever lonely." I was to hear the same story over and over during my stay in the valley. Was loneliness the price of our "progress" in the West?

Fearful of fleas and lice, that night I slept on the stone veranda of the government bungalow while the Tikomorans bundled together for warmth under their blankets in a single bed. A cold moon beamed a luminous white light over the valley. The falling temperature stilled the sound of avalanches from the opposite bank.

In the morning, the doctor sent over fresh eggs for our breakfast. After a lavish repast of onion omelet and rice, we set off on foot for Keylong - twenty kilometers upriver. Hugging the left bank of the Chandra, we trudged through the wild and beautiful valley past mid-day, arriving at the outskirts of the town in early afternoon.

The large village of Keylong is splendidly situated high on the right bank of the River Bagha about five kilometers above union with the Chandra. Flat-roofed clay houses were strung out above brown fields that sloped down to the river below. The village was enclosed by high snow-capped peaks on either side of the steep valley. Clinging to the hillsides far above them were small monasteries. Prayer flags fluttered from their distant rooftops.

After settling into the otherwise empty government rest house in the village, I walked down the road to pay a courtesy call on the local District Commissioner. Delighted to welcome a foreign guest, especially one who spoke English, he regaled me with stories and histories of this remarkable valley.

"In the nineteenth century," he explained, "the Reverend Mr. Hyde, a Moravian missionary and his family settled in Keylong. They only converted twenty-nine people to Christianity in as many years, and most of these reverted to Buddhism after they left. But the Moravians changed the life of this valley and made it one of the most prosperous regions in India. They planted forests for wood, built latrines and showed the people how to prepare compost heaps for gardens and fields. They taught them spinning, carding and knitting wool, and how to build chimneys for tiny stoves to warm the huts during the eight month winter. Above all, they brought the potato from central Europe."

The next day I visited the small library in Keylong, a legacy of the British. There I read a report on Lahoul by the British commissioner writing in 1869, ninety-nine years before my visit.

"There is a strong neighborly feeling here and there is little wrong doing or strife," he wrote. "Living in a local household, one does not hear an angry word or quarrel for days on end." He described the women as "soft and gentle in manner with a shy and modest demeanor. Seldom is a woman's voice heard in anger or argument."

However, this peaceable state of affairs was evidently considered less than perfect by the writer, who noted with chagrin that these same women "hold the marriage tie in very little regard. And treated as they are by the males at whose disposal they are completely, one can only be surprised at the levity of the wife."

Unlike their cloistered sisters of the plains, the women of these remote valleys were apparently protected from the puritanism enforced by both Hinduism and Islam. This was perhaps because they were enclosed by high mountains that protected the valley from invaders.

"Chastity has never been a strong point here," continued the report disapprovingly. "It is but too true that the ideas of both sexes with regard to the sacredness of the marriage tie are not in accord with the view of more cultivated races."

I wondered as I read his words what the commissioner would think of the condition of the marriage tie among "cultivated races" especially in the "advanced West" a hundred years later.

Buddhism flourished in the remote valleys of Lahoul and Ladakh from the fifth century. The area, sometimes known as little Tibet, was protected by high mountains from outside invasion until the thirteenth century when the valleys were conquered by the Mongol emperor Kublai Khan. Four hundred years later, Spiti was occupied by the adjoining Buddhist kingdom of Baltistan which ruled the region until the seventeenth century. Tibet then briefly regained control. Soon after, the Muslims invaded, converting the Baltis, now citizens of Pakistan, to Islam. In contrast, in Lahoul, which remained in India, Buddhist culture continued unbroken to the present. Now, with the road, hospital and schools built by India, old ways were changing. Still, the long, isolated winters preserved the native language, Lahouli, and religion, Mahayana Buddhism.

The following day, Tikomoran, the guide and I left a delighted Tikomoran the porter in the rest house to nap while we climbed up to visit the magnificently situated monastery at Kardung. Perched on a ridge at nearly l2,000 feet beneath the snow-covered Rangcha peak 4000 feet above, the monastery was only forty years old at the time of our visit and housed thirty lamas and nuns. Each had his or her own cell. Kardung *drukpa* (monastery) is of the Red Hat sect of Buddhist lamaism. Although nuns and lamas were considered equal, as in the rest of the world, some were more equal than others. Lamas could marry and nuns could not. Amorous interludes apparently occurred, however, and the local doctor told me it was not rare for a nun to bear a child.

When we arrived at the lamasery, we were welcomed by a sweet-faced woman around thirty years old. Her smooth brown skin stretched tightly over high cheek bones and a splendid broad forehead. Her head was shaved bare and she wore the faded saffron robes of a monk. Smiling gently, she led us through the three floors of the *gompa* (temple) and waited patiently as we examined the relics preserved there. There were ancient skulls, thigh bones, *thankas*, masks and silk-clad statues of the Tibetan Buddhist trinity (Buddha, Mila Ripa, Chenresi). The nun-guide answered my many questions and waited quietly while Tikomoran translated. Faded wall frescos depicted sexual acts of consort and *shakti* on one wall and the life of Buddha on the other.

After our tour of these somewhat startling images, Sister (as I called her, for I never learned her name) invited us to her cell for tea. To reach her quarters, we followed her through a labyrinth of narrow alleys between the multiple two-story clay buildings. Then we entered a courtyard where a bent old woman, barefoot, with shaved head and dressed in a saffron cloth tied over one shoulder, greeted us. Another nun, sturdy and fortyish, stood rinsing a tall wooden tea urn at the water tap beside our nun's dwelling. This Sister smiled but did not speak.

We followed our Sister up a notched ladder to the second floor of the silent building. Entering a tiny low-ceilinged cell just large enough for the three of us, she invited us to sit down on the earthen floor. The room was furnished only with a low clay stove in the center. One wall was pierced by a small window that provided soft light from the courtyard. The dirt floor was swept clean. Dried marigolds were thrust in a small glass jar on the window sill. Beneath them was a cupboard with two dishes, four cups and saucers and a teaspoon. Our hostess wiped their surfaces with her thumb and knelt to blow up the coals in the little stove.

Then she left with a large copper pot to draw water. I leaned back and tried to imagine how it would be to live always in this kind and silent place. When Sister returned with water and sticks for the fire, I asked her, through Tikomoran, to tell us something of her life.

"Because of polyandry, many women go unmarried here," she explained. "Our parents decide when we are still quite small which girls will enter the nunnery."

"And how is it for you? Are you quite happy here?" I asked.

"Oh yes," she smiled, "I am. I have a small garden and I work in the fields at harvest-time." Her family gave her a modest stipend. And like the lamas, she received money for food in return for prayers and *pujas* (religious ceremonies) performed in village houses that call for a nun or lama to pray for family members at times of sickness, weddings, births and deaths.

When the water began to simmer over the small clay stove, our hostess rose and shook powdered tea from a box on the shelf into the open kettle. With a long-handled copper ladle perforated with many small holes, she stirred the brew and poured in thick yellow buffalo's milk from a small earthen bowl. Silently, she disappeared again for a few minutes and returned with a plate with three large baked dough pretzel-like pastries. The tea was ladled into the cups and the pretzel-shaped snacks were passed around.

Sister now sat down in a half lotus position facing the stove in the center of the floor. Her fine face was luminous in the firelight. Her eyes were tranquil and gentle. She radiated the calm serenity I had so joyously recognized in other "enlightened ones," other "realized beings." Free of fanaticism or proselytizing, there was no exclusiveness to Sister's liberation. Perhaps most important, once liberated, there was no need to bow to any outside force or conform to any ritual. Serenity and happiness seemed to come from within - perhaps by opening up some new perceptual channel within the brain and mind.

"Do you ever feel lonely or long for companionship through the long winter?" I asked.

I think the question, translated by Tikomoran, had no meaning for her. Instead of replying directly, she told us of the joys of her life. Selected for the nunnery while still a child, she experienced no sudden conversion, no spiritual illumination and no tortured asceticism. Buddhism, like Hinduism, but in contrast to Christianity, Judaism and Islam, recognized no dualism between soul and body and required no belief in an external god. After achieving "enlightenment" through meditation, Buddha told his followers that true satisfaction lay in embracing "the middle way." This, I remembered, consists in knowledge of the four Truths.

The first of these is the truth of pain: Birth is pain, old age is pain, sickness is pain, death is pain - in short the aggregates of grasping are pain.

The second is the noble truth of the cause of pain and this is craving. The craving of passions, the craving for continued existence, the craving for non-existence.

The third is the noble truth of the cessation of pain. This consists of the remainderless cessation of craving, its abandonment and rejection.

The fourth truth consists of the means of arriving at the first three, namely, The Noble Eight fold Path: right views, right intention, right speech, right action, right livelihood, right effort, right mindfulness, right concentration.

Historically, this ethical teaching moralized the Indian doctrine of *karma*, which like the doctrine of rebirth, was adopted from Hinduism. *Karma* no longer meant a requisite number of sacrifices and gifts to Brahmans, but became in Buddhism an idea beyond ritual. Instead of judging merit by performance of religious rites, *motive* became the criterion of moral action. I wondered whether the serenity in this small woman's eyes sprang from compassion, non-attachment or the particular rapture that reportedly results from right meditation. I suspected it was from right motive. But I did not know the words to ask.

As dusk approached, Sister lit a candle. The small flame turned our seated shadows into giant Buddha-like images on the wall. I wondered for the thousandth time whether religion and mysticism originate in new sensory channels normally closed but that open during meditation, prayer or following use of mind-bending drugs.

And was mental illness related to these experiences? I remembered talking one evening years before with a severely schizophrenic young patient in the silent cafeteria at St. Elizabeth's Hospital in Washington D.C. Suddenly she stopped talking and listened. "Don't you hear the planes coming?" she asked fearfully. The empty room was absolutely silent.

Then, a full two minutes later, I heard the sound. A plane was flying over the city. Some of my other patients had similar extrasensory or hyper-sensory experiences. Some heard the sounds of the sheets rustling down the hall where nurses were making the bed.

"The nurses are trying to arouse me by rubbing the sheets," complained one young man. Another patient told me that the room lights were suddenly blindingly bright or that my face turned into that of a savage animal. Was this a sudden access to a real world out there closed to the rest of us by well-developed brain filters and gates? These are non-questions in the East. There, the answer is always "both."

After half an hour, we rose to leave. Sister led us down a long dark hallway that opened onto the flat roof of the next dwelling. The sun was setting. Prayer flags waved gently against a bright crimson sky. We stood silently for a time watching the glow on the flanks of the great snow peaks. As the light faded, the mountains turned white and cold again. Bowing our thanks to Sister, we started quickly down through the gathering dusk.

In the terraced fields below the monastery, women still were bundling great piles of fodder to carry down to the village. The "ho-hoing" sing-song shout of the yak drivers drifted up from the fields where plowing would continue until dark. As we rounded a corner on the steep trail, a pair of bellicose, shaggy dzos suddenly appeared, walking single file. I jumped hastily behind a rock, much to the amusement of a very small boy who was herding the shaggy giants, stick in hand.

High on the hillside on the other side of the valley, the prayer flags of Shershun lamasery floated against the sky. By the time we reached the bridge and started the climb up the opposite bank toward Keylong, the first stars gleamed above the giant *chorten* outside the village.

That night, I slept dreaming I had lived forever in that magic place.

Next morning, after breakfast of *chapatti* and instant coffee, Tikomoran the guide and I set out for the Shershun monastery, 3000 feet above us on the opposite hillside overlooking Keylong. The little town bustled with activity as we walked through in the early morning light. Women in traditional costumes of brown wool carried bundles of faggots, patted dung pies for fuel against the walls of houses to dry, carded wool or stood knitting at their doorsteps. Men and boys laughed and washed themselves at the outdoor faucets. Several teenage boys, wearing Western shirts and trousers, stood about on corners making loud comments as we passed.

"They are not polite, these fellows," Tikomoran muttered. "They are too rich and too idle."

As we climbed above the town, we looked down on the flat-roofed houses, the post office and on the schoolyard where about forty 6-7 year-olds sat on the ground cross-legged in respectful rows chanting their lessons. *"This too will pass,"* I thought to myself, remembering the disorderly "modern" classrooms back in the U.S.

The two-story mud houses grew further apart as the steep path left the village. Children in ragged pajama-like outfits played tag on the rocks, herded goats and sheep or carried jugs of water. Yaks, who cannot live below l0,000 feet (they develop enlargement of the liver according to the local doctor), plodded torpidly along the terraced fields dragging huge wooden plows to the singsong shouts of their drivers. Women called out greetings to us from a stream bank where they were scrubbing clothes. An old man and woman, picturesque in Tibetan cloaks and peaked hats, stopped to show us what they were knitting as they walked. Stockings of gorgeously colored and patterned wools, they were a legacy, an example, of the great gifts the Moravian missionaries had left behind.

After climbing for several hours in bright sunshine, we reached the first *chorten* (*stupa*: a mound commemorating the Buddha's death) of the lamasery. Shershun, at l3,000 feet, clings to a hilltop overlooking a wild and barren valley beyond. Far below, the Bagha torrent was like a silver thread. Above us soared magic snow peaks. The monastery was silent and peaceful. Above the cluster of flat-roofed two-story buildings, covered with prayer flags, a huge *chorten*, newly whitewashed, dominated the hillside. The scent of sunshine on warm earth mingled with the odor of burning juniper. The golden dome on the *gompa* reflected light and peace. I felt as thought I'd come home to a previous life that was truly mine.

We sat in silence gazing at the mountains and valleys until Tikomoran, impatient for me to see the temple, spotted some movement below. He hailed a figure in a faded apricot robe emerging from one of the multi-storied clay dwellings. Walking toward us was a shaven-headed nun of perhaps fifty years with a simple, open face. After greeting us, she called an old lama from inside the building. A little regretfully, for I was entirely content to just sit empty-minded in this place forever, I rose to follow them inside the temple.

Like most such temples I visited in Lahoul, this *gompa* was a three-storied building of solid clay. We left our climbing boots, huge and clumsy next to the lama's worn sandals, outside the doorway on the ground floor. The lama led us into a dark passageway where several dozen copper prayer wheels were mounted between the high walls. Inside the small low building was a large, brilliantly decorated prayer wheel, at least ten feet high. With a wide smile, the lama showed me that by turning it, I could cause a gong to ring loudly. Then he unlocked the heavy door to the temple with a large copper key hanging on a braided rope under his cloak.

We followed him up a dark stairway of packed earth into a large altar room. Against the far wall, a long low shrine featured a giant serene-faced Buddha in a yellow silk gown. On either side, he was flanked by statues of the great Tibetan teachers, Chenresi and Mila Repa. In pigeon-holes on the walls on either side of this Trinity, the long narrow volumes of the Mahayana Doctrine were wrapped in faded red satin.

Our lama pointed out the *Kanjur*, l08 volumes of the precepts, and the *Tanjur*, the commentaries, *sutras* (prayers) and charms. On a low table before the statues were *phurpas*, the daggers used by lamas to kill demons. Beside them were half a human skull and a brass encased thigh bone, said to be from a virgin female. These objects were used in tantric rites practiced by certain lama sects that emerged from the supraposition of Buddhism on the ancient animist and Bonpo religions of these parts.

I was surprised to find three Hindu gods - a grotesquely leering Kali, a three headed Brahma, and dancing Shiva - flanking the giant Buddhas. The lama explained, "Buddhists of north India worship God in all his forms." Indeed, in Buddhist Nepal I had often seen a figure of Christ among the other deities on similar altars.

The lama lit three of the 108 butter lamps on the altar. I put a five-rupee (about seventy-five U.S. cents) note in the empty shell. Then, following the lama, I knelt, as I do to the gods in every religion, and touched my head to the floor before the shrine.

The large room was exotically decorated in oriental style. Red lacquered pillars, lavishly painted with birds and flowers, supported a roof under which a cloth of faded flowered silk hung over most of the chamber. A huge leather drum was suspended between two slender poles near the windows. Two rows of long narrow benches were placed on reed mats and faded rugs. Before them, trumpets, gongs and tea bowls of the daily service were at each now empty place (evening prayers would start at sunset). On the walls, quite fresh and new looking frescoes depicted the life of the Buddha. Another fresco depicted a grinning Kali, Hindu goddess of evil. Shakti (the active energetic aspect of a god, personified in his wife) was in blissful connubial embrace with her consort.

Leaving this chamber, we climbed steep wooden stairs to the floor above. We entered a similar room where grotesque masks were hanging on the walls. A small altar held dusty figures of the Buddha, saints and teachers. After inspecting these, we followed our aged guide up a ladder onto the roof. There was a stupendous view of the valley and of the Kardung Monastery on the opposite hilltop below the ice and snow covered Goshang peak. The feeling of exaltation was overpowering. *No wonder,* I thought, *that men, and women too, believe in gods.*

I asked the old lama about his life here. Speaking to my guide in Hindi, he explained that his order was part of the *Drukpa* or Red Hat sect. *Drukpas* strike a balance between meditation, family life and work.

"Some family men come here for meditation through each winter and return to work in their fields when the snows are gone," he explained. "Many lamas are married and life is not all prayer and solitude." Indeed, I had heard that ritual dancing festivals held in the fall were enlivened by much *chang* (an alcoholic brew made from barley).

Both the lamas and nuns who live here were "on call" much like doctors for the surrounding villages. They prayed at the bedside of the sick, attended births, deaths and marriages. *Pujas* (special prayer ceremonies) were held at the beginning of the sowing season, at harvest, at dedications of new buildings or the appearance of omens, both good and evil. Sick people were treated with prayers, chants, incantations and ritual burning of concoctions of herbs. People who received these services paid the nuns and lamas with small amounts of money, or food and *chang*. Much of the latter two were eaten and drunk at the ceremonies.

If there is a death in the village, the head lama is called. Leaning over the body, he whispers, "You are dead" three times. Then the dying man's soul sees the body of the beast of the year he was born. There are twelve of these in the Tibetan calendar: rat, ox, tiger, rabbit, dragon, snake, horse, sheep, monkey, bird, dog, pig. Lamas then read prayers in the house for three days. Meanwhile, much *chang* and tea are drunk. Formerly, the bodies were broken up and fed to the birds. Nowadays, the body is burned while drums are beaten loudly to keep demons away. The house where a death has occurred is plastered with fresh dung. Barley flour and *chang* are sprinkled on the floor. The body's bones are collected in a bag. Sometimes they are thrown into the place where the rivers Chandra and Bagha meet.

Occasionally both lamas and Hindu brahman priests were called in to perform the death rites. Death held no fear for either religion, except of rebirth! *The opposite of Christianity,* I thought with wonder.

The old lama told us a story. "Once upon a time there was a terrible drought in this valley. The streams dried up, crops died and men suffered. The village people asked a *saddhu* (holy man) who lived in a cave close by to come and help them. The saddhu demanded a sacrifice. First he asked for a dog. 'No,' said the village elders, 'the dog guards the house.' 'Then give me a cat to sacrifice', said the saddhu. 'Oh no,' said a man, 'the cat lies on the hearth and keeps the mice from the grain.' The saddhu turned to the man's sister. 'Then you must sacrifice this woman,' he said. Both brother and sister agreed, but the woman begged the saddhu to bury her with her breasts out so she could suckle her children. This he did. She died in two days.

"From that day forward two springs gushed forth from the ground at that place. They can still be seen there today."

The old lama pointed his finger toward a low hill. My fantasy of liberated women faded. I did not ask whether the lama too, thought it better to sacrifice a woman than a dog or cat. Through Tikomoran, I asked him why more villagers had not been converted by the industrious and praise-worthy Moravian missionaries during their long years of proselytizing and good works in the valley.

"The Christian idea of only one son of God is foreign to us," he explained. "We believe that we are all, including God, a part of one eternal substance. The idea of a Jesus who dies to save mankind from sin is meaningless to people whose religion teaches that death is only the departure of the soul for another body. Our religion teaches that only through death without rebirth can perfect happiness - the end of suffering - the end of clinging - be achieved."

As dusk fell, I rose reluctantly. We retrieved our shoes. Accompanied by the lama, we walked slowly back down the hillside through the cluster of monastery dwellings. An elderly nun, her robe faded to pale saffron, barefoot and gnarled as a witch, climbed up from the forest, bent double under a load of faggots. We passed beneath the giant *chorten.* The lama told us it contained the body of a famous saint placed in an earthen jug along with several varieties of grain, oil, a lamp, salt and seven cups of water. Inside were also bits of gold, silver and prayers inscribed on paper.

"These people worship the devil," the competent English nurse at the mission hospital in Kulu told me a week or so before, her calm intelligent eyes suddenly flashing with anger. If so, it seemed to agree with them.

We bade the old lama goodbye and descended through the cluster of dwellings surrounding the gateway. An old woman, wrapped in a brown wool blanket, ran from the house and tenderly bent over a weeping two-year-old as she picked him up from the dirt courtyard. A young man, thirtyish, in faded jeans and white T-shirt followed her. Seeing us, his whole face lit with a smile. He walked over to the gate to exchange greetings. Much to my surprise, he spoke English as well as Hindi and Lahouli.

As we exchanged *namastes* with folded hands, I was struck by his eyes, which had that strange clarity and serenity that only much later I learned to recognize as the special gaze of the "liberated ones," Realized Beings.

The young man's name was Norbu. He was a monk in this lamasery. The child was his. The old woman - she was only fifty - was his mother. When I told him I was an American, he seemed delighted and invited us to take tea in his room.

We followed Norbu into the narrow hallway of the many roomed dwelling and up a wooden ladder into a tiny chamber furnished only with reed mats on the floor. After inviting us to sit down, he slipped out the door.

We sat on the mats and looked around the small room. In addition to the floor mats, a small red and blue striped cotton rug and two metal trunks completed the furnishings. Three photos were stuck on the mud plastered wall: one of the Dalai Lama, another of the old abbot of this monastery, now deceased, and a third of a large family, his own family, in Lahouli dress. On the opposite wall was a 1979 calendar from the Tibetan Medical Center in Dharamsala printed with both English and Tibetan dates. A pair of black cotton trousers hung on a nail on the third wall. A green and red cotton cloth sagged limply over the ceiling. A single small window behind me looked out on the great peaks across the valley where the Kardung Monastery nestled against the snow line.

Norbu returned after a few minutes with a plate heaped with brown crisp baked circlets of dough similar to the giant pretzels we had eaten the day before at Kardung monastery. Then he hurried out again, returning with a cauldron of strong tea, sweet with sugar and fresh milk. Speaking a mixture of English and Hindi, he told us about himself.

A monk since childhood, Norbu was unusual in having graduated from the secular school in Keylong in addition to pursuing his religious studies in the monastery. Although he was a monk, he also worked part time as a translator of Lahouli to English or Hindi in the civil office in Keylong. He also farmed several acres of barley on the hillside and kept goats and chickens. Married and father of two sons, he wished for nothing.

"My life is going smoothly and there is nothing I need. This is the goal of life – not to desire too much. Desire leads to unhappiness."

Through the small window beside me a shaft of rosy light fell across the plain little room from the glow now touching the great peaks across the valley. The moment was so silent yet so golden I was afraid to speak. Norbu rose to fetch more tea. When he returned, I asked him to tell me how he spent his days in the monastery? Reading? Writing? Meditation?

"Yes, all of these," he replied, smiling, "but *Samadhi* (meditation) is the most important."

Apologizing for my ignorance, I asked him to explain about meditation, what it was, why it was thought to be so useful to empty the mind, our most creative possession.

Norbu paused a long time before he spoke. His eyes were on the mountains where the crimson glow of sunset slowly changed to pure crystal white.

"The satisfaction to be found in meditation is superior to any other," he said finally. His eyes left the little square of window and met mine steadily. "Especially it is superior to clinging and attachment. Coupled with doing for others, it brings infinite peace."

He paused, then continued, "*Compassion, non-attachment, meditation*, these are the essential trinity of Buddhism. They represent an enormous moral leap from Hinduism from which they sprang. For Hinduism, and perhaps Christianity as well, rely heavily on the influence of *Karma*, one's actual deeds in this life, for determining how well or how badly one will fare in the next. Non-attachment is the antidote. Indeed the abolition of suffering, clinging to nothing, we can lose nothing."

What a liberation, I thought, *but then what would happen to the world?*

"And meditation, what is it?" I asked. (Once, many years before, I had been initiated into TM (transcendental meditation) by a well-loved Indian colleague. However, the hocus-pocus of the mantra and the uncomfortable sitting posture bored me to distraction).

Norbu smiled gently. "You sit quietly and follow where your mind goes," he explained. Once again his serene gaze passed over my head to the window and the mountains. Surprisingly, his serenity was contagious. I felt infinitely satisfied. Only later, when I learned to recognize this same strange contentment in the presence of other "liberated beings," I began to understand the powerful transference that Enlightened Ones can evoke from those who crave similar happiness.

Variously called "energy vibrations" or "aura," this magnetism is perhaps born of our need for guidance so we can approach worlds and concepts of which we are only dimly, inchoately aware. Thus, the power of the guru, the priest and the charismatic leader. The parallel to psychoanalysis was also compelling. But psychoanalysis, unlike my young *bodhisatva*, (pursuer of Enlightenment) seemed to be a ritualization of narcissism, a process dedicated entirely to the self. Buddhism is almost exactly the opposite – dissolution of the self in union with the universe. Still, I thought, both are focused on self, not on the rest of a needy world.

We talked on for almost an hour. Then Norbu asked me to meditate with him. Sitting very erect and quiet with his eyes open, he stared straight ahead. Instantly, I saw him go far, far away from where we sat. Tikomoran closed his eyes. I couldn't be sure whether he too was meditating or just dozing off. Somewhere in the back of the house a woman called to a child. Although I still didn't know how to meditate, I felt unattached, happy and as though I could sit there forever.

It was dark when we rose to leave. I had not felt such a pang at parting since many years before on my first trip to the Himalayas. That time too I turned my back on the earth's highest mountains and went back home to work and family. Apparently, I was still not yet ready to let go of striving (for what, fame? Certainly not fortune, a desire to make a better world?) Once again as we stood in this high, infinitely moving space, I turned around and started the descent for home.

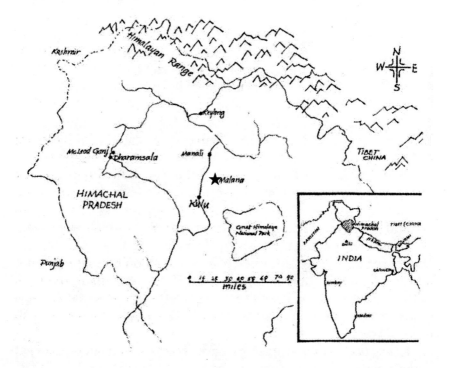

Chapter III

MALANA: WHERE I WAS AN UNTOUCHABLE

"The evil men do lives after them; the good is oft interred with their bones."

-*Shakespeare*, Julius Caesar, *Act III*

"Enjoy every day because not every child grows up to be a person!"

-Amos Oz

The first dwelling we reached was large and strongly built of dark brown wood. Ragged children stood silently around it gazing at us. When we drew closer, they ran speedily back toward the building. There were a number of extremely strange looking people sitting on the floor of the low veranda.

Outlandishly dressed, with long black uncombed hair, wild, rough men in soiled white homespun suits or shawls suddenly stopped whatever they were doing as they caught sight of us. They stared incredulously. Peals of coarse, unpleasant laughter and unfriendly shouts followed. A particularly blowzy female, whose open to the waist blanket dress exposed heavy pendulous breasts, shrieked with laughter as she clutched her nursing baby.

It is hard to say who was more shocked, them or us. Even my guide, Zing, although he claimed to have been here before, seemed nonplussed. I felt as though I had suddenly entered the back ward of a mental institution of thirty years ago - the soiled blanket dresses tied on every which way, the wild staring eyes, the rude remarks, the total absence of any social niceties were beyond anything I had experienced outside of an asylum for the insane.

It all started the week before. I was sitting in the living room of Dr. Kay's small apartment in Manali, a town in the Himalayan foothills of north India.

"If you really want to study the religious impulse," said Dr. Kay, "You must visit Malana. It's one of the strangest places in India, with a religion all its own."

It was early dusk. We were drinking tea in the doctor's small apartment above the government medical dispensary in Manali, the first town on the River Beas after it escapes, foaming and frothing, from the snowbound foothills of the western Himalayas into the Kulu valley. I arrived from the Keylong valley where I had been visiting remote Buddhist monasteries on the northern slopes of the great Himalayan wall. As I usually do, I stopped to make a courtesy call on the government physician, always a source of local lore and nearly always happy to welcome a traveling member of our trade.

"If you go to Malana," Dr. Kay continued, "you must carry all your own food and bedding for they will give or sell you nothing. Most important of all, cows are sacred - don't wear or even carry - anything made of leather or they won't let you near the village."

I gazed out the open windows of his apartment. Just below, the main road through the town was filled with a variety of foot traffic - mostly people from the surrounding hills. Women, wearing gold rings through their ears and noses were bent under loads of grass or hay. Men wore homespun off-white wool knickers, round brightly embroidered pillbox hats and long-sleeved shirts. Their dark western-style vests or suit jackets were purchased from the truckloads of second-hand clothing that arrive all over the third world from the affluent west. Urban men, wearing black suit jackets and factory-made cotton pants, their flat Mongolian faces alert and watchful, pushed through the crowd. Turbaned Sikhs, Spitis, Tibetans and tall Lahoulis lugged children, water jugs, piles of blankets, huge sacks of grain or skins of headless whole sheep, legs tied with thongs and bodies bulging with grain.

Two *Harijan* ("untouchable") women from south India, infinitely graceful but painfully thin, strode past. Their heavy silver ankle bracelets were like leg irons and their heads were straight and steady under heavy loads of handmade bricks. There was even a pair of Western hippies - the boy full bearded, wearing a white *lungi* (pajama-like shirt); his companion oddly indecent in tight white muslin trousers and bra-less beneath a gossamer thin Indian shirt. I turned back to my host.

"Stranger than where I've just been?" I asked, disbelieving. For a week I had been in the Lahoul valley, across the ice-covered Rothang Pass to our north. At 13,300 feet, the Rothang is an icy but penetrable barrier between the Indian subcontinent and the hidden valleys of Lahoul and Spiti which like Ladakh, were once part of Tibet. I was visiting remote Buddhist monasteries, among a people and in a valley very different from any I had known before. Now I felt as though I'd just returned from another planet. Still under the spell of these remote eyries, it was difficult to return to earth.

Dr. Kay's wife brought tea, cups and a plate of sweets on a tray of polished wood. She sat down beside me on the divan. A slender woman, her pale skin guarded from the sun, she wore a filmy rose chiffon sari. Only half concealing her fragile form, her dress seemed somehow incongruous in this Himalayan hill village where sturdy, dark-skinned women wore long, heavy, blanket-like gowns of brown homespun wool and orange and black shawls.

"Although I have never been there, it is said to be one of the most interesting towns in India," she murmured. After pouring tea, she turned to continue what must have been her daily pastime, gazing silently out the window at the teeming street below.

"What's so remarkable about Malana?" I asked. Dr. Kay lit an American cigarette and settled into his cane chair.

"I also have never been there," he replied. "But my brother, a psychiatrist in Dharmsala, has visited several times. He says it's one of the most primitive and isolated civilizations in the Himalayas - their language, religion, clothes, customs - all completely different from any other place. If you go there," he continued, "you must carry all your own food and bedding, for they will not give or sell you anything. Most important of all, cows are sacred. Don't wear or even carry anything made of leather or they won't let you near the village."

I gazed out the window and wondered how much stranger this north Indian province, Himachal Pradesh, could get. I watched as a robust little tribal woman, the edges of her ears circled with dozens of tiny gold rings, trudged past on wide bare feet. She carried a huge load of grass on her head and a sleeping baby wrapped snugly on her back. A bearded *sadhu*, pipestem thin legs like crooked brown twigs, stopped. With quiet dignity, he extended his begging bowl with a claw-like hand toward the hippie couple. They stared at him through glazed, stoned eyes. The old sadhu sank down wearily on his haunches in the shade.

I was intrigued by the mystery of Malana. Dr. Kay promised to find a guide if I wanted to go there. The very next day, he told me of a man who knew the route to Malana, some Malana language, and a little English who would be willing to accompany me. I was delighted.

On the following morning, a young Lahouli of thirty or so, dapper in pink denim jeans and shirt, presented himself at my door. He told me his name was Tenzing. Not wanting to compete with Sir Edmund Hillary's Tenzing Norgay of Everest fame, I asked him if I might shorten it to Zing. He agreed.

After rudimentary conversation, limited by the fact that we shared a vocabulary of only about fifty words, we set off to the bazaar to shop for our trip. Rice, glucose cookies, lentils, powdered milk, sugar and tea. Pointing to my leather boots and shaking his head in the unmistakable gesture for "no," Zing led me to a table piled with cheap red cotton tennis shoes. I bought us each a pair.

The next morning, I left the comfortable room I was renting at the upper end of the town. Carrying a large heavy pack of food, and a sleeping bag, I also carried assorted medicines and bandages in case the Malanese requested some doctoring. Reluctantly, I left behind my good leather boots and wore the new red tennis shoes. Zing was waiting outside, wisely wearing his own sturdy leather boots.

We set off on foot for the bus station in Manali. When we reached the station, we shoved through the crowds surrounding a decrepit gray bus. Zing hoisted our packs onto the roof and disappeared into a small shop to buy tickets. Although it was five minutes before noon, the scheduled departure time, only two people were on board the bus. There was no driver to be seen. I sat down contentedly outside on the steps of a tea shop to watch the action.

One of the most delightful aspects of bus and foot travel in rural India is becoming accustomed to never hurrying, as everything occurs one or two hours later than expected. Moreover, even if you miss the bus it doesn't really matter, as there is always another, if not today, then surely tomorrow. In the meantime, the sun is warm and life an unending series of surprises.

A procession of short brown men with burlap covered bales on their backs trudged past on flat bare feet. Two little girls in miniature versions of their mothers' brown blanket dresses, their small flat noses pierced with gold rings, ran by chattering gaily. Each had a baby brother or sister sleeping peacefully on her back.

Learning to sit quietly, doing nothing, without either boredom or frustration was a new way of life for me, one of my most precious gifts from India. There was no past and no future. My own existence seemed no more and no less than this moment and the passing crowd.

Across the road was a sturdy Tibetan girl in the traditional ankle length, *chuba* over a blue cotton blouse and the traditional green, red and white striped wool apron wrapped from front to back. She stood behind a makeshift stall piled with heavy machine-knit winter sweaters and caps. Manufactured somewhere in India, they were sold in the markets all over south Asia by the energetic Tibetans. Three Nepalese women stopped to stare at me and laugh, their eyes sparkling with friendly amusement. Two tall blond Westerners smelling strongly of *ganja* (marijuana) passed in flapping white Indian shirts, trousers and rubber sandals. Part of the generation of wandering hippies, they were treated with derision and amusement by the locals because they dressed badly, because their men and women touched and caressed in public and because they didn't work.

However, Manali is very popular with these young Westerners, especially Europeans. In the '70's, local families would put them up in their homes for as little as ten dollars a month and sell them plenty of "weed" for even less.

An hour went by before the bus driver suddenly emerged from the ticket office in a mad rush to depart. Passengers were now hustled and scolded aboard until every seat was full. My fellow travelers were small brown men in cotton breeches and *kurtas* (long shirts). Women wore Kulu-style blanket dresses and pill-box hats. With a clash of gears, we lurched off at twenty kilometers an hour over the rough twisting road that followed the River Beas south.

After nearly two hours of winding through the valley, we reached the town of Kulu. I looked down from the dusty bus window on long rows of open stalls where clouds of flies swarmed over piles of grapes and bananas. Grains and spices glowed in bins open to the sun. During a long stop, I drank two cups of sweet milk tea brewed by a charming boy of eight. In the back of the tea stall I exchanged pleasantries with his old father who spoke excellent English with what seemed to be an Oxford accent. Rumbling off again, we soon reached the town of Buntar at the confluence of the Beas and Parbati rivers. Zing rushed off the bus, scrambled to the roof, and threw down our packs.

Glad to be off the jerking, noisy, evil smelling bus, I hoisted my pack on my back and trotted after Zing as he strode rapidly through the town. We reached a narrow suspension bridge across the Beas, a remarkable affair of ropes supporting a double track of narrow planks spaced for the wheels of autos and wagons. When we reached the halfway point on the bridge, a jeep started to cross from the opposite side and met us head-on in the middle. Other foot traffic, including a small herd of sheep, was just able to squeeze past the jeep and the flimsy side rails of the bridge but my pack was too full and thus too wide to slip through.

"Too damn much stuff," I whispered under my breath.

The driver of the vehicle and his companion, both in tan army fatigues, refused to back off. A motorcycle and two bicycles behind me turned back, their owners muttering what I supposed to be oaths in the local language. Behind me, a young woman in Nepali dress with a sleeping infant on her back, grinned, encouraging assertive action. My newly acquired Asian serenity deserted me. Instead of giving way gracefully to the motorized vehicle, as all foot traffic customarily does in poor countries, I stood my ground.

The jeep honked furiously. I gesticulated, first angrily and then obscenely. The young soldiers in the jeep inched forward toward my toes, threatening but cautious. Behind me an old man bent double under a heavily packed goatskin stopped to watch. There was a standoff. Fists were raised on both sides. Insults were exchanged in Hindi and English. Zing, who had managed with his smaller pack to squeeze by the vehicle, came back to rescue me, as every good guide must. He signaled that I should pass my pack over the rail of the bridge past the side of the jeep. Then I was able to squeeze between the wretched jeep and the railing. The Nepalese mother followed me, shouting with laughter.

Mercifully, Zing now hoisted my heavy pack on his back, leaving me his lighter one. We continued our promenade on the other side of the river past the sagging thatched huts and shops of the old bazaar. I cringed as a child of not more than three or four shouted, "Hippie, hippie!" as I passed. I was, after all, fifty-five years old, a professor of two respected disciplines, drug-free and covered from elbow to ankle in clean shirt and trousers. Zing comforted me in broken English.

"The pack it is," he explained.

Another even more ramshackle bus was waiting down by the river bank. There was no sign of the driver, so I strolled down toward the shore. The acrid smell of urine and excrement discouraged contemplation of the broad and shining confluence of these sacred rivers descending from the pure snows to the north.

I returned to the bus and climbed aboard through the rear door. The vehicle was empty save for a couple seated halfway forward on the right. Their heads and shoulders were pressed close together in embrace. It is so rare, so unheard of, to see a man and woman clasped together in public in India that I took the seat behind them out of sheer curiosity. The girl was small and fragile, with long, sleek black hair hanging loose over the seat back. She pulled away from her friend, revealing a cameo-like oriental profile, delicate as a flower. Her companion was a red-bearded scruffy young man who looked back at me with wonderfully serene blue eyes. We exchanged greetings. The beautiful girl was Ceylonese and her burly friend was from the Bronx. They were on their way to bathe at the holy shrine at the hot spring of Makrinana.

During the next hour, the old bus slowly filled with a variegated crowd. There were barefoot farmers in soiled *dhotis* and ragged turbans, school children in neat uniforms, hill women with loaded baskets on their backs and a Hindu sadhu (holy man) in a faded apricot colored robe. Suddenly the sky darkened and the wind blew ominously. Waiting passengers hurried into the bus clutching huge parcels, but no rain came. Finally, we were off. The sides of our vehicle nearly scraped the houses on either side of the narrow alleys through the town.

The road to Jari wound steeply uphill. The bus strained noisily with effort. Dust poured in through the open windows. Soon everyone was coughing and spitting and banging the windows closed. The air quickly grew unbearably hot and stale, thick with fumes from the straining engine. As our vehicle negotiated a series of hairpin turns, most of the passengers under age ten began retching and vomiting on the floor. I passed around precious bits of Kleenex and my water bottle. Every few minutes the bus stopped for more people to get off or on. Although the children on the bus looked quite pale and miserable, the men continued laughing and joking. Tribal women gossiped happily, each holding a baby pressed tightly to her breast.

At last, exhausted with heat and thirst, we arrived in Jari. My neat traveling costume of blue trousers and matching cotton shirt had turned tan with finely powdered dust. When we got off, Zing climbed to the roof of the bus and tossed down the packs. A cloud of dust from the first pack flew in my face, blinding me. As I held out my arms to catch the second pack, it bounced on the road, spewing sweaters and toilet articles. A crowd of villagers gathered to watch impassively. When I reached down to retrieve the scattered bundles, the bus let out a nasty backfire, belching dust and fumes in my face as it screeched off.

I gave silent thanks that it was Zing's clothing that was strewn in the road and not mine. Then I saw the ruptured paper sacks of rice and lentils spilled out in the dirt beneath his socks and sweaters. Too tired and stiff from the journey to care, I trotted over to my own dusty bag and carried it to a squalid little teahouse, where I croaked hoarsely *"Chai, chai, meerbhany!"* (Tea, tea, please!).

By the time tea was brewed by the unkempt looking proprietor, Zing had retrieved his clothes and about half the rice. I was busy waving flies off his cup, having instantly downed my own and ordered more. Scrawny chickens pecked desultorily at our spilled provisions in the road.

We drank off several cups of the sweet milk brew and attempted to exchange greetings with the sullen villagers who stood silently watching us. After half an hour of being stared at, I paid the proprietor and we shouldered our packs to go off in search of the government resthouse.

Down a steep lane behind the village, the government bungalow was beautifully situated with a wide veranda overlooking the valley and mountains. Best of all, a water tap stood close by. Unfortunately, the bungalow was locked and the water tap dry. I threw my pack down on the porch, stretched out beside it and closed my eyes, leaving Zing to cope.

When I opened them again, the sun was disappearing behind the dark hills and the air was chilly. From a ramshackle wooden dwelling nearby, curious villagers were staring down at me from the square hole in their house that served as a window.

The government *chowkidar* (caretaker) arrived and turned on the water. Apparently pleased to have a foreign guest, he led me inside to inspect the flush toilet, the function of which he proudly demonstrated. There were electric lights, but no fuel for cooking. The two rooms were dark and musty with disuse. The beds, covered with cotton mattresses, looked suspiciously flea-ridden and less inviting than the veranda. I signed the visitors' book and paid four rupees for both of us, about twenty-eight U.S. cents. I was more than a little surprised to discover that although Jari was the jumping-off place for the climb to Malana and other remote valleys, no foreigner had signed in for at least the six years of the book's existence.

After sunset, Zing and I climbed back up the hillside to the open shed-like tea house in the middle of the town. The same untidily dressed man brought us the only items available, *chapattis* and small bowls of fiery curry. A foraging tour of the village turned up no rice. We found and bought the few packs of glucose cookies in the shops. Returning to the rest house, I laid my sleeping bag out on the veranda. Zing settled down inside on one of the beds, clearly puzzled why I avoided the relatively luxurious indoor quarters.

Next morning we rose before dawn, washed, dressed and packed up before the town awakened. In the absence of fuel, we breakfasted on the glucose biscuits and water, then hoisted our packs and set off for Malana. Halfway down the steep hillside to the river I knew I was in trouble. I could feel every rock and pebble through the thin rubber soles of my new Indian tennis shoes. I was carrying Zing's pack, as it was much lighter than mine, but with no belly band, it rubbed steadily and abrasively against my hip bones. When we reached a wooden bridge, I stopped for the third time to shorten the straps before beginning the long ascent up the opposite bank.

Now we started climbing. The trail was good and the morning fresh and cool. Zing in the lead, we followed the Malana River upward. Swollen with melted snow, the river descended at the same sharp incline that we were climbing. Alternating between steep falls and roaring torrents, sudden broad pools of quiet water appeared and became a murmuring stream where the trail flattened out. On one of these small plateaus was a charming meadow where wild-looking children were sleeping beside a flock of goats. A few yards further on a family of gypsies called to us in a strange tongue from their campsite by the river. Through the silver mist of early morning, I saw an old woman stirring a witch's cauldron over a blazing fire. Once again, I was overwhelmed with a sense of entering another world.

As the trail rose, we entered a deodar and pine forest so dense that the sun, hot now in the clearings, felt barely warm. After two hours of steady climbing, we suddenly came face to face with the strangest humans I had ever encountered on any trail anywhere in the world.

They were wild-eyed people - four or five men followed by an equal number of women. Indescribably dirty, they were dressed in rough - handspun wool blankets. None replied to our greeting. They simply stared with wide, mad eyes. I stepped off the trail in the brush to let them pass, smiled and folded my hands, giving cheery *namaste*s. No one returned my greeting. They just stared, evidently as astonished as I was. As soon as we had gone by, they burst out laughing and chattering in a strange tongue. I looked back. They all stood in the path, still staring at me with those mad glittering eyes.

"Malana people," Zing explained, disparagingly.

After another hour of climbing it grew very hot. My canteen was empty. I stopped to fill it from the wide torrent that rushed down over giant boulders beside us. As we rested, a middle-aged man in dark cotton trousers and worn jacket carrying a home-made leather knapsack caught up with us and sat down to talk. Zing passed around cigarettes. I shared out the last packet of Gluco wafers. The stranger spoke Hindi. An herb gatherer of Ayurvedic medicines, he was on his way to Malana to buy medicinal plants collected by the villagers. I asked him to tell us something about the place.

"There are really three Malanas," he began. "One is at 8000 feet, one at l0,000 and one at l2,000. The highest one will still be buried in snow. It is only used in summer when the animals are taken up for pasture. The people of the lower village marry only with those in the upper ones. No outsiders are welcome and none of the village people ever leave. There are no schools and no teachers."

"How about a doctor?" I asked hopefully, thinking I might be welcome if my credentials were known. The herb-gatherer replied that he thought there was a dispensary but that the villagers didn't like doctors or any other strangers. When we rose to continue our climb, he joined us.

"I hope you brought your own food," he continued.

I thought ruefully of the spilled rice and wished we had tried a little harder to find food in Jari the night before. However, Zing seemed confident that something would turn up, so I didn't worry long, although my stomach was already groaning with hunger. In five hours of steady climbing, we'd each eaten half a dozen Gluco wafers. I had drunk enormous amounts of water. Out of the shade, the sun was burning hot. Throwing caution to the breeze, I knelt down and lapped water greedily from the foaming river. After two more hours of climbing straight up, I had all but given up hope of ever reaching Malana or anywhere else. Suddenly we emerged from the forest. The steep narrow canyon of the river widened out onto a terraced hillside.

There was Malana, an incredible sight. Forty or fifty two-story houses built of alternating rows of mud—plastered stones and huge horizontal timbers clustered in no apparent order on a hillside. Below them the hill sloped abruptly down to another river at least two thousand feet below. There, a similar but smaller village clung to the steep apron of a high green hillside. I looked up and beyond for the third Malana, but there were only black mountains, their summits covered with snow. Beyond them, even higher, magnificent snow peaks rose to l5,000 or l6,000 feet.

The village before us was entirely silent. Zing took off his pack, sat down and untied the strings of his leather boots. Then he hid his boots carefully in the crotch of a giant oak. Still natty in gray wool socks and his pink denim trousers, he shouldered my pack again. We headed for the village. Wisely, he had apparently left the red tennis shoes I purchased for him at home.

Malana was picturesque enough with its large unpainted wood dwellings, but it was eerily silent. As we approached the first house, we were spotted by a child of around ten, ludicrously clad only in a burlap sack tied with a rope around the waist. He, or she had long matted hair and the same mad staring eyes as the folk we encountered earlier on the trail. The child ran, apparently terrified, toward the center of the village.

As we came closer, women and children, some similarly dressed, others draped in long soiled homespun blankets, appeared on the broad wooden second-story decks of their dwellings. Silently, they stood staring down at us with hostile eyes, clutching their babies and never returning our smiles or greetings. No one uttered a sound as we walked on. A few thin goats looked up briefly. They also stared unblinking at me before resuming their search for bits of grass. I wondered if we would be pelted with stones, as had happened a few years before when I walked uninvited into an old quarter of Herat in Afghanistan.

Somewhat daunted and just a little afraid, we continued cautiously toward the center of the village. We were followed by a growing crowd of boys and girls who came running from every direction to stand and stare at us. There was not a single greeting, not a single smile—a most uncomfortable feeling. I asked Zing to inquire about the dispensary where I hoped we might find a more congenial or at least a more articulate welcome. He spoke to one of the older boys, who shook his head uncomprehendingly. Zing's Hindi, Lahouli and Pahuri seemed to be having little effect.

"Ask him for the school," I whispered. A school is always my second backup, as teachers in India uniformly spoke good English. For the first time, the boy smiled and marched on ahead of us, his bare feet apparently impervious to the sharp stones on the path. In a few minutes we reached a new looking two-story wooden building with a wide veranda on the ground floor. I collapsed on this wide porch and gratefully threw down Zing's pack against the wall. When I turned back around, at least fifty children of all ages had gathered about twenty feet away from the edge of the veranda. They stood staring at me in solemn rows, the boys on one side, the girls on the other. More were coming at a trot from all directions. A few older men came along more slowly and stood with the boys. No one spoke as we gazed at each other.

After several minutes, Zing walked to the edge of the platform and announced loudly in Pahori, the mountain language of the Kulu valley,"Mem Sahib doctor es."

This proclamation was also received in stony silence. Suddenly, I remembered the balloons in my pack and hurried over to take them out of the outside pocket. I tore open the cellophane packet and came over to the edge of the porch, holding out a red balloon toward the nearest small boy. Fearfully, he shrank back in the crowd, his eyes never leaving my face. I blew up the balloon and stepped off the veranda toward the girls. The whole group shrank back. I sat down on the edge of the veranda and waited. Still no one spoke. Zing lit a cigarette and held out the pack toward an older man standing beside the troop of boys. The old fellow, thin and dressed in homespun breeches and shawl, clasped his hands behind him and stepped back, not uttering a word.

Never before, anywhere in the world, had I seen a poor man turn down a cigarette.

It was a good opportunity to examine each other. While most of the children stared at me silently, one or two of the girls began laughing and pointing at the apparent peculiarities of my appearance. Meanwhile, I had time to acquaint myself with the local fashions. The older girls were dressed like their mothers in soiled ankle length bulky blankets tied at the waist with rope. Their black hair was unkempt and untidily gathered in a single braid. Several had bright red spots painted on each cheek and in the middle of their forehead or chin. One wore a dingy little pillbox hat of brown homespun faced with red velveteen. All were barefoot. All stared steadily. Many girls had sleeping infants strapped on their backs.

Teenage boys in ragged trousers with a wool shawl pulled over a long cotton tunic stood in a separate group. Their short hair, evidently cut around a bowl, framed narrow faces and receding chins adding to their general look of idiocy. Larger boys elbowed smaller ones aside for a better view of us. Not one, however, approached within five yards of the veranda. Several times I called loudly, "Doctor, doctor, medicine," hoping someone might be sick and thus be more tolerant of our trespassing. But all kept their distance, never taking their eyes from my face.

Suddenly, a tall, thin, dark middle-aged man in black trousers and a soiled gray cotton shirt came running up the hillside. Skirting behind the crowd of boys and men, he came toward Zing who was sitting beside me on the corner of the porch. Although this new stranger looked at us, he was not staring. His eyes met mine with a gaze that was entirely different. His expression, if not welcome, was at least recognition, however tentative, of one human being for another of his kind.

"*Namaste,* hello," I said mildly, hoping he would not be as stunned at my ability to speak as the others appeared to be. The man clasped his hands in greeting and smiled broadly, revealing a few brown and broken teeth. He picked up the abandoned red balloon, blew it up then let the air escape and threw it on the ground in front of the clump of boys. Instantly, a ragged youngster snatched it up and clutched it tightly in his fist.

I handed the stranger the whole package of balloons lying beside me on the porch. He threw them one by one on the ground between us and the children. Each time, a child ran forward to retrieve it with a joyful shout. Then some of the older girls began to look interested. The schizoid staring left their eyes and they moved a little closer. One or two actually ran up for a balloon and grasped it tightly against her chest before running back to the others.

When the package was empty, our new friend introduced himself as Sanja Ram, the village chowkidar (local government representative). Happily accepting a cigarette from Zing, he threw several more on the ground. They were speedily retrieved by the elders standing by. Sanja Ram explained that we and all our belongings were untouchable to these Malana-ites. To approach any closer to us would defile them dangerously.

I nodded and smiled with relief — at least it meant we must be quite safe. Unless, of course, they decided to stone us. Sanja Ram laughed and shook his head.

"They don't like strangers," he said in passable English. "But if you don't touch them, and especially if you don't touch their temple buildings, they won't hurt you."

We asked whether there was any shelter where we could sleep and cook our rice. The chowkidar hospitably invited us to stay with his family. Gratefully, we shouldered our packs and followed him across the wide dirt path from our veranda refuge. Sanja Ram explained that the building where we had been sitting was the half-finished schoolhouse.

We walked through the main group of houses in the village down the hillside beyond followed by a troop of children. Many of them had an infant tied on their backs with a dirty blanket. Other children turned to stare and then ran away fearfully as we approached. Our status was considerably improved by following this genial sponsor. As the village chowkidar (government paid representative-cum-watchman), Sanji Ram was the intermediary between the villagers and all their external affairs. As we walked, he told us about the place.

"There are forty-four houses here," he said, "ten or twelve people to a house. There is no school or teacher yet, but the government wants to send one. The people don't want a school."

"What do they do for a doctor?" I asked

"There is a doctor, but he has gone off on a visit. He should be back in a few days." explained Sanja Ram.

Later I found that Malana's doctor was of Ayurvedic persuasion. This traditional ancient school of Indian medicine is based on the use of herbs, heat and cold and various exotic items, such as rat or bat droppings. Apparently, this gentleman, although paid by the government, was not often in residence. Nor was he consulted by Malana's citizens when he was there.

Sanja Ram's official post as the village chowkidar gave him a certain cachet, if not prestige. As the village clerk, he kept the vital statistics and collected taxes. His father held the job before him, and he himself had held the position for more than twenty years. As his father was not born in Malana and did not worship Jamlu, the Malana god, he was considered an outsider and was therefore an untouchable. Although Sanja Ram and his children were born in the village, their family background and lineage made them untouchables too.

A few children followed us at a safe distance as we walked across a wide open arena at the center of the haphazard jumble of houses that comprised the town. The clearing was flanked by two large three-story wooden buildings with wide slanting slate roofs and an arcade of wooden arches over the verandas extending from the first and second floors. Slender, spindle-shaped wooden pendants were suspended in a delicate fringe along the whole length of the overhanging roof edge. Sanja Ram cautioned us to keep our distance from the log veranda.

"Temple, don't touch!" he warned.

A crowd of ragged men, engaged in some sort of game with small sticks and stones, squatted on the temple porch. They stopped their game and stared at us silently. Some women and girls stood around in front of the temple, their thin arms and legs protruding from long heavy sack-like dresses. Each had a child slung like a bag of flour on her back. They sniggered and stared rudely as we walked by. Several shouted questions to Sanja in their strange hoarse tongue. Sanja answered cheerfully enough, his voice suggesting a certain deference. Later, he told us he was explaining our presence and agreed to keep us in line.

"Temple, don't touch," he hissed again as we passed a large square platform made of flat slabs of gray slate held together with mortar. He repeated the warning again as we passed a small dwelling without windows. Walking on, we passed more of the two-story houses constructed of alternate layers of horizontal timbers and mud-plastered stones. The second story of these dwellings extended chalet style out several yards over the ground floor where their animals were housed at night. A notched log leaning against the back of the house served as a ladder to the balcony and living quarters on the second floor.

At the far corner of the clearing, a ragged old man crouched by a pile of reeds. He was weaving them into a *kiltas*, the large cone-shaped backpack basket used by Himalayan people all the way from Baltistan in western Pakistan to eastern Nepal. Against the outside wall of the next house, a small dark man in a torn suit coat and homespun gray knickers sat on a broken stool at a cracked loom, tying a frazzled thread of wool. Beside him a girl of ten or so, a baby slung in a blanket on her back, sat on the packed earth, spinning from a long upright pole covered with raw yellow wool.

Sanja pointed to the largest of the buildings and explained, "In here is the god Jamlu. Even I have never seen him and I have lived here thirty-nine years. On Sunday they will take him out and parade him through the village. A goat will be sacrificed." He beckoned to Zing and suggested it would be politic for him to offer a cigarette to the temple caretaker, a dark rat-faced little man who stood frowning and silent outside the building. Taking two cigarettes from the offered pack, Sanja threw them on the ground near the little man's feet. Grunting approval, he picked up the cigarettes and placed one between his lips and the other in the pocket of his ragged jacket. The cigarette was startlingly white and clean against his brown skin and jet-black mustache. Only the snow peaks above the hills seemed of equal purity.

Smiling broadly and soothingly, Sanja Ram now explained that I was a doctor, visiting from America, and wanted to see the inside of the temple. Discussion was brief and one-sided. Although I could not understand a word of their strange tongue, the unkempt village elder was unmistakably saying there was no chance at all of going inside. Sanja tried to soften the man's vehement unfriendliness.

"Maybe later," he said to me, smiling. "You know, even I cannot touch their temples or enter their holy places." He stepped back deferentially to give the frowning priest in his scruffy suit plenty of room to pass without touching us. We did the same. The little man walked arrogantly down the middle of the path, avoiding our eyes and keeping a wide space between us, evidently in fear we would defile him by coming too close

A soft drizzle began to fall as we passed through the last village clearing. Two little boys, not more than three or four years old, left off their play - making small bonfires - to turn and stare at us. An old granny, the very picture of a witch, dressed in a sleeveless tunic of brown burlap, dashed out and picked up the smallest of these toddlers, evidently in fear we would defile him by coming too close.

Several boys and men left off their game of throwing little rocks in a square in the dust to stare. They made rude sounding remarks and laughed unpleasantly as we passed. The sky darkened. Clouds covered the sun. The dismal rain fell harder. We walked on past children of undistinguishable sex, each with a baby on its back. All ran away with a frightened expression as we approached.

At last we came to a long low building of dark wood, open on one side. A thin middle-aged woman, whose expression was softer and gentler than the harsh staring faces of the others, sat at a hand loom. A glowing orange-red scarf of Kulu valley design grew under her fingers. She looked up and smiled with her eyes.

"This is my wife, Mariya," said Sanja Ram.

For the second time since we arrived in Malana, I felt the warm message of friendship that passes from one human being to another through the eyes. With a start, I realized the enormous importance of eyes in establishing human contact. Eyes relay an instant signal of safety and friendship or of suspicion and dislike before a word is spoken.

Sanja explained who we were and that we were going to stay at their house. Mariya seemed delighted. Rising graciously in her ragged Kulu costume, she moved the loom to a dark recess in the back of the building and followed us through the rest of the village to their little cottage at the far end of the town.

Sanja Ram's house was set on a small plot of cleared land next to the last Malana-style house of the town. His house looked out on the path leading from the village to the terraced hillside below and was smaller and even more ramshackle than its neighbors.

A stream of women and girls, carrying huge loads of faggots on their backs, approached from around the bend of the steep path below. They stopped to stare at us unsmilingly, forcing us to step off the track so they could pass. When at last we reached Sanja's porch, I felt limp with relief. The seven-hour climb up to Malana was hot, fatiguing and painful for my poorly shod feet. The gauntlet of dislike we had run in the village was tense and unpleasant. I felt as though I had emerged from the back ward of a hospital of deteriorated, unpredictable psychotics. I was startled at how much I hated not being liked and accepted.

After piling our packs in a corner of his porch, we followed Sanja into the dark little house. Mariya immediately set to work stirring up the coals under a heap of ashes in a fireplace on the center of the floor of the back room. Soon she had water heating in a large blackened pot suspended over the blaze. The dark kitchen quickly filled with wood smoke.

Sanja Ram's two children now appeared. Sheelah was a thin girl of fourteen wrapped in a sleeveless brown blanket dress over a soiled dark cotton shirt. Myla, a five-year-old boy whose spindly legs and body seemed too frail to support his large well-formed head stared at us gravely. Both children were barefoot and anemic looking. After greeting them, I squatted down Indian style on the veranda supporting my back on the sturdy wall behind me. I closed my eyes while the two children stood in front of me and stared.

After four cups of sweet milk tea my spirits rose. Despite the drizzling rain, I began to look about the cottage with more interest. Our host, Sanja Ram, had lived in this village all his life as had his father and grandfather before him. Yet, for the Malanaites, he was untouchable, just as we were. As such, he was of great use to the little community since he was their only contact with outsiders and with the government.

Although Sanja was thin and obviously poor, his single-story cottage was reasonably well built and tidy. A small courtyard at the front was fenced with sturdy horizontal timbers to hold the family livestock - six lean and milkless cows. The little veranda was swept clean. Inside, the entryway led to two rooms. There was a large kitchen to the right with the clay fireplace for cooking in the center, but no chimney. Some, but by no means all the smoke escaped through a small window on the far side of the room.

The family of four slept on the floor of this room. A second room, furnished with a *charpoi* and reed mats, served as a sitting and guest room. Toilet facilities were the field behind the house. Beside the back porch, water ran in a wooden sluice from the hillside above.

The chowkidar's job was like that of a town clerk. Sanja kept track of births, deaths, deeds of land transfer and taxes. For this, the government paid him fifty rupees (about seven U.S. dollars) a month. Sanja supplemented this income by selling milk when his cows were not dry and by gathering medicinal herbs. He seemed glad to have us as guests. The whole family feasted on our remaining rice and lentils. After the meal, I was ready for a walk in the town.

Zing had had quite enough sight-seeing and seemed content to sit on the porch silently, not only that afternoon but throughout the length of our stay. This ability to sit totally without occupation for hours on end is a trait I have both envied and deplored among nearly all developing-world village people I have known.

Although theoretically on search for similar tranquility, I was restless. Taking my small movie camera from my pack (this was before the days of small TV cameras), I suggested to Sanja Ram and Sheelah that they show me the town.

As we walked into the village, Sanja Ram carefully instructed me what not to touch: temples, people, unidentified stone objects or anything I wanted to give away. The townsfolk, in their second exposure to this strange lady, now in the company of the town chowkidar, seemed somewhat less astonished. Women shouted and joked with Sheelah from their verandas. Men and boys asked Sanja in their strange tongue who I was. He told them that I was an American doctor. No one seemed impressed. I was not permitted to enter any building or dwellings. Children ran to a safe distance before turning to stare at me. Mothers herded toddlers out of my contaminating proximity.

I suggested to Sanja that we go to the bazaar to replenish our food supplies, entirely consumed at lunch. He assented eagerly, pointing out, however, that there was no bazaar. There was only a single shop to serve the entire village.

We stopped in front of a two-story house, indistinguishable from all the others in the little community. Sanja pointed to a room on the corner of the second floor, indicating that this was the village store. However, neither he nor any member of his family was allowed to enter. Naturally, it was off-limits to me as well. Instead, we stood waiting below the wide veranda that surrounded the overhanging second story of the house. A wild-haired woman with a swaddled infant sucking at her breast shouted down to ask what was wanted. Sheelah shouted something back.

After ten minutes or so, the *sojee* (storekeeper) came up the path. He was a wiry little man of around fifty with a small black mustache, dressed in a dark vest faced with red velveteen. He muttered a few words to Sanja but carefully avoided eye contact with me.

Sheelah placed a rather dusty dark amber glass bottle on a flat rock behind him. Speaking in Hindi, she asked for oil, rice and dahl. Without a word the *sojee* picked up the bottle and walked to the corner of his house. He climbed the notched log ladder to the wide veranda above. I started to follow as I wanted to see what was in the store. Immediately, I was called back by Sanja Ram, just as a huge black mastiff with a spiked collar rose with a low growl from behind the building.

Another woman, also carrying a baby, appeared on the veranda. Staring down at me nastily, she shouted something to Sheelah and laughed. Sheelah replied, as she did to everyone, in a tone of sweetness and humility. Although I could not comprehend one word of their language, the wild women's tone was clearly rude and unfriendly.

"Can't we go into the store to shop?" I asked Sanja.

"No," he answered, smiling. "Even I have never set foot in there, and I have lived here all my life." I wandered about, kicking the ground with my wretched cloth tennis shoes and trying to suppress a rising sense of outrage. I felt like stomping off haughtily telling him to keep his blasted rice and *dahl*. With no other source of food available, however, this seemed excessively arrogant.

Sheelah's cheerful voice at my elbow inquired in a mixture of Hindi and English whether I would also like to buy some tea and sugar. Grateful for her amiability in this dismal village full of suspicion and dislike, I agreed eagerly. Even if this one family's friendship meant I must feed them all, it was worth it to have a friend.

After ten minutes more, the little storekeeper finally emerged onto the balcony above. He crouched down to weigh the rice on an old-fashioned balance. Standing in the cold drizzling rain below, I felt senselessly chagrined and angry at being treated as an inferior at being forced to stand outside in the rain, humbly awaiting disposition of food at the pleasure of this rude, ragged fellow. Finally, he descended the ladder and placed our purchases on a large rock near the house. Then he laid a small slip of paper next to them, securing it under the partly filled bottle of cooking oil. Sheelah walked over, picked up the paper and handed it to me.

"Forty-eight rupees," she said anxiously, knowing it was a month's wages for her father. I held a fifty rupee note to the little storekeeper. He stepped back locking his hands behind him. Taking the note from my hand, Sheelah placed it on the rock. The *sojee* then stepped forward, put it in his pocket and fished for change in a dingy leather pouch. Two worn paper rupees were placed on the rock. Sheelah picked these up and handed them to me. By this time I again found myself unreasonably seething inside.

"So this is the tiniest taste of what it feels like to be an untouchable," I said to Sheelah.

Not understanding, or perhaps understanding too well, she smiled with no trace of bitterness. Then she led the way down the hillside toward her home at the edge of the village. Hostile stares and rude remarks followed our passing.

In the gray drizzling light, tiny children in rags still were building small bonfires and feeding them with bits of wood or dung. An untidy old crone in a burlap wrapper knelt warming her hands beside a fire kindled by a pair of four-year olds. Troops of little girls with babies on their backs followed us at a safe distance. They shrank back or ran off with fear in their eyes if I attempted to approach them. Men spinning yarn or weaving stared down suspiciously from the balconies of houses as we passed.

I suddenly remembered I was carrying my small movie camera under my raincoat. These village scenes were certainly worth remembering. Pointing to my camera, I asked Sheelah if she thought people would object to pictures. Sheelah turned to one of the village elders who had stepped back under the protection of the overhanging roof of his veranda to give us a wide berth as we approached his house. Much to my surprise, the man assented cheerfully to her request. Then, although all conventional manners were absent, and no one had returned my greetings or cheery smiles all that long afternoon, both children and adults now crowded forward and posed for pictures. Indeed, they were so interested in staring at the camera it was hard to film them while they carried on with their usual activities. Although they stopped dead in their tracks and faced the camera when they caught sight of me, their unfriendly faces softened a little and some even smiled faintly in the manner of photographic subjects everywhere.

The light faded rapidly now and it became damper and colder. Rather reluctantly, I returned to the chowkidar's dank little house. There, we *harijans* - untouchables - sat through the dusk drinking tea while I asked Sanja Ram questions about the town and its history. Sanja, himself isolated from the mainstream of village life, and no scholar, was, however, an eager and intelligent conversationalist.

"No one really knows quite where the Malana people came from or how long they've been here," he told me. "Their god is Jumdugga and no one is allowed to see this god except themselves.

I asked him about the teachings of this religion and the village culture, but he could tell me little. Apparently the rules of the culture were extraordinarily rigid and their traditions were designed to protect the group and their beliefs from disintegration and from contamination from the outside. Drinking and stealing were heavily fined. Marriages were forbidden except within the village.

Several weeks later, I read about the Malana people in the District Commissioner's library in Kulu. The slender volume *The Himalayan Districts of Kooloo, Lahoul and Spiti* was written by the British Resident Commissioner Edwin Harcourt a hundred years before my visit:

> "Malana is perhaps one of the greatest curiousities in Kooloo, as the inhabitants keep entirely to themselves, neither eating nor intermarrying with the people of any other village and speaking a language no one but themselves can comprehend."

And,

> "The people are all densely ignorant, no one in the place being able to read or write. Their faces have a startled and frightened look; the nose projects over the vacillating mouths, which with the narrow chin gives a character of feebleness to the entire face."

Like Sanja Ram, Harcourt also failed to see the gold image of their sacred god. His account continued,

"There can be very little doubt that this god was presented to them by the Emperor Akbar."

Akbar was the great Moghul conqueror and enlightened Islamic ruler of all of north India in the sixteenth century. In the splendid period of his reign, all religions were tolerated. Many Hindus held high office and marriages between Hindus and Muslims were encouraged. Perhaps this is why the religion of Malana is neither Muslim nor Hindu, but an amalgam of both.

I asked Sanja Ram to teach me a few words of the strange Malana tongue. I found it completely different from Hindi, Urdu or any other Indo-Aryan language I knew anything about. I learned to count to five only with the greatest difficulty: *id, nish, shjun, pooh, nahar.* Rice was *lar,* mother was *va,* water was *tee,* and I was *goo.* My guide Zing, a Ladakhi, recognized a few words that were similar to his own tongue.

Harcourt's chronicle described the unique rules used by the villagers to settle civil disputes.

"In former times when a dispute could not be settled amicably by the tribunal, it was the custom for each claimant to bring a goat to the proceedings. The thigh of each animal was cut open and each claimant placed poison in his own animal's wound. The victorious decision went to him whose goat died first."

As dusk fell, a parade of the strangely dressed inhabitants climbed up the path leading to the village from the fields and forests below. The women, shapeless in their bulky blanket wraparounds, wearing dirty gray pillbox hats over their untidy black hair, carried huge bundles of firewood or large baskets of fir cones on their backs. Men carried wooden plows and piles of fodder. Barefoot boys and girls herded flocks of sheep, goats and cattle before them, prodding and swatting at them with long sticks.

As it grew darker, I heard the sound of singing from the direction of the temples in the center of the town. Hoping that the gathering darkness would shelter me from their hostile stares, I couldn't resist leaving the untouchables' porch. I followed the last of the villagers returning from the fields toward the center of town.

A fantastic scene greeted me there. In the large square of beaten earth that lay between the two great wooden temples was a blazing fire. On both sides of the leaping flames, long lines of village girls, their arms linked around each other's shoulders, were bobbing in a wild sort of dance accompanied by loud chanting and singing. Their eyes sparkled with joyful excitement and their strange heavy costumes flew as they rhythmically bowed, stomped and raised their feet in unison. Their dance was strangely reminiscent of a maniacal caricature of a western chorus line. Instead of kicking, however, they lunged in concert, all bending their right knees at the same time. Then, planting one dusty, bare foot ahead, bowed forward, all chanting a repetitious litany that sounded like "Roh-shan Malana" over and over.

As it grew darker, the scene grew more dramatic. Villagers gathered around the periphery making a wide circle around the fire. Huge logs were thrown on the blaze. The brilliant flames illuminated balconies and verandas of the wooden dwellings and the strange temples that surrounded the open pavilion. A gray-bearded shepherd led his flock of goats to the edge of the clearing where the animals knelt or lay down calmly to watch the dancing. Firelight reflected from their unblinking pale eyes. Another old fellow walked past, carrying what appeared to be a headless, fat sheep. Legs tied with short thongs, it was a whole sheepskin sewn up and stuffed with grain.

As the dancing grew more frenzied, men on the sidelines unrolled goatskins from their backs and sat on them cross-legged around the fire. The two lines of dancers continued to lunge and plunge before them. Singly or in groups more villagers gathered on the sides of the clearing. Some men carried giant burning wood torches, lighting the scene with Wagnerian splendor. Another flock of goats and sheep entered the circle from the opposite side and lay down in the shadow of the largest temple.

Groups of men and women sat on the ground around smaller bonfires at the periphery of the circle rather like customers at a nightclub without chairs or tables. Meanwhile, the weaving, swaying, singing line of dancers in the center became more and more energetic and excited.

At one end of the clearing the chowkidar, Sanja Ram, arrived carrying a huge drum. He shouted for a cigarette. Someone threw one on the ground for him. He quickly picked it up and lighted it. Then he set up the drum in front of a man of forty or so with a sloping forehead and glowing eyes who sat at the far end of the circle near the fire. This man began pounding on the drum, slowly at first and then faster and faster. Women, nearly all carrying sleeping babies in their arms or on their backs, gathered at the edge of the circle, their brown faces calm and peaceful in the firelight.

Several men seated close to the fire struck up curious instruments made of two long metal rods with multiple pairs of castanet-like circles mounted on them. The men now began to sing in fine, sweet tenor voices. Firelight lit their rapt faces. The two lines of girls, who had been plunging and chanting around the fire without ceasing for several hours, gradually withdrew to the sidelines.

The men's singing began slowly, always keeping time with the rhythmic beat of the drum. As the tempo quickened, a young man seated in the circle suddenly jumped up and began to dance alone - a wild Afghan-like dance of enormous grace and vitality. Arms straight out, body and head slightly forward, he circled madly between the ring of faces and the leaping fire. A second man sprang into the arena - not quite as graceful as the first, but even more energetic. He whirled and dipped against the brilliant orange light of the flames as the drums led the singers to chant faster and faster. I found myself clapping with everyone else in time with the hypnotic music, and my heart pounded with the same beat as the drum. Suddenly, a girl whirled into the circle from the sidelines. Her woolen wraps flew as she, by far the most graceful of the lot, bowed and swayed at dizzying speed and in perfect harmony with the pounding beat of the drum.

It was an unforgettable scene. The great tongues of fire created fantastic shadows against the looming dark temples. The rough brown faces of the villagers in their bulky costumes were softened by music and rapt with pleasure in the orange firelight. Blazing torches flickered over the calm visages of goats that lay watching the dancing with quiet absorption. A full moon rose over the great white peaks surrounding the valley.

As the music and the dance reached a crescendo of excitement, suddenly two more girls appeared. Unlike their ill-clad, blanket wrapped sisters, these two wore long-sleeved filmy dresses of pure white and startling cleanliness. The circle around the clearing widened as the men pushed back to give them room. The dancer in the circle retired to the sidelines as the new pair of white-clad dancers began to whirl and leap in the center of the clearing. The excitement of the new performers was contagious. The men's voices grew hoarse with chanting and singing. The small bonfires at the periphery slowly died out as the groups at the side drew closer to the main event. Small children slept on their mothers' backs, firelight warm on their peaceful faces.

I sat on a stone wall just outside the circle as inconspicuously as possible for fear of being driven off. A young woman seated herself only a foot or two away looked at me and smiled, the wild, wide-eyed look of the day now gone. Sheelah and her mother brought me a blanket and sat down close beside me. Teenage boys and girls in their loose blanket costumes were rolling about on the ground, tackling and tickling each other good-naturedly. As the drum beat grew faster and faster, an occasional pair ran off into the shadows outside the circle.

I had been sitting on the stone wall for nearly four hours. With the sun gone, it was now cold in the valley, 9000 feet high. Stiff and chilled, I finally rose to return to the untouchable house. Sheelah and Mariya followed. I unrolled my sleeping bag on the veranda and snuggled down to dream of the *Gotterdammerung* like scene, the fire, the goats' strange eyes, and the whirling dancers. The beat of the drums still pounding in my ears lulled me to sleep.

At dawn the next morning, I crept quietly from the porch and went around to the back of the house to take advantage of the open-field-cum-toilet in relative privacy. I washed and scrubbed in the clear water flowing from the sluice mounted by the porch. The six cows, their udders as dry and empty as the night before, watched me solemnly.

Happy for a few moments of solitude, I sat on the steps and gazed out over the silent village. The curious houses and rude temples were shrouded in a fine mist that also concealed the distant peaks surrounding the valley. The little village seemed to be floating on a bowl-shaped island on a sea of gray cloud.

Half an hour later, Mariya tiptoed out from the kitchen where she, Sanja Ram and the two children all slept together on thin bamboo mats on the dirt floor. Smiling as always, she began her sixteen-hour work day by drawing water. Then she blew on the embers beneath the ashes in the fireplace and fed the fire with a handful of fir cones. Zing was up next, emerging from the guest room that I, fearing fleas, had avoided in favor of my air mattress on the veranda. Sanja Ram and the children soon joined us. Mariya ladled out cups of hot sugared tea, the family breakfast.

After tea, I asked Sheelah if I could accompany her to her daily chores. She seemed puzzled but delighted. First, we drove the six dry cows out of the yard and down the path between the terraced fields. The sun shone brilliantly in a pure blue sky. We followed the cows down a steep path across a torrent where a stone mill for grinding barley was enclosed in a small wooden lean-to. As I stopped to watch the water-driven stone whirl above the horizontal paddles, two villagers driving a cow and some goats gesticulated angrily at me to move off the path so they could pass. A man in flapping rags ordered Sheelah and me to step aside into the weeds or rocks as if he was a lord and we were dogs. This scene was repeated several times as we descended toward the pasture and these people exercised their caste rights of preeminence.

Only once I held my ground, enduring hostile stares from older men and taunts and shouts from boys. Even women laughed derisively and brusquely ordered us aside. They were not very formidable looking people, being small in stature and with plain undistinguished features. However, their obvious hostility was a little unnerving and gave me an uneasy feeling in all our encounters.

After we had seen the cows safely to their pasture, I invited Sheelah to climb with me high above the village where we could find enough privacy to bathe in the clear stream as it tumbled from high on the mountainside. She agreed eagerly. We found a large warm rock to sit on. I pulled off my shoes, socks, shirt and trousers, took a bar of soap from my rucksack and proceeded to scrub myself. Sheelah watched every move as I shed successive bits of clothing to wash and then covered myself as modestly as possible. After wrapping a towel around myself, I washed all my clothes and laid them on the warm rocks to dry. Then I turned to Sheelah.

"Now it's your turn," I suggested in my abominable Hindi, handing her the soap.

Sheelah laughed with pleasure and was soon scrubbing and rubbing at her scaly brown arms. I watched in some amazement as her dark hands turned pink and her nearly black legs and feet became a pale golden brown. When her arms and legs were quite clean, I pointed to her heavy wool blanket dress. After hesitating for a moment, she peeled it off, followed by her filthy blouse and baggy trousers. Since she had no underthings, I put on my own nearly dry clothes and threw her the towel. After wrapping up in the towel, she scrubbed her own garments vigorously with the bar of soap. Then I washed and braided her hair. When I gave her a clean red *kurta* from my pack, she was delighted, slipped it over her head, and pulled on her almost dry trousers. She folded her damp blanket dress carefully. When we climbed down the stream bed to the path below, Sheelah enjoyed the admiring glances of the village women who made surprised comments about her appearance as we passed.

Mariya, Sheelah's mother, was hurrying down the path carrying Myla Jr. as we approached the cottage. Worried since we had been gone so long, she smiled with pleasure at Sheelah's fresh happy appearance. Once again, we mounted the trail to the village, stepping aside when men and boys overtook us. Sheelah blushed and gave an angry retort in response to their gruff sounding remarks, but refused to translate them for me.

When we reached the cottage, the spicy aroma of dahl drifted over the untidy dung-filled yard. Sanja Ram knelt before the fire, stirring a large pot in the dark smoky kitchen. All the supplies we had purchased the day before were cooking in two big black pots. Mariya and I beamed at each other, our eyes meeting in maternal pleasure as she passed heaping plates to the children and Sanja Ram.

After lunch, Sanja Ram asked me diffidently if I would be willing to see a "patient." In the house next door lived an old woman who had fallen off her balcony the week before and "split her head open to the bone."

I said I would be glad to examine her and dress her wound but wondered how I could do either as an untouchable. We picked our way over fresh cow dung in the back yard and climbed over the wall that abutted directly on the open courtyard of the neighboring large two-story dwelling. The solid old house of heavy beamed wood faced a courtyard of hard packed dirt where an old woman, all in black, sat on a low wooden stool holding her head on her knees. Beside her stood a man of around forty in baggy homespun trousers and black coat. Behind him, two wide-eyed children, barefoot and in rags, stared shyly.

"This is the woman who is hurt," said Sanja Ram.

I looked up at the balcony, twenty feet above, from where she had fallen the week before. A young woman holding a baby at her breast peered down curiously. Two children of six or seven clutched the folds of her blanket dress. Approaching the old woman, I looked at the chowkidar and asked if I could touch her.

"Jee," he nodded in assent, "you can."

I knelt down, folding my hands in *namaste* before reaching out to probe through her matted hair for the wound. At the very top of her head I felt a large scab of congealed blood and dried dung applied as a plaster. I asked for *garam pani* (warm water). Sanja translated to Malanese. A young man waiting under the veranda ran inside. I suggested we bring the clean boiled water from the kettle in Sanja's house but the chowkidar pointed out that it would not do. As he was untouchable, his water was unclean.

From the veranda, the younger woman, my patient's daughter-in-law, called down something to the chowkidar. Translating, Sanja Ram said the woman wanted me to look at her eyes. I agreed, hoping that while waiting for the boiled water I would have a chance to enter a typical Malana house. That was to remain out of bounds, however. Here, and wherever I was called to come to see patients in the village, the patients were always brought outside.

The woman came down the notched log stairway while nursing a grimy infant swaddled in layers of homespun cotton. She stood silently looking at me. But the wide-eyed look of suspicion and hostility I had received from everyone in the village the day before was now quite gone. She pointed to her eyes anxiously. Gently,

I pulled the lower lids down, exposing fiery red conjunctivae. It was the type of inflammation common in women who spend many hours each day crouched over smoking cooking fires on the floor of their unventilated "kitchens." The redness and pain are usually easily relieved with cortisone eye drops. Convincing them that prevention was better than cure, however, was a more difficult, usually impossible task.

I climbed back over the wall to Sanja's cottage and rifled through my pack for eye drops, bandages and soap. When I returned the boiled (and boiling) water was ready. First I attended to the old woman's scalp wound. The entire family plus a few neighbors gathered to watch. Daubing gently at her scalp with warm water and the antiseptic Phisohex, I finally succeeded in getting rid of enough cow dung, clotted blood and matted hair to get a good view of the deep infected wound. Although I could not feel a fracture, there was too much swelling to be sure. The old woman didn't flinch as I cleansed the wound and dressed her head with a sponge soaked in betadyne. I covered the affected area with a roll of gauze - startlingly white in this untidy place. For the first time, the men smiled.

Then I got up and put a few drops of the cortisone eye drops into each of the daughter-in-law's reddened eyes. Sanja Ram translated for me as we explained the cause was from smoke and rubbing her eyes with dirt-blackened hands. I talked about chimneys made of tin cans. Then I gave her the small plastic bottle of eye drops and the bar of soap. All year I save up the tiny bars of soap in the bathrooms of hotels I happen to stay in for just such an event. Easy to pack in large numbers, they are also welcome gifts in strange villages that have no soap at all.

We climbed back over the wall followed by the older of the two men. Back in the dung-filled courtyard of his untouchable house, Sanja Ram pointed to him and translated his request.

"This man has stomach-ache. Can you give him something?"

I felt a sudden rush of happiness. I was accepted. After gleaning a few particulars of this stomach complaint, not apparently very serious, I handed out several attractive looking anti-spasmodic tablets. During the rest of the afternoon and evening, a steady stream of villagers came singly or in groups to our mud and dung-filled courtyard. I asked Sanja Ram and two of the men to lay a couple of reasonably clean boards across stones in the dirt. This became my examining table. Belly-aches, scabies, infected flea bites, cuts and coughs were the usual problems. Malnutrition of the very young children seemed universal. Their dirt scaled little pipe-stem limbs broke my heart.

No one in this village kept chickens or raised fruit or vegetables. Dahl, a spicy puree of lentils, plus rice and *chappatis* washed down with tea was the diet of young and old alike. Although there were large numbers of cows about, few gave more than a cup or two of milk a day and most were dry at this season. The Malana religion, although demanding the sacrifice of goats or sheep, forbade eating meat.

When I walked through the village to the store that afternoon with Sheelah, the hostility against me seemed slightly less than on the previous day. Once again we ordered rice, lentils, oil and tea, the only eatables available, and waited down below. The storekeeper, taciturn and unsmiling, left his loom, climbed to the veranda and disappeared inside.

I wandered up the hillside and watched an old man skillfully weave a great cone-shaped basket of reeds. Half a dozen barefoot little girls of around ten, dressed in grubby blankets or burlap sacks, each with a small brother or sister tied on her back, gathered to watch me from a safe distance. When the *sojee* finally descended with our purchases, Sheelah called to me. Again he placed our bundles and bill on the rock. I reached out to hand him the money.

Although I'd examined him, including his belly, the day before as he lay on the rude planks in our backyard, now I was once again untouchable. Sheelah indicated that I should place the money on the ground. I did so. The *sojee* picked it up and ascended the notched log to the second floor for change. When he reached the doorway overhead, I shouted up to him and pointed first to my head and then to his, shouting, "Topi, topi," which means hat in Hindi.

Sheelah translated that I wanted to buy a Malana hat like his. Still silent and unsmiling, the *sojee* disappeared inside. Again, I waited restlessly below. Meanwhile, the ragamuffin children of the family gathered. They ran up and down the notched log ladder staring at me and shrieking with laughter. After waiting ten or fifteen minutes, I turned to Sheelah in disgust. Picking up the packages of rice and lentils, I mumbled, "Let's go," and strode off impatiently.

As I walked through the village once more I felt as though hateful eyes from every balcony glared down at me. The setting sun turned the sky beyond the great snow peaks brilliant pink. I stopped with a thrill of pleasure, momentarily relieved of the ache of being a social outcast. A line of ragged men carrying a heavy wooden plow passed me. The oldest one stopped and shouted at me angrily.

"*Mulai budina*" (I don't understand), I muttered in Nepali, the first local language to surface in my confusion.

"*Chelas!*" (Go!), he shouted, pointing in the direction of the untouchable cottage. There was no mistaking his meaning. Once again, I became irrationally, almost furiously angry at being treated so contemptuously.

"*This must be how many blacks feel every hour and every day in the U.S.*" I thought suddenly.

"*Idderow,*" (Come), called Sheelah anxiously as she ran up behind me. I tried to suppress my rage by remembering that this little village had its own life and customs. They had not invited me to come here. I turned back irritably. Sheelah was holding a typical Malana wool cap trimmed with red velvet in her hands.

"Twenty rupees," she panted, handing it to me. "*Sojee* for you make it." Only a dollar and forty cents. Inwardly I cursed my inability to develop the patience of the East, to simply stroll along in harmony with whatever happens. The seemingly long wait that made me so impatient was the short time it took the *sojee* to make the hat.

I clapped the wool *topi* on my head and walked back with Sheelah to the store. Wonder of wonders, when the storekeeper saw me he smiled broadly for the first time. I realized how pleasant, how necessary, it was for me to be liked and accepted. How intolerable and infuriating it was to be treated with scorn and contempt.

Thanking him profusely, I politely placed two ten rupee notes on the ground between us. The storekeeper picked them up, smiled again and said something to Sheelah.

"He makes these hats from cloth he weaves himself," she explained. "It took him so long because he finished this one just for you."

Walking back to the cottage with the hat, slightly too small, perched on my head, I had the feeling of being somewhat more tolerated. A few of the laden villagers who passed us on the trail even smiled or gave friendly sounding grunts.

All afternoon I prodded and listened to bellies and chests on the rough planks of my outdoor clinic as the six cows looked on placidly, defecating, urinating and chewing bits of straw.

The next morning after breakfast tea, Sanja Ram announced he had been asked to bring me to a house behind the temple to see a sick infant. We walked into the town, stopping in front of a large house where half a dozen villagers were waiting for us. We were left to stand outside at a safe distance from the dwelling while a small boy climbed up the notched ladder to the second floor to announce our arrival. A woman wrapped in the usual pile of untidy blankets came down carrying an infant swaddled in heavy wrappings. Although he was six months old, the child surely weighed less than ten pounds. He cried constantly. The mother strongly resisted undressing him so I could examine him. I pulled the filthy rags around him aside bit by bit, examining him as best I could.

Painfully scrawny, the child looked starved. The mother herself, thin and empty breasted, understood little of my explanation, translated for her by Sanja. The very concepts of supplementary feedings, boiled milk, eggs and soft-cooked grain were beyond her. A crowd gathered and listened impassively to the translation. It seemed a favorable situation to talk about nutrition, kitchen gardens and the value of chickens, of which there were none at all in the village. When I finished, no one asked a single question or commented with as much as a single word.

"Do they understand?" I asked Sanja Ram.

"Oh yes," he replied. "But it is their way not to speak."

Quite a crowd had gathered around us by this time. An oldish man in the Malana uniform of worn baggy trousers and dark western type secondhand jacket stepped forward to ask Sanja Ram to bring me to see his wife. We walked up the hill through the town, a troop of children following at a safe distance as usual. In an open shed a middle-aged woman sat on a stump holding her head in her hands. She shrank back as I approached and would not permit me to touch or examine her. I explained that I could not treat her without some kind of examination. No compromise could be reached, however. I gave her husband a few aspirin tablets and walked back to our untouchable house.

More patients had gathered in the cow yard. All through the afternoon the villagers straggled in. Strangely submissive as patients, the hostility and suspiciousness of the days before had disappeared as miraculously as their mad, piercing stares. It was as if the whole population of the village, so angry and psychotic looking only two days before, had now taken a good dose of tranquilizers.

That evening Sheelah swept the cow yard clean and laid a fire in the center. We were joined for our evening meal of rice and dahl by half a dozen relatives of Sanja Ram who had walked up from the valley below. There was no dancing that night, but twenty or thirty young men of the village gathered in Sanja Ram's back yard. I fell asleep on the veranda to the sound of their singing.

The next morning was Sunday. We were all up early for a special festival. According to Sanja Ram, the god Jumduggu (Jamu) would be taken from the temple to a high hilltop where a goat would be sacrificed. After our usual breakfast of sugared tea, I loaded my camera and walked with Sheelah and Sanja to the edge of the village. A crowd was gathered in front of the largest temple. The men, solemn faced, passed steadily in and out of the building. The god never appeared. No women were allowed inside the temple.

Finally, the procession began. The priest, a bearded, white-haired man dressed in a dirty ragged gown, carried a long crook. Uttering strange, hoarse little cries, he undulated with rhythmic pelvic thrusts in front of a smoldering pot of ashes on the ground in front of the temple. All the men in the village were gathered in a circle around him. Two were holding the tall musical instruments of multiple castanets from the night of the dance. Several had long wooden trumpets. One fellow carried the large skin drum attached by a thong around his neck. A terrified goat on a short tether struggled vainly to break away from its owner.

After ten minutes or more, the old priest stopped chanting and wiggling his hips and turned to lead the procession of men and boys through the town toward the hillside. Behind him came the drummer, pounding away rhythmically and then two men shaking the castanets. Two old men blew on the wooden trumpets. The plump white goat was followed by a sinister-looking fellow with a bushy mustache and a great curved knife. Behind them, in ragged file, trailed all the men and older boys of the village. First they all marched around the temple. Then they proceeded through the open square in the center of the village to the outskirts of the town. In single file, they ascended the steep hillside toward the mountains. Women and children followed to the edge of the village. There they stood watching from rooftops and verandas as the procession of men and boys climbed slowly up the hillside. In the lead was the now docile goat, which proceeded, like the rest of us, blindly along to its fate.

Camera rolling, I squinted my eyes against the sunlight to see the sacrifice. After a long ceremony at the top of the hill, the man with the scimitar made a violent chopping movement. The goat fell, spurting blood. There was a great shout and the crowd closed about it so I could see no more.

Half an hour later, the parade descended again, everyone smiling and satisfied, carrying pieces of the butchered animal. The boy who had led the goat up the hill now carried the empty skin and staring head. The man at the front of the procession entered the temple. The rest scattered in the square. The god did not appear at all.

We returned to the chowkidar's house to find half a dozen more relatives waiting eagerly for our arrival so the noon meal could begin. The fourteen of us made short work of the day's pile of rice and dahl. Mariya continued cooking and filling plates without stopping to eat. The smile never left her face. The relatives ate hungrily, stopping only to lick their fingers appreciatively. Everyone talked in their strange mountain language of which I understood not a word. The thought of a night with a dozen or more of us under one roof did not especially appeal to me. With many thanks, Zing and I packed up our gear.

Accompanied by the chowkidar and Sheelah carrying Myla, we walked back through the village toward the trail to Jari. My feet had recovered from their bruising and the pack felt good on my back. When we reached the center of the village, carefully avoiding the sacred temples and the heaps of special stones, people gathered to watch us silently. Strangely, their eyes no longer seemed to stare with the mad wild look of three days before. Their dress, so outlandish on first encounter, now seemed quite normal. A few people even waved farewell and smiled in response to our goodbyes.

As we reached the center of the town, a woman suddenly ran across the open clearing with her hands cupped before her. She lay a heaping pile of brown sticky stuff on a rock in front of me. Motioning to me to take it, she stood by and watched. It was *giri*, raw, dark brown sugar, tasting like sweet molasses. I took as much as I could in both hands, bowed my thanks to her, and carried it like an offering through the town to where Zing's shoes were hidden in the forest beyond. Then we said fond farewells to Sanja, Sheela and tiny Myla and gave them the sugar to take back for tea.

The following week in Kulu, I read about Malana in Harcourt's journal in the small English library, opened for me by a cooperative official.

"These strange and isolated people," he wrote in 1876, "are densely ignorant, a people with perpetually wild and frightened eyes."

His visit must have been even shorter than mine.

1986   January 31. Space shuttle Challenger explodes killing all 7
       astronauts.

       February 18. Oil price drops to $15.00 a barrel.

       March 21. American planes bomb base in Libya.

       October 2.   Tibet: Six Buddhist monks demonstrating
       against Chinese occupation killed.

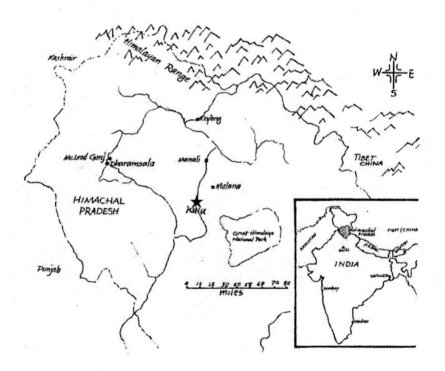

Chapter IV

AN ASHRAM IN KULU

It all started by sheer coincidence. I was climbing through heavy snow heading south for the Rothang Pass from Keylong in northwest India where I had been visiting remote Buddhist monasteries in the Lahoul valley of the Himalayas. It was early May but the valley was still isolated by deep snow that buried the road to the north Indian town of Manali. Struggling up the steep mass of fallen rock and ice that marked the final hundred feet of the north slope of the pass, I was breathing hard under a loaded pack when I heard a very American voice shout greetings above me.

A blond young man wearing thin white cotton trousers and wrapped in a brown wool blanket stood watching our party of three ascend the final few steps to the summit. At last, we reached the top - a glorious snowfield at 13,000 feet. The snowfield formed a pass between the 16,000-20,000 foot Himalayan peaks behind us that separate the Tibetan cultures of Lahoul, Spiti and Ladakh to the north from the rest of India. I looked back to see where we had come from.

For someone like myself, caught in a lifelong love affair with high mountains, it was a glorious moment. There was a stupendous view of the shining wall of snow-capped peaks to the north. Miles of white snow-filled valleys stretched between those far off jagged peaks and the pass where I stood. Hidden in the desolate looking valleys between were the isolated villages of Lahoul and Spiti. I turned round to gaze toward the gentler southern slope. A broad expanse of unbroken snow lay ahead toward the still invisible verdant valley of the River Beas. Beyond that, 300 miles south was the scorching Indian plain.

The owner of the American voice approached us. We exchanged greetings, *namaste*'s, the traditional Indian greeting, followed by "hellos" and "where-are-you-froms?" His name was Steve. Having spent the previous night in one of the rest houses in Marhi, this morning he climbed to the summit of this pass for a day's outing.

Remarkably, Steve was from Portland, Oregon, my own hometown, half a world away. A lawyer who gave up a dull government job in Washington D.C. eight months earlier, he, like me, was engaged in a love affair with the mountains of north India.

It was a perfect May day with a cloudless sky and unlimited view. The day was also free of the famous savage wind that on occasion hurled unlucky travelers to their deaths from the very spot where we stood. Somewhat to my surprise, the summit of the pass in this remote place was crowded. Warmly clad men, women and children sat in the snow enjoying a midmorning repast before continuing their journey down the slope I had just ascended. They were all from Nepal, traveling north to work in India's Lahoul valley.

Fortunately, Steve, my new acquaintance, spoke their language fluently, a legacy from two years in Nepal in the Peace Corps ten years before. As we all sat in the snow beneath the tattered prayer flags that marked the summit of the pass, we were soon involved in animated conversation with the ebullient Nepalese. They were easily distinguished from the local Indian and Kulu people by their dress, stocky build and flat round faces. A single epicanthal fold of the upper lid shields their eyes from the wind and sun, giving them a faintly oriental appearance. All were from Taplejung in northeast Nepal, one of the loveliest but poorest countries on earth.

Every year, they left their homes in the valleys below the highest of the Himalayas to travel by foot and bus to summer jobs on the roads of India. With apparent ease, they were going to traverse this 13,000 foot pass in deep snow with fifty pounds of bulky baggage, often including children, on their backs. They were also very proud. Many seemed reluctant to admit that poverty had driven them from their farms and villages in Nepal to haul dirt and rocks for six or seven rupees a day (then worth 85-95 U.S. cents) in neighboring India.

After a brief rest in the sun on the icy summit, the Tikomorans, my guide and porter, although content to nap for hours at the top of the pass on our way to Keylong the week before were anxious now to move on for home   After a short stop for an unsuccessful attempt to sell their sun glasses to the Nepalese, they started off with unaccustomed energy down the south slope ahead of us.

When we reached the village of Marhi we descended icy steps into a tunnel through the snow that led into a small snow-buried hotel. We stamped snow from our boots in front of a blazing fire. As my eyes became accustomed to the change from brilliant sun on snow to the dark interior, I recognized the Indian officer I had met at the army camp on this slope the week before. He was taking his noon tea before the fire. We sat down to join him. After exchanging the usual pleasantries, I asked the officer why these Nepalese were pouring into India.

"It seems incongruous to me that India, land of mass unemployment and underemployment should be importing foreigners to work on its roads," I said. "It's not as though you're short of laborers like the Swiss or Germans who must import workers from Spain and Italy."

The Indian lieutenant explained. "Madam, we could use 10,000 people if we could get them. Our own people from the plains can't work in this climate and altitude." It was true that few points in the Lahoul-Spiti valley are less than 10,000 feet high. "The Nepalese are willing to come here for six or seven rupees a day because in their own country they can make only two or three for the same work. Thus, both they and we are satisfied."

We finished our tea and bid the genial lieutenant *au revoir* and *donnybad* (thanks), for he insisted in paying for our tea. Then we continued the descent to Manali. We walked more rapidly now over an easier trail. My porter and guide were far ahead of us and hurrying for home.

The snow gave way gradually to dark wet earth. Blades of new grass and tiny blue flowers covered the floor of the valley. The surrounding hills were soft and rounded, green with pine and cedar trees. Waterfalls fell on all sides from the melting snow above into enchanting meadows where horses and goats grazed. In front of an open cave in the rocky hillside a shepherd and his son sat before a blazing fire. When we stopped to greet them, they offered us chunks of uncooked meat from a freshly slaughtered lamb. We sat down with them to exchange what pleasantries we could in fragmentary Hindi and Pahari (hill language). Then, much to their amusement, we insisted on skewering our bits of meat on sharp sticks and roasting them over their fire. The shepherd offered Steve a pull on his pipe, a long curved ram's horn. I gave his son a balloon. A poor gift, but one that unfailingly delights both adults and children.

As we continued our descent, I explaiined to Steve that I had gone to the monasteries of Keylong to learn more about Buddhism and the goals of meditation. Although I was deeply impressed with the serene equanimity of Buddhist monks and nuns who lived in these remote aeries high on the mountains, I still could not understand what was so satisfying about the meditation process. Indeed meditating seemed a rather puerile waste of mental abilities.

"Why should anyone want to make their mind, that marvelous instrument of thinking and creativity, a blank? I asked. "The mind is certainly man's most remarkable possession and thoughts are its product. What does one achieve by turning it off?"

Steve, who seemed to know more of the subject than I did, agreed, confessing that he too was baffled by meditation's apparent charms. Yet, we both were fascinated and drawn to the quiet happiness we saw in the faces of those who had found *The Way*.

As the sun sank low in the sky, the route descended more steeply. Then suddenly the mountains were behind us and we reached the motor road I looked back to see if my porters might be behind us, as we had not passed them. Then we were surprised to hear the sound of a car approaching. A gray sedan came suddenly around the curve heading for Manali. Instinctively, my thumb went up and the car stopped. From inside, three cheerful Westerners greeted us warmly. They were Canadians, members of a Kulu ashram dedicated to meditation! After a day's outing on the snows beyond Marhi, they were now homeward bound and happy to give us a lift.

The driver was a man of around 30 who wore a full curly brown beard, white pajamas and turquoise beads. Beside him sat a tall clean-shaven man of 25 or 30 with blue eyes of startling clarity. On the back seat a tanned middle aged man dressed in spotless white shirt and trousers moved over to make room for us. We piled in gladly. As is so often the case when I travel without plans, coincidence makes them for me much more satisfactorily. These new friends seemed to have just the answers I was seeking. All three were in India to enter more deeply into the practice of meditation. Almost before we had settled ourselves in the back seat, we were all into a discussion of mysticism, yogis, and routes to enlightenment.

Our new friends were far from novices in these disciplines. They were leading members of the ashram of Swami Shayam, a well known guru in the village of Kulu 20 miles below Manali. Although at present they were disciples of this Swami, they had been through numerous other meditation trips, ashrams, and yogis from Vancouver, B.C. to Varanasi in India.

Except for the driver's rather unpleasant habit of drinking his own urine every morning they all seemed quite normal. "The Prime Minister does it, it's very healthy," he explained. Like the monks and nuns in the lonely monasteries of Keylong, the serene eyed young man in the front seat had a face as radiant as a clean-shaven Christ. We got on.

Halfway to Manali, we stopped at a *chikhana* (teashop) to wait for the Tikomorans. We continued our discussions free of distraction of motor and road. After nearly an hour, the Tikhomorans caught up with us. We had another round of tea and then set off, squeezing the two delighted porters into the back seat between us and stowing the packs on the roof.

It was nearly dark when my new friends dropped the Tikomorans and me in Manali. Steve continued with our new friends to the ashram. I promised to visit them soon.

Almost two weeks later, I arrived in Kulu by local bus. After signing the register at the old Imperial Hotel where I was evidently the only guest, I had a cold water bath. There was no hot. Needing time to change gears in preparation for the ashram, I sat down at a small table on the veranda and drank several glasses of lemonade while gazing contentedly over the bucolic valley carved by the river Beas in its rush south through the Himalayan foothills.

Neatly planted fields of maize and barley glowed in the sun. This gentle Kulu valley was originally called Kulanthipatha "end of the inhabited world." Now, with its paved roads, chugging buses and crowded villages it was far from that. Nevertheless, I felt intoxicated with freedom. Was the ashram to be the threshold of a new doorway?

I followed the lemonade with a cup of sweet milk tea and an excellent omelet. Then I inquired the way to the ashram.

"It's just a few furlongs up-river," replied the hotel proprietor, a huge Sikh in white *dhoti* and purple turban. He directed me to stow my gear in a musty little room at the back of the hotel. I walked out into the hot morning sunlight and followed the road by the river past the scattered houses of the town.

I quickly reached the ashram. It was almost indistinguishable from the other dwellings along the road. A dozen or so small buildings were on the hillside and several larger buildings nearby descended down the slope to the river. Walking down a wooden stairway beyond a narrow unmarked gate, I walked past an open shed where two soft-eyed cows gazed at me mildly. A newborn calf staggered to its feet on the clean straw. Reaching the door of a two-story cedar dwelling at the edge of the bank high above the river, I rapped gently.

A graceful, smiling Indian girl in a yellow cotton sari opened the door. I asked for Scott, the young man of the serene blue eyes. Although it had been nearly two weeks since my encounter with Scott and the other meditators below the Rothang Pass, I was evidently expected. The girl, who turned out to be the Swami's daughter, went off to look for my friend. I stood on the veranda overlooking the sparkling river, feeling happy. In a few minutes Scott appeared, carrying two glasses of tea, his remarkable eyes still clear and shining.

We took up our conversation where we had left off two weeks before. After we finished tea, he led me to a large building across the yard above the river. There I found the Swami, legs crossed, sitting on a crimson cushion. He was a small, stocky man with graying beard, dark penetrating eyes and a full almost sensuous mouth; he projected instant warmth and kindness. He folded his hands in *namaste* and then extended both of them to me.

"I have been expecting you," he said in softly accented English. "You are welcome here, Jan. I have heard so much about you from Scott and John. I am happy you could come."

I folded my hands and bowed. A slender young man in white trousers and embroidered Indian shirt slipped in quietly, bringing cushions for us to sit on. I sat down on a pillow and forced my legs into some semblance of a lotus position. Then I looked hopefully toward Scott who seated himself farther back in the shadows of the large room. A blond, barefoot girl of around twenty dressed in a long white gown walked in softly, carrying a tray with teapot and cups. Swami nodded and directed her to serve me first and then Scott. She poured the tea for us and then, radiating pleasure, respectfully bending her knees, served Swami. Outside, the river rushed past, cleansing itself of glacial debris on the warm rocks before reaching still pools below the rapids. I hoped that could happen to me.

I explained to Swami that although I was a teacher of medicine of the mind and brain, I had really come here as a student to learn about meditation and meditators.

"I want to know what is so remarkably satisfying about silencing thoughts," I began, rather clumsily. "And I'm eager to learn what so many young Westerners - many of whom have tried psychiatry as a way to solve their problems - are getting from meditation!"

The Swami nodded as though he already knew why I had come.

"Tell me where you have been," he said quietly, "and what you have learned there."

For almost an hour we talked of the pilgrimage I had just made to the monasteries in the mountains far north of the high pass, and of my short stay in the remote village of Malana where I was an untouchable and where the people worship the strange god Jumdugga.

"I'm seeking the reasons people believe in gods," I finally concluded. "Everywhere it is so - why are they so sure? I'm beginning to feel there is a special sense I have been deprived of and that I must understand."

The Swami laughed and clapped his hands. With his twinkling eyes and his long gray beard he reminded me of Santa Claus dressed in a white *dhoti*.

"I cannot explain to you why and what is meditation," he said gently. "But I can teach you to know for yourself. Meditation transcends fear and gives total self-confidence. When you meditate all your stresses will go away. All your tensions will be reduced. All agitation is eliminated."

Swami paused, gazed out the window for a few minutes, drank off his cup of tea and poured another. Then he adjusted the white cloth robe over his knees and continued.

"There are many roots to the pure consciousness achieved through meditation. Most of my people learn by concentrating on the source of their own breath. This is a good device for focusing attention and preventing wandering of the thoughts."

He asked me to close my eyes and try.

"Attend very closely to how your breath rises and where it rises. Then pay attention to how it leaves the body. Gradually your mind will be freed. Meditate on the eternal flow of world consciousness and do peacefully whatever you want. As long as you do not see your own restlessness you will think that the whole world is without peace, but when you look within and you find yourself tense, agitated and peaceless, then you will not say that it is others that have a similar state. You will start making efforts for your own improvement and with this formula the world will also gain."

Now Swami closed his eyes and sat breathing quietly. Sitting before him in this silent place, fragrant with the faint scent of incense and full of the meditation of others, I easily slipped into attending to my breath entering and leaving, chest rising and falling, breath going in and out, in and out.

"Is that all there is to it?" I asked when Swami spoke to me after ten minutes or so. Scott laughed gently behind me.

Swami rose smiling and replied, "Now, Jan, we have just begun."

I was intrigued with the breath watching. It reminded me of methods of internal conditioning first expounded by the Russian physiologist Pavlov and his followers to bring autonomic and physiologic processes such as skin conductance or blood pressure into consciousness. I had even experimented with a similar idea in the electroencephalograph (EEG) laboratory years before. By making the movement of the EEG pens audible, I tried to make my epileptic patients aware of sudden abnormal electrical discharges in their own brains. It was not very successful.

Theoretically at least, concentration of attention on the origin of each breath could also increase perception of some aspect of the neural events that precede each breath, signals normally ignored or inaccessible to conscious awareness. The Russians call this *endogenous conditioning*. The sound of our own heartbeat, normally imperceptible, becomes clearly audible in a totally soundproof room. It seemed plausible that exclusion of usual percepts and random thoughts might allow access to previously ignored stimuli from both inside the body and brain as well as the external world.

Swami again instructed me.

"While meditating, you observe the breath going and coming from within. This is a direct indicator that you are the breath in its deeper sense. If it stops, you are no more. Concentrate and perceive to what extent the breath goes in and out. As you reach the extreme end of inhalation and exhalation, remain breathless for a while. Watch when your diaphragm feels like drawing the air again and watch very attentively." Again, we closed our eyes and breathed together. Although I experienced nothing, it was a little easier to concentrate on the rise and fall of my own breath.

"If you will do this for at least one hour, I am sure tremendous concentration of mind will take place and no unnecessary flow of random thoughts will come. If you sit down long enough, continuously in this way, you will experience the state of *Samadhi*, where there is only *Awareness* and absolutely nothing else."

This was much easier than concentrating on the mantra "Om" as I tried to do years before during transcendental meditation, which I soon abandoned out of sheer ennui.

"You will be so full of dynamism that any time you think to undertake a task you will be able to do it with greater efficiency than ever before," explained Swami. "Having gained this state of awareness, the mind and body coordinate in super efficiency and the result of thinking and performing actions will become more satisfying and fulfilling."

When I finally opened my eyes, Swami was watching me closely. Then he rose, folded his hands in *namaste* and walked with dignity out of the dark shadows of the large hall into the dazzling light outside.

Scott and I followed behind him at a distance. The sun's brilliant light blinded me after being so long in half darkness.

Scott and John invited me to lunch with them in their apartments in the building just across the lawn. Seated on the floor on large blue cushions, we dined on *chapattis*, *dahl*, and vegetable curry. After lunch, John suggested that we go for a swim in the river.

"Then I'll show you a small house you could use, if you would like to stay a while and learn more about meditation," he offered. I happily accepted.

All afternoon we sat on the stones by the river, sometimes talking, sometimes silent. That evening, refreshed from a bath in the icy river and my first steps, or rather breaths, into meditation, I attended my first *satsung* - the daily meeting of the guru and his disciples for meditation, singing and a "sermon."

The assembly hall was full when we arrived. A crowd of pale young men and women sat on the floor in lotus position, straight-backed, eyes closed; all were in deep silence. At the far end of the room Swami, his legs also folded beneath him, sat facing them on the dais, with closed eyes. As we entered the room, Swami opened his eyes and beckoned to me to come sit beside him.

No one as much as peeked from under their closed lids as I tiptoed toward the front of the room and squeezed into the corner on the floor close to his platform. Almost at once, someone passed me a large pillow which I eased onto gratefully, slightly mortified that my knees, although very serviceable for mountaineering, were too stiff to reach less than six inches from the floor when I attempted the lotus position.

I closed my eyes and tried to watch my breath, but found the scene before me much more absorbing. Thirty-five or forty young westerners, both men and women, sat in semicircular rows before me. Their eyes were closed, their faces serene. Many held a *malla*, a string of orange beads, in their hands. Some were slipping the beads one by one through their fingers. Like the rosary, the one hundred and eight beads of the *malla* serve Hindus and Buddhists as a marker for prayers.

Most of the young women were long-haired, blonde, slender, clad in ankle-length white or pale blue gowns. The men, dressed in white cotton trousers, Indian shirts and a wool blanket or shawl over one shoulder, were mostly bearded but not scruffy. The youngest in the gathering was a man of about twenty with a shock of long golden hair. The oldest was a woman of forty or so with a ravaged face and dark eyes hidden in deep hollows. Except for the rise and fall of their breathing, no one moved. A quarter of an hour passed in this fashion.

Finally, the Swami slowly opened his eyes and rubbed them with both hands. In a quiet voice he asked for a *bhajan* (religious song). Slowly, everyone opened their eyes and gazed at Swami. A blond Nordic woman of around thirty commenced singing in Hindi. The others followed, their faces beaming with joy. Swami rocked back and forth, singing lustily.

After several *bhajans*, Swami gave a long dissertation on a passage from the Bhagavad Gita, which he read first in Sanskrit, then translated and discussed in English. I was too busy watching the intent faces of the ashramites to pay much attention to the passage that apparently centered on the theme "thou art that."

There were only two Indians in the audience, Swami's daughter, the girl who greeted me when I arrived that morning, and her brother, a dark-bearded friendly young man. The rest were westerners. As I discovered later, nearly all were Canadians.

I found the sermon hard to follow, almost sophistic, and either excessively subtle or altogether banal. Everyone else seemed vastly interested, however. I attributed my failure to appreciate its meaning to inexperience and ignorance.

When he finished, Swami presented me to the group, explaining that I was a psychiatrist interested in trying to understand meditation and their experiences with the life they were leading in India. He invited them to share their feelings and perceptions with me. Swami's words were a great boon for me. Pandora's box opened and it was up to me to sort out the jumble of ideas I found inside.

Many members of the ashram now crowded forward to tell me what was happening to them here. As I tried to scribble hasty notes, someone thrust a cassette recorder in front of us and I was able to sit back, ask questions, and listen.

Graham, a young American who arrived only a day or two before, sat down beside me. "I would like to tell you what happened to me today in meditation," he said softly. "The thoughts, the colors, the vibrations and the energy must become words." The young man's eyes glowed with wonder as he continued.

"I went down by the river and sat under a tree. As I entered into meditation I felt energy rise first in the back of my head and then in a band at the level of my eyes. My thoughts were bright colors, moving patterns. My *mantra* was a breathing violet spot in the very center of my perception - right between my eyes. For a few seconds in deep stillness, I felt my own true self being revealed to me. Then there was pure unstruck sound; pure existence. I opened my eyes to stare at the river and the valley. I saw the sky. I saw all and nothing. I breathed deeply and felt complete peace. I pressed my palms to my eyes and suddenly 'whoosh'- a wave of most brilliant pure blue swept over my mind."

Graham looked so exalted, so dumbfounded, that I had to believe he wasn't making this up. There were many similar stories.

The forty ashram members were for the most part natives of Montreal, Vancouver, Toronto and the northeast provinces of Canada. Most had come to this place to stay three to six months or for as long as their resources would allow. A few, like Graham, were Americans who had wandered in by chance or by hearsay, as I had. No one was really sure how long they would remain. I had the feeling most of them would like to stay forever. But they were "here and now" people who evidently didn't waste much time agonizing over future plans and decisions. *This was the first lesson I learned from them.*

After many weeks of traveling among the bronzed Afghans, Pakistanis and Indians, the Canadians seemed startlingly pale, anemic, almost ill-looking. Obviously, they had not been doing much sun-bathing. But there was a special happy radiance in their eyes. Like Scott's, their gaze was direct and clear, without a trace of the glazed, drug-dulled vagueness of the many hippies who roamed these parts.

Although all were free to explore the fascinating villages of hill people around the valley, their time seemed wholly devoted to the routine of daily meditation, *satsung*, and simple household chores. There were also individual meetings with Swami, the high point of their experience. *Satsungs* were held every day and sometimes continued for as long as twelve hours or more - meditation periods alternating with long readings and discussions led by Swami. In between sessions, they retired to their individual rooms, walked along the road, read, talked, and shared experiences. Each member engaged in solitary meditation for two to six hours every day.

I was impressed and intrigued by what I heard. The next day I moved into John's small house, a mile south of the ashram. It was located beyond the village in open country on a knoll surrounded by green fields that looked down on the rushing river Beas. Beyond, the hills on the opposite side of the valley rose steeply to a backdrop of snow-topped mountains. Every morning I walked the mile to the ashram past fields where brown-skinned peasants bent over the endless tasks of planting, weeding and harvesting the barley. When I reached the ashram and its pale inhabitants, it was to enter another world.

On the afternoon of my second day in Kulu I made my first attempt to meditate alone. After lunch, when everyone dispersed to their quarters to avoid the heat, I climbed down the bank to the sparkling river. The shore was lined with large boulders. I slipped off my sandals and lay back against a sun-warmed stone, my eyes on the ridge of mountains beyond which lay a land I had yet to explore. I closed my eyes and tried to concentrate on my breath.

"In ... out, in ... out, in ... out."

I couldn't keep continuous thoughts from streaking past. It was hard, almost impossible, to focus only on the rise and fall of breath. I kept trying and failing and trying again until suddenly colors began to change behind my closed eyelids. The sunlight, which had been bright orange red, turned black, blue, then pale brown. I saw a small mound rise in this umber, desertlike landscape and grow steadily into a slender white pyramid. Dark, almost black hillocks appeared on either side and gradually became brilliant red. In the valley between, the pyramids dissolved and the background changed to dark blue-green. An ever-changing series of grottoes appeared, almost exactly as if I was swimming underwater over a Caribbean reef, except that there were no fish. Caves, polyps, tunnels of green and purple caused me to hold my breath in excitement and strain my eyes to see what would unfold next.

After a while I opened my eyes. It was gone. There was only the slate-gray river foaming white over rocks, and beyond, the rounded hills enclosing the narrow valley. At last I had seen, if only briefly, a vision. I felt marvelously excited. That evening, Swami explained that this was a relatively common experience for beginners.

"That you saw it is actually where the concept of the Third Eye - the eye that allows us to see the unseen - comes from," he explained. "But it's only the very beginning of meditation."

On the following afternoon I climbed again down the boulders beside the river. Once again I leaned back against the warm stones and closed my eyes. I watched intently through closed lids as I felt my breath coming and going. After about ten minutes, a shape appeared. At first, it was just a small hump in the dark landscape behind my eyelids. It grew into a face lying horizontally in *bas relief*. As I searched its contours I recognized it as a three-dimensional replica of a Kollwitz self-portrait I have always cherished. Then I was back underwater again, exploring slowly an ever-expanding series of brilliantly colored grottos that widened and narrowed before me. Some had red centers that grew larger and larger, then vanished. Suddenly, although my eyes were still closed, the fantastic voyage ended.

"Beginner's luck," John assured me that night at supper.

"That's the beginning of the course, not the goal, Jan," said Swami. "Now you're enrolled in the freshman class."

With real anticipation I returned to my rock in the river the next afternoon. Nearby, a group of school children played tag on the grass and a *Harijan* family hung rags to dry in front of their tumbledown hut. The river sparkled in the sun. Looking north, I could see a straight white ridge of mountains above the Solang Nala beyond which lay the remote valleys of the Western Himalayas where I had found such peace and tranquility a week before. Could I, through meditation, capture that treasure and carry it with me forever?

I closed my eyes and concentrated on my breath. At first, thoughts kept intruding. I counted, concentrated, whispered, "in and out, in and out," to myself, fighting the persistent intrusive stream of conscious ideas. Then suddenly the river was silent. The red sunlight through my eyelids disappeared. A series of large room-sized sienna-hued spaces lined with flat stones rose before me. It was rather like looking into the ruins of dwellings at Pompei or Mohenjadarho. I strained to see what was on the floor of these rooms, but could never reach that level with my eyes. A strong breeze came up outside and the colors seemed to streak and swim as though I was seeing the wind. Finally the breeze became so strong it blew gusts of sand against my eyelids. Reluctantly I opened my eyes and rose to leave. The children stopped their game of tag and surrounded me, begging for money.

On succeeding days I could scarcely wait to find time for my meditation hour.

Alexandra David-Neel, a remarkable Frenchwoman who spent fourteen years studying with the lamas of Tibet and Sikkim, described the experience of meditation vividly in her book *Mystery and Magic in Tibet*: "People who habitually practice methodical contemplation," she wrote, "often experience when sitting down for their appointed time of meditation, a sensation of having put down a load, or taking off a heavy garment and entering a silent, delightfully calm, region. It is the impression of deliverance and serenity which Tibetan mystics call *niampar jagpa* 'to make equal,' 'to level' - meaning calming down all causes of agitation that roll their 'waves' through the mind."

This all without benefit of drugs - even the altitude, a modest 5,000 feet, could not have been responsible for my hallucinations. In the years that have elapsed since those exciting days, I have tried in vain to achieve a similar quiet of mind and expansion of space. Sometimes I even wonder whether it was only the effect of my malaria pills!

Although only the "elementary course," the hallucinations were fascinating. They have been variously attributed to depletion or accumulation of carbon dioxide from so closely attending to breathing and thus overriding ordinary automatic respiratory regulation. However, when I experimented with breathing much faster or much slower during the visions there was no change. One day I thought the edges of the expanding and contracting balls of light were pulsating at the rate of my heart. On another I saw a faint network of blood vessels and I began to suspect that what I was seeing was simply the content of my own eyeball, a possibility partly supported by the fact that passing my hand in front of my eyes changed the depth of color. Swami, however, assured me that even men without eyes report these same visions. Much later, Scott showed me pictures drawn by an artist who must have had exactly the same visions during his meditation that I had - the same caves, the same pyramids, the same fantastic sense of swimming under water past brilliantly colored rock and sea plants.

The similarity of our hallucinations reminded me of a patient I had once taken care of at St. Elizabeths, a government mental hospital in Washington D.C. Extremely ill with chronic, unrelenting schizophrenia, he also experienced florid auditory, visual and kinesthetic hallucinations. One day he stood staring at a weird picture on my office wall of shapes and figures painted by another very psychotic patient, muttering, "there it is, there it all is."

The woman who painted the picture later jumped to her death from the roof of a state mental hospital to escape the voices and visions that tormented her relentlessly. The young man recognized that the visions she painted during her psychosis were also his own. I wondered if the similarity of their experiences tells us something about how our brains are wired? Or might it mirror actual other-world perceptions discernible only during mental derangement, hallucinogenic trips, or meditation?

"Both," replied the Swami when I asked him this question.

It is an answer that has never left me - "Both," - one of Mother India's replies to all of life's dilemmas.

On my third night in the small house by the river, as I lay down to sleep under a sky full of stars, I asked myself for the hundredth time, "Who are these ashram acolytes and why have they come here to live in cramped little cells under burning tin roofs in summer, or in the freezing cold of a Himalayan winter?"

University graduates, college drop-outs, engineering candidates, artists, teachers and social workers; they had not been satisfied with their plans or professions back home and were fed up with what they called the "Western Movie."

"Most grown-ups that we know in the West, including my parents, aren't getting much fun out of life," said Jane R.

Jane dropped out of college in her third year to "find herself." "They work at jobs they hate, they quarrel, watch television, and worry about money. That's not a very good life to aim for."

Jane, like most of her fellow ashramites, is involved in a different scenario, one that is perhaps an inevitable sequel to what they so disparagingly reject. Theirs is a conscious, rather humorless search for personal happiness, fulfillment, and "liberation." Many of them have been at it for years.

"We are here with the Swami because in his space we are perfectly happy," said Doreen, a delightful young artist from Ottawa.

"My life has a new vitality and purpose since I joined Swami," agreed Helen, a physical therapist from Montreal. "Can't you feel the energy in his space?" she asked with perfect seriousness. "It is the space of a Realized Being."

Helen found a source of unwavering love in the Swami and she seemed to revere him almost as she would God.

"Through contact with *him*, his vibrations, his aura, I'm a better person, and I myself have a chance to become liberated and a fully realized being," she explained.

I was overwhelmed and inundated by their bliss. I spent hours listening and talking with them, trying to discover how they managed to get such a "high" on this drugless trip. Patiently, they tried to put their feelings into words for me and I began to understand.

Meditation seems to achieve its benefits by emptying the mind of its usual endless ruminations. Concentrating on a few syllables of a mantra (which is often just a single sound such as Om or Eym), focusing on one's breathing, or simply on emptying the mind of thoughts, causes something new to happen. Although initially such focus of attention or mind stillness is difficult to sustain without continual mind wandering, gradually, with much effort for some, easily and quickly for others, the intruding thoughts are excluded. Then, when the mind is still, perception seems to open to other sensations never before experienced. These may be visions, tactile sensations or emotions.

With proper preparation and guidance the process proceeds smoothly and pleasantly almost like a well-guided drug trip but without the loss of control or dazed sensorium. On the contrary, as concentration increases, perception and thoughts become increasingly clear. New channels of awareness open. With the guru's guidance, the successful meditator realizes that his new sensations are glimpses of infinite reality of the "oneness of man with his environment and all other creatures."

This realization itself was a source of blissful happiness to each of them at the moment of insight. More important, as realization emerged, anxiety and fear slowly receded. An immense sense of inner understanding imparts self-confidence, contentment, love and compassion to all aspects of daily life. At least, that's how they explained it to me.

Listen:

Sidney is twenty-seven, employed as a computer programmer by a large corporation in Ottawa. Four years ago while he was still in college, he met Swami at a meeting in Canada.

"I was doing okay but I wasn't satisfied or interested. I didn't want to get off on the typical western trips - job, house, wife, kids, all that. Then, after being with Swami for several months in an ashram in Canada, I felt satisfied and ready to learn. My professors were never able to answer my questions. Swami always did or tried to. I came here to learn how to be happy. Swami helps you find what you're doing that is wrong without curtailing your freedom. Freedom is being able to be satisfied in a lot of different situations. Whenever your mind is not sure, suffering occurs. The more I expand my mind through meditation, through *Satsung*, the more I find I can deal with everything. I don't ever find myself getting unhappy anymore. I have found a whole new perspective."

Martin is twenty-eight I talked to him one afternoon as we sat on the veranda of Swami's house high above the river. He has no regular job but goes home "to the West" every year or so and stays until he can make enough money to return to the ashram.

"I stay here in Kulu to get more grounded in the feeling of oneness, to stop seeing duality," he explained. "Meditation causes the mind to be at ease, still, less agitated. There is less distortion in *the space*."

I asked him about his plans for the future. Smiling gently he replied, "I have no plans except to stay here as much as I can. Some day I'd like to teach meditation in the West, just like most of the people here."

Each evening, I had dinner with Swami. Afterward, I returned to the small house over the river. Two servants who came with the house hovered about me so protectively that I usually left early in the morning and took my breakfast at the hotel near the ashram. One morning I was sitting there at a small table on the veranda when Mary, a girl of twenty-six with large trusting brown eyes, asked if she could join me. I signaled to the landlord's young son, who served as waiter, to bring us a fresh pot of tea. Then I leaned forward to listen to her story.

Back in Canada, Mary was a successful artist. She had heard the Swami speak in Toronto two years ago. Soon afterwards she sold most of her paintings and traveled to this ashram in Kulu. She had been here ever since. Her face and eyes glowed with happiness. She had no plans for leaving, no longer painted, often meditated four or five hours a day.

The dark-eyed small boy brought pots of tea. Mary continued her story.

"Through meditation the pure screen of your mind allows you to see," she explained. "If I were a fully *Realized Being* I would carry this clarity all of the time. The state of meditation redirects your energy instead of letting it dissipate. Most people use only about ten percent of their brain capacity at any one time. If I can function fairly well with ten percent, think of what I could do with another ninety!"

She paused and I leaned back, remembering hearing the same argument from friends of mine who were in psychoanalysis in the '60s. Mary's face radiated warmth and satisfaction, but I could not detect a trace of fanaticism in her soft eyes.

"But it seems so self-centered," I interjected feebly. "Have you or any of the others who stay here ever thought of volunteering sometime to help the poor in this village as a teacher or in some other way?" (Me, always the bleeding heart.)

"First we have to get our own heads together," explained Mary. "How can we expect to help other people until we understand ourselves?"

I was to hear almost exactly the same phrase repeatedly from many others.

Kim, a striking brunette of twenty-eight, was a graduate student in the university when she heard the Swami at an evening lecture five years before in Montreal. Instantly, attracted by his message, she followed him to Kulu. She had been here ever since. One afternoon, she invited me to her apartment on the hillside across the road from the ashram. There were only two rooms, a closet-sized kitchen containing a tiny alcohol stove, pots and pans, spices and bags of rice. The other small room was for sleeping and meditating. Smiling pictures of the Swami beamed from all the walls. Her sleeping chamber was almost filled by a wide platform as long as the room and jutting out to the door. Comfortably padded with blankets and bright colored cushions, it served as a place for meditation by day and a bed by night. A fresh flower was placed in a glass of water in front of Swami's framed picture at the head of the bed.

"I can't always follow where Swamiji is coming from, but I feel happy when I'm near his space," she told me. "Like I'm sitting there with a hundred questions in my mind and he answers them all, one after another without my even asking. So he's able not only to see his own mind but others also."

As we sat quietly together on her wide pillow-strewn pad, I tried to understand. Then I asked her if this happiness of hers would persist if Swami died or otherwise disappeared.

Kim smiled and replied, "Of course. Swamiji prepares us for this. I can't separate meditation from Swamiji, but I know that meditation is a way of increasing my intuition and enhances my whole life. My perspective on everything has changed. My perceptions are more acute. My energy level is higher. As your mind expands into a whole new life style, the most important things are contact with the guru, then meditation, and finally the need to look after your own health."

The health thing was big here. Good simple food (no meat of course: this is a Hindu ashram; killing animals for food is forbidden), plenty of rest, no drugs, moderate exercise. All of these were emphasized by Swami, who insisted that each member of the ashram maintain his own kitchen and cook for himself.

One blazing hot afternoon, I climbed the steep hillside across the road to visit Karen, a dark heavy-set girl of around twenty-five years. Her specialty in Canada was *reflexology*, a particular kind of massage that claims to achieve healing by rubbing various parts of the foot. Each part of the foot is supposed to correspond to a specific bodily organ. Karen had invited me to come to her cottage for a demonstration. We sat on mats on the floor. She asked me to put my right foot in her lap. Then she told me her story.

"Until two years ago I was a graduate student in physiology," she began, while rubbing my much-calloused toes vigorously. "I was not very happy. In fact I was frequently very, very depressed. Then one night I heard a lecture by Swamiji. It inspired something in my mind and suddenly opened a well of happiness. He opened my emotions to joy and bliss. Now I have to have to have that *space*. If I have it, anything else I do is beautiful."

I winced as she pulled particularly hard on my great toe. A warm and loving light beamed from her large brown eyes. Her plain face glowed with happiness.

"What's so important about Swami?" I asked, hoping to avert her forceful exertions on the ball of my foot.

"I can trust him. He's intelligent. I get high just from absorbing his space. It's the *praana* that's in a fully *Realized Being* which is being picked up by all of us around him. That's why we're all here."

A wide-eyed hawk swooped lazily overhead, searching, searching, always searching.

Far below where we sat talking, Swamiji left his chalet and strode down the path toward his family dwelling on the other side of the road. Carol, a Canadian woman with long silky golden hair and the face of an angel, hurried from her tiny hut toward Swami's private aerie carrying a large feather duster to tidy up while he was out. Her son, a lad of nine or ten, followed her halfway across the field and then stopped to climb on an ancient tricycle near the water tap. Swamiji, majestic in a long white cotton robe, stopped to pat the boy on the head. Then he walked firmly on down the hillside. Carol had lived in the ashram longer than anyone else except Swamiji - seven years or more. Her son had most of his schooling from itinerant members of the little colony. At first this seemed rather shocking to me. But as time went on I found it was not hard to accept and even envy all of their happiness.

Perhaps Dan was right. With only one life to live, why should we all elect the "Western Movie"?

Who was this Swami Shayam, this miracle worker?

One night while Scott, John, Swamiji and I sat on straw mats under the stars eating a spartan dinner of *chapattis* and *dahl*, Swamiji told us his life story.

Born to a farmer's family in a small Indian village in Uttar Pradesh, he was the oldest of four brothers and one sister. From early childhood, his life had been seasoned with religious training. The family's own guru, a devout and scholarly old man, visited the household regularly each week to instruct the family in the Hindu epics, prayers, and meditation. As Kundi, Swamiji's daughter, stepped quietly into the pool of candlelight to collect our plates, Swamiji laughingly recalled those early days.

"I remember being required to come in from play to participate in prayers and lessons when I was only six or seven," he said, eyes twinkling with amusement. "I took much more joy in those lessons than in school. The schoolteachers considered me something of a scamp."

After completing his secular studies, Swami took commercial courses at a business college and within a few years was installed as a speed shorthand expert in the Punjab legislature at Chandighar. Soon he established records for his proficiency. After work he taught religion. For a time he joined Maharishi (of transcendental meditation fame) but found his operation "too commercialized, too sensational, too large."

"My own little circle grew. Soon a few foreigners began to attend our sittings. One night on a pilgrimage in Rishakesh I was conducting a *satsung* outdoors in the shadow of the great mountain. There was a visitor there from Calgary."

Swamiji paused now for a long time. When Kundi approached from the shadows, he asked her to bring tea. Evidently it was ready, for Evan, a bearded young Canadian immediately hurried toward us with the teapot. He served us silently. Everyone in the ashram (with the possible exception of Swamiji's wife, a heavyset, dour, definitely Unrealized Being) seemed to take an almost reverential joy in serving Swami. The same generosity and courtesy were extended to me on the many occasions I was asked to be his guest. Now Swami continued.

"The man from Calgary begged me to bring my message to Canada. I had no reason to go. I was content, so I said no. This man was very disappointed. He returned to Calgary, but continued to write that I must join him in Canada, that I was much needed there. I was in conflict with myself. All of my friends urged me to go. They gave me many reasons, many arguments. They even offered to pay all my travel expenses. I had no desire to go, but I agreed to meditate on the question."

Several days later the Canadian sent Swamiji a round-trip plane ticket to Edmonton. Yielding at last, he flew to Canada and traveled by bus to Calgary. After a few days settling in at the home of his host, Swami became distressed. He found himself altogether isolated from the work he thought he had come to accomplish. His host, however, insisted that he sign a contract before commencing his lectures. Unwilling to commit himself to an extended contract, Swami refused. He felt like a prisoner in the house which was far out of town in a strange land. One afternoon, when his host was out, a woman came to visit. Swami asked her to drive him to town. He packed his belongings and thus escaped. Swamiji, who was not Swami then but simply Mr. Shayama Charan Scrivastava, determined to return to India.

"Before leaving however, I thought to see something of the country. I asked the woman to drive me to a bus depot. There I bought a ticket to the West."

Three days later on a hot July evening, Swami arrived in Vancouver, B.C., and checked into a cheap hotel. Tucking his passport and wallet under the pillow of his bed, he padded down to the common bath at the end of the hall clad only in *dhoti* and sandals.

Swami laughed as he recalled that fateful evening. "Suddenly while I was sitting in the bath, I had a strange feeling that all of my belongings might be disappearing. I got out of the bath and hurried back to my room. Everything was gone - valise, clothes, even the money and passport I had hidden under the pillow."

Once again his eyes sparkled as he shook his head back and forth in the Indian way. "I was left with only my *dhoti*, a shawl and the pair of sandals I'd worn to the bath."

Now Swami paused. We felt the magic of the sudden darkness. The air was fragrant with juniper smoke and the soft tenderness of spring. Stars glowed in a velvet sky which slowly began to lighten above the black shoulder of hills to the east as the moon rose and lent a luminous beauty to the shining river below. Swamiji filled each of our cups with more tea.

"What then?" I cried impatiently, for Swamiji had the real story-teller's knack of making every tale, however simple, come alive with expectation and excitement. He laughed and went on.

"What then? You may well inquire. There I was without a rupee in a strange town 12,000 miles from home. What to do? I sat down and meditated, asking my god, what shall I do? After an hour of quiet meditation I heard the voice of my guru and I could even see his face."

"I have sent you to work," he said, "and now you are leaving. I want you to do the work for which you came here."

At that moment Swamiji's American career began and Mr. Shayama Charan Scrivastava became Swami Shayam. Clad in *dhoti* and sandals, all that remained of his clothing, he became an instant sensation. Larger and larger audiences were drawn by the same charisma that now brought his disciples from far-off Canada to Kulu in the valley of the Beas. Soon his lectures and *satsungs* were being broadcast on Canadian radio and television. Ashrams were established in Vancouver, Montreal and Ottawa. Swami gazed up at the canopy of stars above us and said gently, "Now we are many."

During my stay at the ashram I asked myself repeatedly what could lead this group of school teachers, engineers, laboratory and office workers to give up their comfortable western homes to gather in this remote Himalayan valley. The answer was the Swami himself.

"Can't you feel the vibrations in his space?" asked Dorothy as we sat having coffee on the veranda of the hotel. It must have been the fiftieth time I'd heard the same sentiment in various terms by my new friends. While I had not had the good fortune to feel special "vibrations," I tried hard to understand what they were talking about.

"Swami gives pure love as Christ did," said one grateful disciple.

Indeed, Swami had an endless series of stories, parables and fables that spelled out a philosophy to live by. The ashram's members were enchanted by his affection, his puns and metaphors. It was as though they needed to love and be loved and had at last found someone who filled that requirement without reservation. One morning after *satsung*, Swami invited me to sit with him in his private quarters behind the main assembly hall. I asked him how it was that he excited such god-like veneration from his followers.

"I would do anything for my people and they know it," he explained. "I am available to them twenty-four hours a day; they have only to ask." Then his irrepressible humor burst forth. "I also have to admit it's a living!"

"Swami's product is happiness through mind expansion," explained Dorothy, coming in with the usual tray of tea and cups. "What do you mean by that?" I asked rather sharply. I was beginning to get a little fed up with the clichés.

"Our minds expand through meditation and healthy living habits," Dorothy replied unperturbed. "His aim for us is the same as his own goal was, to become a fully Realized Being."

"But what does this mean and how do you do it?" I persisted, unable to share her perfect confidence.

Dorothy smiled serenely, "Wait and see."

At *satsung* that evening Swamiji told a story.

"Once upon a time, there was a merchant who went to his *Guruji* (honored teacher) and said that he must have help to complete his work. He would give anything in the world if a good helper could be found. Guruji listened to him and then called for a ghost.

When the ghost came, Guruji instructed him to give every assistance to the merchant. The ghost agreed but extracted a promise in return. 'I will work untiringly for this man as long as he has work for me to do, but when he runs out of work I will eat him up.'

The merchant agreed willingly, saying that he had more than enough to keep the ghost busy for a lifetime. The ghost followed the merchant to his village where the merchant put him to work harvesting wheat. Within one second, all the fields were harvested. The delighted merchant was amazed and told the ghost to grind the wheat. Within another second all the wheat was ground and in bags. The merchant was even more astounded and told the ghost to deliver the wheat to its various addresses throughout the world. Two seconds later the job was done. The merchant was then beside himself.

'I have no more work for you,' said he. 'Then I will eat you,' said the ghost. 'Oh, no, no,' said the merchant, 'let us return to Guruji. There must be some other solution.'

Guruji heard the dilemma. Turning to the merchant, he said, 'You have made a promise; now you must be eaten.'

'Please, no! I had no idea this ghost could complete everything so fast. It would have taken anyone else years to do the job,' cried the merchant.

'But you made a bargain,' said Guruji. 'You obtained the power and you must know how to use it. I will give you a secret,' said Guruji. 'Take this ghost home and tell him to climb the tree in your yard and then climb down again. Keep him busy at it.'

The merchant did as he was told. He instructed the ghost to climb the peepul tree in the back yard and when he reached the top to come down again. The ghost did so ten, twenty, a hundred, a thousand times. Then the ghost begged for release.

The merchant said, 'Let us strike a bargain. I will let you stop working, if you'll agree not to eat me.'

'Done,' said the ghost, and he left.

Swamiji paused and gazed benignly on his audience.

"You also have the power," he said firmly. "Know how to use it."

He rose. We walked outside where the evening star shone over the dark hills across the river. Someone brought chairs for us and we sat down near the bank.

"Swamiji," I began, using the affectionate familiar address of student to beloved master, "I wonder if you will allow me to ask a potentially embarrassing question."

The Swami's deep brown eyes looked into my face intently for a moment before he smiled and replied, "Anything, Jan."

"It is this," I began rather lamely. "These young men and women, especially the women, adore you, love to be close to you. You are the centerpiece of their lives. Have you never found that a sexual love affair might emerge from these attachments?"

Swami looked thoughtful. "Yes, of course I am aware. Once or twice I have even had late callers to my room. Then, very gently, very kindly, I must send them away or take them back to their own place. But this is an aberration. I could never take advantage of them because they must trust me."

"I asked the question because I'm searching for the source of your power here," I explained. "The more I've seen of this ashram, the more I am impressed that you're carrying on marathon group psychotherapy. You've gained a magnificent transference from your members to yourself. Meditation takes the place of free association or talking about feelings."

Swami laughed aloud with pleasure at the challenge. Then he turned to me very seriously. "The trouble with you psychiatrists is your preoccupation with the past as an item of importance without changing the level of manifest reality. This is really a mistake. It's no use to get in there and try to sort out all that past as it will elude your every attempt to do so. This is the failure of western methods. Through meditation you reach a state of pure being where you can transcend the past, where there is no perception whatever on the manifest level. Once reached, there is a carryover of energy to other channels and a special kind of radiance emerges."

I looked across the lawn. Cows slept beside the little manger bathed in pure white moonlight. A dozen members of the ashram had quietly joined us and sat cross-legged on the ground listening. Kundi brought a shawl and slipped it around Swami's shoulders. In all my hours of conversation with members of the ashram I never heard anyone being put down or anyone trying to do so. No one was ashamed. Few were guilty. No one wanted to die. No one still hated his family or at least was interested in talking about it. I contrasted my life in the ashram with my work in western psychiatric hospitals. There, we either subdued fear and delusion with drugs or turned patients into intensely narcissistic human beings dedicated to self-examination, self-expression, and self-aggrandizement.

These people were on a different journey. Most seemed satisfied to go on as they were indefinitely. There was much talk, strange to me, of energy channels, the rising of *Kundilini*, special spaces, vibrations, and astral travel. Yet no one was crazy. All cared for their own needs in a strange land, were happy in their life together. All were seeking answers beyond themselves. It was more than I could say for "the Western Movie."

On my last night in Kulu, Scott, Swami, a few others and I sat up drinking warm milk and talking by the river bank until it was nearly morning.

"The goal of meditation is happiness," said Swami. "In meditation you become Jesus Christ, Mohammed, Krishna, Buddha. While western psychotherapy seeks to improve attachment of man to his fellows, Self-Realization counsels him to search for inner peace and oneness with nature. This will bring a searchlight so powerful, so radiant and satisfying that the ashes of regret and guilt in which so many wallow will lose all importance."

Although the moon was still overhead in the western sky, its light was pale and cold now. In the east the horizon was becoming light again. Swami rose and looked quietly over the river. Surprised that I felt neither stiff nor cold although we had been sitting through the entire night by the river bank. I stood beside him looking at the impassable heights to the north.

"It is man himself who is God," said Swami. "Man creates, or removes darkness and suffering. The highest thought is that of serving humanity. As your consciousness becomes fully expanded, you will be able to look after all humanity and will wish to do so. Most of all, never lose trust in man, for man is God himself."

I knelt a moment to touch Swami's feet, the Indian way of showing respect. When I rose, he embraced me and kissed my cheek. We said goodnight, although it was already morning.

1981   20 March. President Ronald Reagan shot by twenty-five-year-old John Hinckley, who was then committed to St. Elizabeth's Hospital in Washington, D.C.

13 May. Pope John II shot by Turkish student in Rome.

29 July. Prince Charles marries Diane Spencer.

6 October. Cairo: Anwar Sadat, president of Egypt, shot by Islamic terrorists during parade of troops.

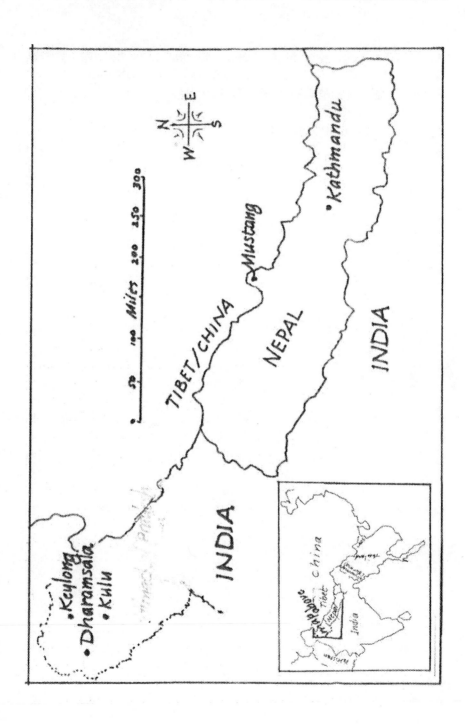

Chapter V

MUSTANG!
UP THE KALI GANDAKI
VALLEY TOWARD TIBET

I met an old man and his eyes were all yellow
I held a young child and her belly was stone
I met a young woman whose child was not coming
I met another whose baby had died
It's hard, hard, hard, hard ......

The man's pleasant voice on the phone at Royal Nepal Airlines told me that no seats were available from Kathmandu to Jomsom for at least two weeks. By that time it would be late May. The monsoon would be under way in the valley, and getting back from north of the Himalayan wall either by air or on foot over rain swollen streams would be hazardous. I persuaded Pasang, the Tamang guide I had hired for the journey, to go with me to the airport at 5:30 the next morning.

"If we don't make it," I suggested, "we'll try for the flight to Pokhara at 7:00 and walk up the Kali Gandaki to Mustang."

Late May can be a dismal time to walk up the valley. A verdant passage in the dry season, the thick forest in the deep gorge would be dank and filled with leeches during the rains that flood rivers and trails every afternoon during monsoon. Bridges are washed out and fording streams is treacherous. No planes fly because clouds shroud the immense peaks on either side of the valley.

By five next morning, a gray dawn was just breaking over Kathmandu. Low dark clouds hung over the sleeping city. The daily morning rainfall spattered lightly on the windws of our taxi as Pasang and I taxied to the airport. Except for a few tousled men washing up at the public faucets, the streets were deserted.

When we arrived and disembarked with our gear, a small group of orange-robed lamas were the only people in the large waiting room of the airport. Laughing and joking merrily, they stood beside conical baskets stuffed with plastic thermos jugs, kerosene lanterns, and blankets. While we waited for the Royal Nepal Airline ticket agent to finish his tea in the back office, the waiting room gradually filled with the usual unusual variety of travelers to be found in Nepal. There were Tibetans in belted cloaks, homespun breeches and embroidered mukluks. Tamang women in long black sleeveless *chubas* and red and black striped aprons stood beside great baskets filled with bundles purchased or bartered for in Kathmandu. Thakalis, who, like Tibetans, are great traders, compared the contents of their bags and boxes, their broad Mongolian faces beaming with satisfaction. A few Westerners wandered in. There were two blond bearded young men with huge canvas packs and bedrolls towering on alloy frames. A western woman in her thirties, neat, with a long blond pigtail and horn-rimmed glasses, bustled about efficiently. She spoke in fluent Nepali to the porters weighing her baskets of household goods, bamboo stools and aluminum trunks.

Pasang and I lolled drowsily at the ticket counter where the English half of the sign over the baggage scales read:

> "Passengers are requested to keep pocket knives, daggers, swords, kakuris, etc., in the checked baggages."

At last the ticket agent arrived. Everyone rushed the counter. When the commotion of ticketing people and baggage subsided an hour later, we had tickets and our packs were weighed and checked through. We were directed to proceed out to the tarmac, where once again we sighted our baggage. We had to identify each bag for security personnel who then marked them with white chalk. I was amused to see there was not a single conventional travel bag in the lot.

The flight from Kathmandu to Jomsom is one of the most spectacular in the world. I stared down at the shining, twisted ribbon of the Kali Gandaki far below. I had walked along those lush green banks, dotted with temples and villages. I remembered the tea shacks filled with laughing porters and the biting taste of home-brewed *chang* (local beer). Rarely, we stopped at a teahouse with imported Indian beer in bottles, icy from cooling in the river that descended from the mightiest glaciers on earth.

There were other memories: scrawny children, crusted with scabies and dirt; a young mother with a breast abscess, a five-year-old whose rock-hard spleen filled her whole belly. After I had examined the little girl the family insisted I stop for dinner. Potatoes were brought from their storage place in the abandoned temple next door and boiled over an open fire in their dark, smoke-filled hut. After supper we drank tea and I sang Clementine. When I told them I was fifty, they said I was the oldest woman in the village and sent for *rakshi* (distilled from fermented barley) to toast me.

Suddenly the gorge deepened to at least 10,000 feet as we passed between vertical walls formed by snow covered flanks of the Annapurna massif to the right and Dauhligiri to the left, each soaring to over 26,000 feet. After passing through that giant ice-walled corridor, we broke into brilliant blue sky as we soared north of the Himalayan wall, beyond the monsoon-soaked valley, into a landscape of parched brown rolling hills.

I turned around to look through the rear windows at the north slopes of the Himalayan giants. My eyes met those of the girl in horn-rimmed glasses. There was something familiar about this competent young woman.

"Look at all these empty seats," I marveled, "yet, they told me yesterday this flight was sold out!"

The young woman laughed and asked who I was.

"I'm a neurologist from the United States - stopping off for a while between worlds," I explained.

"That's a coincidence," she replied. "Five or six years ago I met a lady neurologist near Skardu in Baltistan."

"But I was up there five years ago myself!" I cried. "Could you be Suzanne S.?"

"Of course I am," she exclaimed, as astonished as I was. Disregarding the bumpy weather, I unfastened my seat belt and ran back for a closer look. We were both amazed and delighted that the world was small enough for our paths to cross once again in another unlikely part of the globe - this time in a twenty-one passenger Fokker flying between Annapurna and Dauhligiri.

Five years before we met in Shigar - a small village on the banks of the Indus on the remote plateau northeast of Skardu in Baltistan. I was visiting a health guard team, Pakistan's version of the Chinese barefoot doctor, with its training director. Suzanne was living with a family in a nearby village where she was taping folk songs and stories of the little-known Baltis. I remembered vividly our trip together to visit a stone age village across the Indus. We were transported on a raft of logs lashed together with leather thongs kept afloat with inflated goat skins at each corner. Bearded old men in turbans stood at each corner propelling the raft with long poles. When we left the village in the sudden darkness of evening, a young woman rushed down to the raft and thrust a dying baby in my arms, begging me to make it well.

Suzanne is an anthropologist and had married since our last meeting in Shigar. She and her husband, Donald, an architect, were on their way to Jahrkot. We soon picked up both the conversation and friendship we left off five years before. By the time we disembarked in Jomsom, we had decided to join forces for the trek north.

Landing in Jomsom is unlike landing in any other airport in the world. The small airfield is at the south end of town, right on the foot trail that follows the Kali Gandaki gorge five days walk north from Pokhara. From the upper end of town, the trail continues on to Lo Montang, forty miles to the north on the Tibetan border. In lieu of taxis or any other motorized transport a pair of yaks and a half dozen donkeys festooned with red tassels were tethered to the barbed wire fence around the landing field. There were no roads, no wagons, not even a bicycle. Close by, half a dozen Tibetan women in long black sleeveless gowns over faded blouses trudged back and forth, carrying huge stones from a heap by the road to the low foundation of a building twenty yards away. After each trip they crouched down so that the men working with them could place a fresh load of stones into the panniers on their backs.

Jomsom is a long narrow village that lies on both banks of the Kali Gandaki in a wide, dry valley surrounded by brown hills. To the east terraced shelves of green slope toward the river and the tiny Bon village, on the far bank. Beyond, the fluted peaks of the Nilgiris rise to more than 20,000 feet. Fifty miles to the south the north faces of the Annapurna and Dhaulagiri massifs, dazzling white in the clear morning sunlight, form a wall between two worlds.

Because Suzanne and Donald were planning on a stay of several months in Jharkot, they had piles of gear and needed porters. Rejecting the pair of yaks and the tasseled donkeys waiting outside the airfield, we set off with as much as we could carry on our backs to one of the small tea shacks that are strung along the foot trail between the airport and the town. En route we caught up with an old Gurung, bent double under an eighty-pound oil drum he had packed up from Pokhara. After a brief conversation with my guide, the fellow's face creased into a wide toothless grin. He would be delighted to porter my stuff on to Kagbeni for twenty rupees. The heavy oil drum he had carried for the past five days would be quickly deposited at its destination in Jomsom and replaced with my pack - feather light at only fifty pounds.

By the time we had drunk several cups of sweet milky tea at the little hotel, Suzanne and Donald found and hired two more porters. We waited for an hour or so for everyone to assemble, meanwhile eating hardboiled eggs and looking unsuccessfully for fresh vegetables. Then, we set off, with Donald and Pasong in the lead carrying their own light packs. Suzanne and I followed, happily carrying only our canteens. Behind us the three laden porters followed. By now the famous wind that sweeps from south to north through the breach in the mountains carved by the Kali Gandaki, was blowing steadily. Warmed by the Indian plain to the south, each day around noon the air is sucked through the mountains toward the cool low pressure area over the high Tibetan plateau. Now it pushed us from behind as we started the gradual climb toward Kagbeni, the northernmost village in which foreigners were permitted in Mustang district just below the Tibetan border.

This whole area was closed to outsiders for most of the past five years because of intermittent warfare between the Nepali army and the Khampas. Th Khampas are Tibetans who have been fighting a guerilla war against the Chinese ever since their country was taken over by the People's Republic twenty years earlier. To avoid trouble with the Chinese, Nepali authorities now forbid this forgotten group of patriots to enter northern border regions of Nepal. Earlier, a number of these Khampas were given American material and moral support during their years of warfare against the Chinese invaders of their country. Several years earlier I had even met a storekeeper in Pokhara who with many others was flown by the U.S. army to Texas in the '60s for training in guerilla warfare. Because of their raids on village food supplies and the complaints of their large neighbor to the north on their return, the Nepali army closed the area and forcibly restrained the Khampas activities. Foreigners were now allowed into previously closed parts of Mustang district.

Passing the north end of Jomsom, we walked by the huge orange *chorten* that stands beside the wooden bridge over the Kali Gandaki. We passed the middle school from where we heard a chorus of boys chanting lessons aloud in the small wooden classrooms. Beyond the village the trail climbed steeply north along the valley wall above the river through one of the most dramatic landscapes on earth. Barren golden brown hills rise to 15,000 feet or more above a flat, wide, rock strewn valley. We were walking along an ancient river bed a full mile across at an altitude of 9,000 feet. The trail followed the east - right bank. The river was milky gray with glacial debris and swollen with melted snow from the mountains and high plateaus of Tibet. We crossed the river bed and followed the trail along the left bank that climbed along a steep hillside high above the torrent. After a mile or so, the path dropped down to the river again. The entire valley floor was a chaos of rock and boulders that marked the site of former streams. When the hillside became impassibly steep, we descended from the narrow trail and walked up the dry river bed over smooth stones. Here we found many round black rocks which when split open revealed the perfect spiral imprint of sea-snails, fossilized remains of the creatures of an ancient ocean erased by the collision of the Indian subcontinent with Asia (and giving rise to the Himalayas).

Although it is a barren wasteland of gray rock and bare hillsides, there was plenty of traffic on this old caravan route to the north. Women in bright Tibetan dress and turquoise ear beads, with chains of silver ornaments and prayer boxes around their necks, descended the path under heavily laden conical baskets. The short copper-skinned men, less curious about us than the women, herded goats that marched in single file, each with a small pair of loaded saddle bags connected by a canvas strap across its back. Many men were bent under huge piles of fodder on their own backs. Others, presumably more prosperous, trotted past on donkeys decorated with red tassels. A bent old Lama wrapped in a maroon wool blanket, wearing a Chinese style straw hat and torn sneakers carried a long walking stick. He glanced up at us impassively as we passed.

After two hours of gentle ascent from Jomsom, we reached a wide tributary of the Kali Gandaki that rushed foaming down a canyon that split the hillside on our right. Suzanne and I sat down on the rocks to take off our boots to wade across, but Pasang insisted in carrying us across, one at a time, on his back.

Several weeks later I followed this stream eastward to where it hurtles down into the valley from Lupra, a tiny village of fifteen mud huts and an enchanting *gompa* two hours' walk upstream.

As we continued north, the valley narrowed again, forcing us back up on the trail that wound along the steep bank above the river. We met a long procession of donkeys, the three leaders decorated with a crown of red tassels and necklaces of large copper bells. They plodded single file down the hillside, each carrying brown and gray striped homespun saddlebags filled with grain. Behind them trailed two dozen more, less festively adorned than the leaders but equally burdened. Behind the last of these patient little animals, a Tibetan man in a long belted cloak, his black hair wound around his head in a single untidy pigtail tied with red wool, walked briskly, carrying a long stick. Behind him, his son, a barefoot youngster of ten in ragged trousers and jacket, smiled at us shyly. They stopped to exchange gossip with Pasang. The small donkeys seemed to need little guidance and continued plodding steadily down the valley.

The wind from the south, warm and dry at mid-day, was much stronger now. It pushed us steadily north, blowing fine dust in our eyes if we turned for a minute to look back at the spectacular sweep of brown hills, and the shining slopes of the Himalayan giants behind. A solitary horseman, splendid in homespun woolen knickers, belted cloak and Tibetan hat, galloped down the gorge on a silver bridled roan. Reining his horse to a stop, he asked us the inevitable *"kata jani?"* (where are you going?). After a few pleasantries, he cracked the horse smartly on its rear with a small twig and with a grin lighting his flat Mongolian features, tore off down the narrow trail. The horse's hoofs raised little puffs of fine dust in the whistling wind. A vast flock of long-haired goats grazed on small hummocks of grass on the rocky hillside above us. A langermeier - the broad winged, red eyed vulture of the Himalayas - cruised lazily overhead. The steady wind swept more strongly up the valley as the gorge narrowed and the vast panorama of barren hills stretched unbroken toward the distant passage to the north.

After another hour of walking, the valley broadened again and two brilliant patches of green appeared like shelves, one above the other on the far bank of the river. This was P'aling, where Snellgrove, the British Tibetologist, stopped to visit the Bon Temples described in his book *"Himalayan Pilgrimage."* Green fields of waist-high barley appeared on our side of the river, rippling in the steady wind like the surface of a sea. Now the valley broadened where the Kali Gandaki is joined by the Muktinath river flowing westward from the sacred shrine of the same name. At the wide delta of their joining, the silhouette of a ruined fort marked the village of

Kagbeni ("Two Rivers"). We were enclosed on all sides by stark steep hills. Behind us, the great snow peaks soared skyward.

Kagbeni is a small island of flat-roofed mud and clay houses surrounded by brilliant green fields of barley. Prayer flags flutter from every roof top. A giant entry *chorten* stands just outside the town. We walked beneath the faded bodhisatvas painted on its peeling ceiling, past a *mani* wall and the first huts at the edge of the town. In an open court yard, mud bricks were drying in the sun. A narrow footbridge led across the river. We entered the main part of the village by a narrow alley paved with huge smooth stones. A tiny calf no larger than a St. Bernard dog lay quietly by the trail and looked up mildly as we passed. The high clay walls on either side of the alley were penetrated from time to time by heavy wooden doors. A train of donkeys, bells jingling and tassels waving, wound toward us. We pressed against the wall to let them pass. The stone paved street then passed the open door of a tea shack-cum-hotel. Men and boys standing at the entry greeted my friends with surprise and pleasure. A youngish woman in Tibetan dress rushed out from inside to welcome them.

Suzanne had spent the previous winter living in a nearby house researching for her doctoral dissertation on the status of women in northern Nepal. No one in the village could really understand how her activities - living in a local house where she visited with local women all day long and wrote by lantern each night - could be called work. She was evidently well liked despite her curious occupation. Fortunately, the halo of good will that surrounded her was extended to me as well. Later, when they discovered I was a "medical doctor," a steady stream of villagers made their way to our door.

After greeting the people standing about the little inn, we continued on through the village. Suddenly the stone paved street widened and led up four or five broad stone steps under an archway beneath an old fort. Donald turned into another narrow alley, pushed open a wooden door in the wall and we stepped into a courtyard flanked on three sides by open sheds. Above them rose the main floor of a large house built of stone and red clay. Half a dozen chickens scurried away squawking as we entered the yard. A young woman in traditional Tibetan black *chuba* and striped apron looked up from a copper vat of roasted barley kernels. When she spotted Suzanne, who had stayed here for four months during the previous winter, she shouted with joy and rushed toward her.

After a long exchange of greetings in Nepalese, Suzanne turned to introduce me to Pima, mistress of this large red house where we would stay.

Pima and Donald exchanged quieter, but no less cordial greetings of reunion. Beaming with pleasure, Pima led us toward the wooden ladder propped against the side of the house, and we followed her up to the second floor. I climbed up last, looking down through the ladder at three tiny furry calves lying quietly on the straw in the shed below. The size of small collies, these docile little creatures are separated from their mothers each morning. They wait silently, patiently, alone all day until the mothers return at dusk from foraging on the barren hillsides.

At the top of the ladder we entered a dark narrow kitchen furnished with a waist high clay stove and a single *charpoi* on which a child was sleeping. Pima ushered us through another corridor into a large room at the back with clean cream-colored mud walls, floor and ceiling. A ledge along one side was strewn with bright Tibetan rugs. She rushed to place burlap mats on the floor for us near the clay oven. On the walls hung a variety of shiny cooking vessels and a narrow wooden churn for making Tibetan tea. A ceremonial hearth at the far end held a huge copper pot of *chang*.

Now our porters straggled in and squatted against the ledge on the far side of the room. Pasang seated himself cross-legged beside us. Pima brought a large teapot full of *chang* and a bottle of *rakshi*. Drinking and talking now began in earnest. For the next two hours, while neighbors and children dropped in to view us briefly, we talked and were served heaping plates of rice and dahl and quantities of *chang*, the local beer made of fermented barley. I avoided the *rakshi*, a rough tasting distillate of chang, which not only is highly intoxicating, but tastes enough like kerosene to be a frequent precursor of the abdominal d*ukha* ("it hurts") so common wherever it is imbibed.

After much good eating and drinking, Suzanne and Donald retired to their large room at one end of the house. Pasang and I followed Pima up a notched log to the roof. Like all Mustang homes, the roof was flat and bordered on all sides by a low wall of stacked firewood. There were two small sleeping rooms built of rammed earth at one end of the roof. Pasang took one and I the other. In my little chamber, faded pictures of the Dalai Lama, of the King and Queen of Nepal in their horn-rimmed glasses, and a paper calendar indicating the Tibetan year 1374 hung on the wall over an ancient charpoi. A pile of soiled blankets in one corner of the dirt floor suggested a potential home for rats or at least fleas - a hypothesis I was to confirm a few hours later.

Pasang lay down on his charpoi and promptly went to sleep. Down below, Suzanne and Donald were sorting out their gear for the trip up the valley to Jahrkot. I settled down on a wooden block outside my chamber to watch the late afternoon sun turn the snow peaks from white to gold. Prayer flags, which had fluttered from tall poles on every roof top in the steady wind of afternoon, were still now as the wind subsided. The sun's last rays caught the gold dome of the temple high above the river.

When the copper color faded from the fluted mountain peaks surrounding the village, I climbed down the notched log to the kitchen below. Pima's stepmother, a toothless old hag, sat on the floor holding the child who had been sleeping on the charpoi. I patted the youngster's frowsy head and went down a second ladder into the courtyard and out the great wooden door to explore the town.

The streets were full of action now. Women and children drove cows and donkeys up the stairs in the narrow streets and into the alleys and courtyards. A man carrying a heavy wooden plow disappeared through a door in the wall across from ours. A caravan of donkeys, bells tinkling, red tassels waving, climbed the stone steps at the far end of the street. When they reached me, the bulging bags hanging across their plump sides pressed me close against the wall. I followed them through the winding alleys to the north end of the town where another *mani* wall marked the upper end of the village. Its smooth stones were carved with the sacred words *Om Mani Padme Hum,* which means, roughly translated, "Indeed, the jewel is in the heart of the lotus." The significance of this divine phrase of Tibetan Buddhism varies from the most abstract and obscure concepts of a supreme deity to the frankly copulatory interpretations of Tantrism. Above the *mani* stones a row of prayer wheels was mounted. Whirling them made a pleasant sound and sent the same precious words, inscribed on parchment within the wheels, to the heavens. On the other side of the path an onion-domed *chorten* marked the northern gate of the town. Soldiers lounged on the stone veranda of a long row of barracks. High above us on the hillside another *chorten*, silhouetted against the sky, seemed to be the last outpost of human endeavor before the barren hills stretched in endless folds to the north.

As the dusk deepened, the gorge of the river filled with hazy clouds. Below, doll-like figures of a donkey caravan forded the river, headed north, and were lost in the vast landscape. Two pigtailed men driving *dzos* - a cross between yak and cow - trudged up the bank toward the village. I sat on a stone, cold now that the sun was gone, but unable to pull my eyes away from the mysterious passage to the north that leads to Tibet. That route, which drew me so strongly, was still off limits to me and to all of us from the West.

Back at Pima's house supper was ready. We dined on *tsampa* -ground roasted barley mixed with goat's milk and washed down with quantities of *chang*. By the time we had finished, the village was silent and dark. Slightly unsteady, I clambered up the notched log to my small room on the roof. The prayer flags hung motionless against a star-filled sky. A near full moon rose, illuminating the ruined fort next door with a soft, mellow light that lent an air of magic to everything around me. Like a stranger from another planet I felt the rhythm imposed by the inexorable cycles of light and darkness, wind and calm in this vast landscape of sky, wind, and mountain. I sat for a measureless time bathed in stillness. Then I entered my little chamber and went immediately to sleep.

About three o'clock next morning I awakened with my left hand burning like fire and my right eye swollen shut. Romantic transcendentalism forgotten, I hastily rose and felt for the tell-tale itching and welts around by waistband. Although I had spread DDT powder liberally on the old mattress, I was clearly being eaten alive by fleas. I bolted from my previously charming quarters, carrying my sleeping bag and a canister of DDT. I shook a generous portion of the latter into the bag, pulled out an old air mattress and an army surplus mosquito hood from my pack and prepared a new bed on the roof. When I awoke next morning the sun was streaming into my eyes and prayer flags were waving gently above my head. The perfect pyramids of Tukchi and the Nilgiris glowed crimson red just beyond the roof edge. If it had not been for my hand, now swollen to the size of a boxing glove, I would have been sure I had died and awakened in heaven.

Beyond the stacks of firewood along the roof edge, I could look down on the whole panorama of the town. The sun shone warmly on flat roofs of nearby dwellings. All, like ours, were piled with neat long rows of stacked firewood along the edges. Prayer flags flapped lazily at the corners of every roof and on the crumbling towers of the old fortress. Beyond, toward the river, the gold roof of the gompa gleamed in the sunlight. Two round chortens at the south end of the village were silhouetted against green fields of barley rippling in the dawn breeze. Far above them, mountains of eternal snow formed a protecting wall, which faded from crimson to purest white as the sun rose. In a special state of blissful content and mindlessness, I sat a long while just staring, feeling loose and happy. The kaleidoscopic colors of my meditation aura came - red, yellow, blue - deep blue even with my eyes closed.

For a moment I understood the peculiar appeal of catatonia and, like my patients, I dared not move for fear it would all go away.

"Doctor-sahib!" Pima's sleek head and smiling face appeared in the square hold of the roof that led down the ladder to the kitchen below.

"Nima Dorche bemarry tsa!" (Nima Dorche is sick!). Already she was lining up patients for me!

Pima is a handsome woman of twenty-six. Two years ago she was married to two brothers. It is the custom in these parts for all the brothers in a family to share a single wife. This prevents the land being broken up into parcels too small to sustain a family. As traditional heir to the father's property, it is the eldest son who marries. In former days the second son became a monk. The remaining sons live with their eldest brother, work for him and share his wife.

The doctor in Jomsom told me of one woman in Mustang who was married to nine brothers. Astonishingly, this arrangement generally works reasonably well. Many times I was told that polyandrous marriages are less torn by jealousy and dissension than polygamous unions. Nonetheless, the custom is slowly dying out, especially in villages in contact with western cultures.

Pima's case was rather unusual. She is an heiress, for her father, a lama of the Red Hat sect (who are permitted to marry) had no sons. Thus, both his house and his fortune came to her when he died. Pima, as a lama's eldest daughter and owner of a house and property, had a very high status in the village. However, she didn't like her two husbands. Instead of living with them she lived in her own house and refused to sleep with them - allegedly for fear of becoming pregnant. Living with her was her sister's child and the lama's second wife, who, although she was not Pima's own mother, was nevertheless treated by her with affection and respect. There were no nursing homes for old folks in Nepal.

The stepmother, a gnarled old creature wrapped in a dirty rag of a blanket, squatted on the floor warming herself before the clay stove much of the day. Hanks of long grayish hair framed her seamed face, as brown and wrinkled as a dried apricot. Black eyes glittering, she hummed and muttered to herself as she rocked her plump little grandchild tenderly or cackled with laughter at our foreign antics. She is considered a witch in the village. Many years before at dusk one evening after a festival, the old lama, her husband, began to behave strangely. As was the custom, he had drunk a great deal of chang and rakshi at a festival. Afterward he appeared to be in a kind of delirium. As he walked from house to house, he bade each of the villagers goodbye. Then, without further explanation, he strode toward the high escarpment of rock over the river behind the gompa and continued straight on over the edge, falling to his death several hundred feet below. His second wife, the old woman, was blamed for witchcraft.

Every day the old widow walked slowly through the town to the river, where she had a little flour mill made of two grinding stones and powered by a water wheel. At the end of my stay she presented me with a cloth bag of whitest *tsampa*, freshly ground.

Pima's head appeared again in the square hole in the roof above the kitchen. She put down a jug of washing water on the roof, beamed and beckoned for me to hurry down. I squatted on the roof behind the low wall of firewood and sloshed cool water over myself, undressing and exposing successive bits of skin while a few curious neighbors watched from nearby rooftops. Two wide-eyed children popped through the hole and gazed at me silently. After a demonstration of the art of bathing, I descended the notched log to the kitchen.

The boy, Nima Dorche, was waiting in dark shadows behind the stove. Nine-year-old son of a family too poor to keep him, he was a kind of a servant in the household. Nima Dorche's skin was hot and dry and his small dirt-caked body was painfully thin. Lungs, belly, throat all seemed in order. Diarrhea was denied. After I dispensed aspirin, I joined Suzanne and Donald for a breakfast of heavy Tibetan wheat bread smeared with butter and cheese from the dairy in Kathmandu. Then I gathered up my soiled clothing from the roof and climbed down the ladder into the courtyard. A startled chicken shook its head distastefully as it pecked at a fresh pile of human excrement in the yard. Nima Dorche, pipestem legs and slender feet black with dirt, was treading in a huge copper cauldron of roasted barley. I realized with sinking heart that this process somehow proceeded the grinding of grain for the *tsampa* I had so relished the night before. Two tiny calves stood alone forlornly in the courtyard, their plump mamas tied in deep recesses of the open shed. I passed through the great wooden door to the street and set out with my laundry for the river.

It was already eight-thirty and the main street was teeming with local traffic. Herds of small cows traipsed briskly down the steps on their way to graze on tufts of grass sparsely scattered on the ocher hills outside the village. A procession of donkeys passed, carrying loads of firewood so wide that they scraped the walls of houses on both sides of the narrow street. Dozens, perhaps a hundred brown and white goats with spiral ibex-like horns went past, followed by barefoot children with long sticks. The goats are kept neither for milk nor meat, but for their ability to convert the sparse tufts of grass on the hills to fertilizer. They are penned into small huts or enclosures each night. In the morning, their spoor is carefully collected from the floors, yard, and even from the cobblestone streets through which they are driven to the hills each day. Then the women carry the droppings in their back panniers to the fields and dump them on the rows of barley. Other girls and women, dressed in long black sleeveless *chubas* over bright blouses, laughed and chattered, bent under huge loads of hay. As I approached the stream that raced through the town to join the river, a line of women bent under backslings filled with mud bricks greeted me with wide smiles as they strolled gracefully across the wooden bridge into the town.

I squatted by the stream and shook my laundry out on the ground. Above, dozens of prayer flags stirred gently on tall rooftop poles. The daily wind began to freshen. Across the Kali Gandaki a patch of green caught the sunlight below P'aling. A sound of gongs came from the temple. Two children stopped to offer me a black fossil stone, relic of the ancient Himalayan sea. The sun grew hotter as I spread my bits of laundry on the warm rocks. The dry wind gathered strength as it worked slowly up toward the gale-like force of afternoon, bringing its harsh, dry currents from the south, only to dissipate, becalmed as dusk fell serene on the high country each evening.

Our days passed pleasantly. I set up my charpoi on the rooftop and sent the guide Pasang back to Kathmandu with a week's pay. Every morning I awakened to find a few patients already standing quietly at the end of the cot waiting for me to get up. After breakfast we held a small clinic in the god room of Pima's house. There, faded bodhisattvas and angels gazed blandly from the walls as I poked stomachs, prodded at aching backs, and listened to lungs and hearts.

The god room was smaller than the other chambers of the house, but still measured an easy twelve feet to a side. On the altar against the far wall there was an enormous gold-painted Buddha at least six feet high, sitting in solemn lotus, both hands raised in the position of teaching. Each day the old woman draped a fresh white scarf over his dusty saffron robe, above which the serene face gazed benignly on all who entered. Pictures and statues surrounded the base of the Buddha. A photo of the Dalai Lama leaned against an ornamental Chinese teapot framed with tinsel and dusty green peacock feathers. Eighteen-armed Chenresi flanked the Buddha on one side and a graceful Shiva danced his cosmic dance on the other. Angels and demons frolicked in small murals painted on the base of the shrine. Eighteen butter lamps were lined up neatly below. Behind them sat a statue of Tara, the enchanting goddess of mercy, and beside her a snarling Kali, destroyer of evil, was decked with flowers over her traditional necklace of human skulls. Chinese style dragons guarded the far sides of the shrine beneath vertical rows of pigeonholes where narrow prayer books lay wrapped in faded red cloths. This house of the old lama had once been a wealthy one, but all the objects had grown faded and dusty with age. Still the god room seemed an auspicious place to give out my simple medicines.

Two days after we arrived, a great *puja* (special prayer by lamas) was scheduled to drive out the caterpillars from the barley fields. When Pima told us about it the evening before, I offered my stock of DDT as a sample of what might be accomplished with modern science. Horrified, Pima, a true Buddhist, shook her head at the thought of actually killing the pests. The *puja* would not harm the caterpillars but only induce them, with gongs, trumpets and prayers, to leave the fields.

The next morning I was again washing clothes on the river bank when the gongs from the temple sounded. I gathered up my damp belongings and headed back to the town to watch the ceremonies. When I reached the house to leave off my wet laundry, a young man of the village was just entering the god room to collect the Buddha for the procession. With the help of the entire household, he loaded the giant statue onto his back, supporting it by passing a strap around Buddha's waist and balancing the load by a tumpline across his forehead. We all followed the young man into the entryway and watched as Buddha, gazing imperturbably skyward, disappeared down the ladder and then bestowed his enigmatic smile on the wondering beasts in the courtyard.

We hurried to the gompa where a crowd of men, women and children had already gathered. Many carried Buddha statues or stacks of holy books on their backs. At least twenty maroon-robed lamas with shaved heads held long slender trumpets or swung small pails of smoking incense. One young man carried a giant leather drum slung from a strap around his neck. Another had copper cymbals. Finally the procession was ready to begin. The lamas set off first, chanting loudly, followed by the music section. Cymbals crashed, trumpets blew and drums beat loudly. Next came the men and women of the village, single file, each bent under a load of gods, goddesses, or a stack of holy books. The entire village appeared to have gathered before the gompa.

The parade passed down the stone steps of the town and streamed toward the northern gate. Women rushed forward to kneel and press their foreheads against the holy objects. More and more people joined behind the single file of marchers as they wound through the village past the long row of copper prayer wheels. They left the town and climbed up a steep path to a ledge high above the gorge and paused briefly before the chorten marking the end of the village. There, all the horns blasted, cymbals crashed, and the lamas shouted prayers. Then the parade snaked steeply upward to a small shrine on the bare hillside a thousand feet above. There they stopped for more chanting and dissonant trumpeting. The cacophony of eerie sounds filled the valley. Then the long line of marchers came down the hillside again and swung along a narrow path in a wide arc around the entire village and its fields. Led by the lamas, the marchers descended the steep bank of the river, waded through the swift clear water and strode up the opposite side.

I sat down to take off my shoes before gingerly picking my way across the rocks in the cold stream. When I reached the opposite side I caught sight of a long line of black plastic pipe leading from far upstream toward the terraced fields on the hillside above. There the parade had now halted, trumpeting and chanting lustily.

I recognized the plastic pipe. It seems that UNICEF, in a massive and laudable effort to provide clean drinking water to the remote villages of Nepal, had at great expense sent hundreds of feet of plastic pipe by plane to Jomsom months before. But it had mysteriously disappeared. Rumor had it that instead of being deployed as intended to bring clean water to the town, the higher caste burghers of the place had commandeered the pipe to irrigate their own fields. Adding insult to injury, they then forced the impoverished villagers to "donate" their labor to install the pipes in the fields of the wealthier citizens instead of for the good of the town.

This example of greed and imposition by the strong on the weak caused great bitterness and added to the already considerable suspicion and distrust of westerners and government projects I found among the poor throughout much of Asia. I regret to say that the UNICEF team, consisting of two plump Indians who rode on hired horses from Jomsom to Kagbeni to inspect their water project a day or two after I arrived, did not discover the whereabouts of the plastic pipe.

I had tarried too long at the river bank and was now far behind the procession. I half expected to see legions of caterpillars line up like lemmings to dive off the ledge into the canyon below, exorcised from the fields by the trumpets, drums, and gods. I headed back to the town. The hills were barren and silent now, with no living thing in sight. The village, golden in the sunlight, floated like a ship on a sea of gigantic brown waves. Trumpets and cymbals sounded far in the distance. Soon the long line of marchers wound back into town, laughing and chattering. The gods on their backs continued to gaze serenely at the sky.

In town, villagers lined the streets to welcome back the gods and marchers. Once again women and children rushed forward to kneel and press their foreheads against the gods and the faded scarlet cloths covering the holy books. Slowly the procession wound back to the temple. Most of the men disappeared inside, while others dispersed to return the household gods and prayer books to their accustomed homes.

An hour later a crowd began to gather in the town square. Well fortified with chang and with lamas, Buddha and prayer books now absent, the crowd formed a wide circle around a large court. A dozen men stepped into the circle, joined arms in the traditional way, and began singing and hissing as they stomped and kicked the paces of a Tibetan dance. Soon women joined in. There was much teasing as the dancing grew more disorganized and the shouts more raucous. Gradually, as darkness fell, the women, flushed with excitement and chang, retired to the sidelines. Goats and children straggled across the open square. A few lanterns appeared and women and girls of the town - all seated together on a ledge at one side of the square - left in twos and threes to prepare the evening meal. Men and boys soon followed. When the moon rose behind the pale peaks to the east, the square was empty.

Next morning I wakened to the sound of an eerie melody. On the rooftop next door, a small man with high cheekbones and flat oriental profile stood sharply silhouetted against the early dawn sky. Both of his arms were stretched out before him. In his left hand he held the shoulder blade of some large mammal, perhaps a yak. In his right hand, a white arrow protruded from a black rag wrapped around a club-shaped object. Etched against the glow of the rising sun he sent his thrilling song over the sleeping valley. I rose, dressed quickly, and walked to the outskirts of the town to watch the sun rise over the great peaks. In the barley fields, the caterpillars were gone.

Chapter VI

"OM," A DISCIPLE OF SAI BABA

To shoot straight is more important than to know how to write.

-Afghan proverb

The struggle is itself enough to fulfill the heart of man; one must believe that Sisyphus is happy.

Albert Camus

"Hi! Do you have a place to stay?"

I heard a clear American voice behind me. It was my first encounter with the young woman who called herself "Om." I was standing at the pink and white gate of Brindavan, Sai Baba's ashram at Whitefield, twenty-five kilometers from Bangalore, capital of the state of Karnataka, in south central India. Hundreds of well-dressed Indian men and women filed by into the grounds of the ashram. As they passed the guard in front of the reception center, they slid off their sandals and added them to the neat rows already there - men's in front of the gatehouse and women's around in back.

I first heard about Sai Baba, a famed holy man of south central India, during a climb over the Rothang Pass in the Himalayas. Returning from visits to the Buddhist monasteries that cling to the mountains beneath snow peaks in north India, I met three Canadians from a Hindu ashram in the Kulu Valley, forty miles to the south. From them I heard for the first time about miraculous deeds and cures of a variety of maladies by Sai Baba, a self-proclaimed reincarnated saint from the small Indian village of Puttaparti.

Several weeks later while rummaging through my gear for unused film, a worn paperback surfaced. On the cover, smiling enigmatically, was Sai Baba's placid round face, framed in a wide Afro hairdo. Vaguely I remembered picking up the book from a pile of dusty secondhand paperbacks in a Manali bazaar weeks before -indeed, before I had ever heard of Sai Baba. Curious coincidence.

That evening, tucked in my sleeping bag on the dirt floor of a village house, I read the Sai Baba story by flashlight. According to this author, an awestruck theosophist from California, Sai Baba demonstrated all the signs at an early age of being an *avatar,* a divine incarnation of God. As a schoolboy he astounded his mates by plucking a variety of sweets and fruits from a single barren tree, or even from the air. He then passed them around to his delighted companions. As an adolescent, he announced to his family that he was a reincarnation of Sai Baba of Shird, one of the most famous *rishis* – miracle-working saints - of India. He astonished his family and fellow villagers by recollecting events and people from his former life and by an uncanny ability to materialize great quantities of *vibutti* (sacred gray ash) from thin air. These miraculous doings gradually overcame the skepticism of his friends and family. His fame began to spread throughout south India. He was acclaimed as a true *avatar,* an incarnation of god. His ashrams in Whitefield and Puttaparti attracted tens of thousands of disciples and visitors every year. Not such an unusual story in India.

A month later I was in Nepal, trying to place a phone call to Dr. I in Bombay from the crowded Kathmandu public telephone office. The only other westerner waiting in the long queue stood directly in front of me. He was a blond, pleasant looking man of around thirty. His name was Karl. As the queue scarcely moved in two hours, we had ample time to get acquainted. Karl, a South African, was trying to place an urgent call to Teheran to the parents of his charge, a young Iranian he had just locked in their room in a hotel nearby.

"His parents hired me as his caretaker," Karl explained. "He was quite okay until yesterday. Then suddenly he became absolutely bonkers."

"What a coincidence that you should be standing in line in front of a psychiatrist," I remarked. Before the queue brought either of us to the window where a cheerful young Nepali agent was leisurely booking trunk calls, Karl told me this story.

"My charge is the only son of a wealthy Indian family. He was diagnosed with schizophrenia many years ago. All kinds of treatments were tried without success in the U.K. and elsewhere. Then, three years ago, on advice of a friend, his family took him to Sai Baba's ashram in Puttaparti. After a series of meetings with

Baba, he became entirely well. He remained well until two days ago."

He paused and looked at me anxiously. "Then, for no apparent reason, he began to be increasingly agitated, talking to voices and running in the streets."

"This is quite astonishing," I commented as Karl finished his story. "Real schizophrenia is not very likely to yield to holy men in my experience! Tell me more about this Sai Baba. This is the third time in a few weeks that, quite by chance, I have heard about this man from Puttaparti."

As with the westerners in Kulu, I again found myself listening to a series of remarkable Sai Baba stories. And as before, my informant was no fuzzy-minded truth seeker. On the contrary, he was a well-traveled university graduate from Johannesburg.

Finally, we reached the head of the queue where we each placed our trunk calls with the ever-smiling young man at the wicket. Then we settled down on the long wooden benches to wait for the calls to go through.

"I know it sounds unbelievable," said Karl, "but I have seen Sai Baba materialize precious rings, statues, and gold lockets from thin air. We have stood with Baba in front of a tree where he asked us what kind of fruit we each wanted. No matter what we asked for he could reach up and pluck it from the tree!" I shook my head in disbelief. Karl smiled patiently.

"I was as skeptical as you are - even more so," he went on. "But I watched the *vibutti* - sacred ash - flow from his hands like water. Many of my friends have pictures of Sai Baba in their homes. These pictures continue to make *vibutti* for years, thousands of miles from India."

Karl sat back, lit a cigarette, and shook his head as if still amazed. Then he leaned forward and went on slowly.

"Three years ago at his ashram in Brindavan, Baba cured my charge completely. At the time, he was absolutely uncontrollable - hallucinating, violent, and barking like a dog, just like today. As soon as he saw Baba he quieted down. After staying at the ashram and seeing Baba several times a week, Baba materialized a talisman for him. He warned him that if it was lost, the illness would return. Well, he lost the talisman just thirteen days ago. This is his first attack since Baba cured him."

"Probably a coincidence," I commented.

"I've been to Baba's nearly every year for the last twelve years," Karl continued. "I was never a religious person before and I was even more skeptical than you are before I went the first time. Now, I have no doubt that Baba is some kind of incarnation of God. The first time I saw Baba, an electric charge seemed to go through my whole body," Karl paused momentarily. "Although I was standing in a large crowd and Baba had never seen me before, he looked at me as though he knew everything about me. Later, when I talked to him, it was true. Somehow, he knew all my past life although he had never seen me or heard of me before. It is the same with everyone."

Three hours later, Karl's call to Delhi went through. He made arrangements for his ward's family to meet him at the Delhi airport the next morning.

By 10 p.m. the waiting room was deserted and my call to Calcutta had still not gone through. Instead, I telegraphed my arrival time to my host, Dr. I., a neuroscientist at the medical college.

Although on the following day, the plane was several hours late, Dr. I. was waiting at the airport. After my lecture and a tour of his institute, I asked him whether he had ever heard of Sai Baba.

"Of course, everyone in India knows about Sai Baba," replied this very capable Canada-trained neurophysiologist.

"And do you believe in his miracle cures, his sacred ash, his plucking of jewels and fruits from trees?"

"Science can't explain everything," was his enigmatic reply. "Sai Baba is now in residence in Whitefield near Bangalore. Since you are heading south, why don't you visit his ashram summer quarters in Whitefield?" *Why not indeed*, I thought. *I have a week until I'm due in Madras.*

I took the evening train for Bangalore. After a night on my air mattress, rattling across half of south India, the train arrived in Bangalore's huge modern railroad station. I asked the polite young man in the station Inquiries Office if he knew anything about Sai Baba's headquarters. Somewhat to my surprise, he immediately handed me a telephone number.

"Yes, Sai Baba is in Whitefield, fifteen miles from here, Madam," a voice in heavily accented English at the other end of the line replied to my query. "The bus leaves for Whitefield from here every hour."

The bus ride tested my determination. After squeezing inside the doorway of the crowded vehicle, I was crammed between a half dozen obese, sweating sari-clad women on one side and the guard rail surrounding the driver on the other. Standing on a thin, loose floorboard, which only partly covered the smoking engine beneath, the soles of my feet were soon burning through my thin sandals. The bus bumped and swayed through the streets, scattering pedestrians, pushcarts, cyclists, and scruffy monkeys.

Beyond the town, the soft Indian countryside was scarred and ravaged by erosion and industrialization. Long windowless factory buildings spewed acrid smoke skyward. Abandoned vehicles rusted in fields of weeds under a merciless sun. A small donkey stood listlessly, tied on a short tether to a stunted tree while his master lay prostrate in a small pool of shade.

After more than an hour of starting and stopping, we traveled the fifteen miles to Whitefield. I stumbled from the bus, dizzy with heat, nauseated from the fumes, and with the soles of my feet tingling from broiling over the engine. After asking directions, I walked the half mile from the bus stop to the ashram. The road was lined with scrawny beggars and peddlers of cheap Sai Baba souvenirs.

When I reached the high pink and blue plaster wall that surrounded the ashram, I stopped at the gatehouse to ask if I could leave my pack-sack. The well dressed overweight man at the reception desk shook his head brusquely. Without a word of welcome, he turned away. I discovered later that I'd committed a major *faux pas* by entering the men's reception entrance rather than the women's. I stumbled back outside, damning the lack of compassion in the ashram of this famed saint. Surrounded by beggars outside, like other ashrams frequented by well off Indians and Westerners, Sai Baba's ashram seemed to be a small island of prosperity surrounded by disease, poverty and indifference.

"Hi? Do you have a place to stay? Have you just come? Can I help you with anything?" The voice was sweet; the accent distinctly North American.

I looked around in surprise to see a startlingly white face that glowed with inner joy. A young woman around thirty years old, her head shaved completely bald, and with pale, serene green eyes stood before me dressed in a monk's pajama-like suit of faded ochre.

"My name is Om," she said simply. "I used to live in Schenectady."

My black mood disappeared at once. In the friendliest manner imaginable, Om took me under her wing and showed me the "ladies area," where I could leave my shoes and backpack. She then urged me to come quickly, for it was time for Sai Baba's afternoon *darshan* (appearance before his followers). We hurried along on our bare feet across the road to where we could get a view of the *avatar*, whose arrival was imminent. Obviously experienced in these occasions, Om pulled me down onto the grass in front of a crowd of women standing along the street leading through the ashram grounds. All were eagerly, silently, worshipfully awaiting arrival of the saint.

As we waited, Om told me her story. Formerly a teacher of anthropology in a New England college, she had joined Sai Baba in Puttaparti seven years before. Last year, after a long series of adventures and vicissitudes, she had at last become a *sannyasi*.

"A *sannyasi* is one who has reached the fourth stage of human development in Hinduism," she explained. "That means you have succeeded, after a long period of preparation and meditation, in renouncing all possessions, gainful work, and worldly ambition. It means you devote yourself entirely to the pursuit of Realization."

Thirty-five years old, Om had been through much of what my friends back in the Kulu ashram called "the Western Movie" before seeking her spiritual journey. "I was born into New York's upper social register," she explained. "Mother and grandmother were Smith, Dad was Harvard. I attended the right schools, the right parties, studied violin at Julliard and anthropology at Princeton."

After acquiring the usual degrees, she got a job teaching at a women's college.

"After a few years I found teaching absolutely stultifying, sophistic, purposeless, without satisfaction. Like everyone else in those days, I got into meditation, took a little acid, smoked lots of grass. Finally I left. I rented a trailer in upstate New York for six months and started serious meditation."

Om stopped talking abruptly. A sudden hush fell over the crowd. The white gates in the high walls surrounding Sai Baba's private estate and mansion opened. A shiny Mercedes rolled out. The guards at the gate stood at attention, and the crowd pressed forward eagerly for a glimpse of the *avatar*.

Om grabbed my arm and pulled me along at a fast trot toward the road for a better view. I was out of breath by the time we reached the corner where the car must stop before joining the main road. As the Mercedes approached, I glimpsed a round face framed in bushy black hair, familiar from the cover photo on the paperback I had read while swatting mosquitoes the week before. Sai Baba was seated in the back seat behind half-drawn tasseled curtains. He was surprisingly small and young looking. His eyes met mine for less than an instant as the car stopped, then turned and headed for the college lecture hall less than two blocks away.

"He saw you. He looked at you! That's so wonderful!" cried Om. Her green eyes sparkled with excitement and her plain face shone with happiness for me. "Let's run quickly to the college and we might be able to see him again."

Caught up in the excitement of the chase, still barefoot, I charged after Om, who was practically flying down the main road ahead of me. Droves of women in brilliant saris and men in white shirts and trousers were hurrying toward the college buildings. No one seemed to notice the long line of beggars, lepers, and cripples crouched along the roadside.

Om reached the pink and blue college buildings before I did and was beckoning vigorously for me to join her on the roadside. Once again we stood in front of a rapidly gathering crowd of women who waited silently for Sai Baba to disembark from the Mercedes. Men, equally numerous, waited on the opposite side of the entry to the building. Baba's small stout figure, clad in a long orange gown, emerged from the car and walked quickly into the building. We had only a momentary glimpse of him before he disappeared inside. I was disappointed that I had not experienced any of the vibrations and electric shocks described by Karl in Kathmandu, the first of so many people to tell me about Sai Baba. Still, there was a sense of satisfaction that I had at least seen the hero of the miracle tales I had been hearing.

A crowd of perhaps 700 or 800 people was gathered in the auditorium of the assembly hall. Men and boys sat on long benches on one side; women and girls on the other. We had no tickets or passes - Om because she's a *sannyasi* and doesn't need one; I, because I'd only just come and was not registered in the school.

We stood outside the building. Loud-speakers mounted around the walls broadcast the proceedings to the hundreds of standees outside. We were separated by sex, men on one side of the building, women on the other. I tried to get up on a step on the outside stairway so I could look in the windows but was quickly scolded off by several obese guardian women in stunning saris.

Imperiously, these harridans pursued me throughout my stay to scold about my clothes, posture, and other petty misdemeanors. Now they placed themselves between us and the walls of the building. We went round to the side and stood on tiptoe, our eyes just clearing the window sill.

Inside, the crowd first sang *bhajans*, (Hindu hymns), led by Sai Baba in a high clear tenor. Next, two students from the college, one boy and one girl, each gave a short speech summarizing the day's class work. Afterward, each received a certificate from Baba. They knelt in turn and pressed their foreheads to his feet. Then an old man in a white *dhoti* gave a long rambling discourse in English and Telegu on the importance of education. Finally, Sai Baba came smiling to the podium. The crowd hushed. I was interested to see that his orange gown had long sleeves that were close fitting at the wrist. Remembering the tales of Baba's supernatural achievements, I couldn't help thinking that his long loose-sleeved gown was well designed for materializations.

Sai Baba spoke in Telegu in a high harsh voice, pausing after every sentence while the old man translated his remarks into English. The tone of Sai Baba's lecture was clearly expository, even exclamatory, and certainly exhortative. It was rather like listening to Fidel Castro's harangues in Spanish, which I also don't understand.

Baba's topic that day had to do with the necessity of eating proper food. "Food is not inconsequential," he shouted in staccato Telegu. "All of the eight types of yoga need food for their very basis. If one does not have purity of mind, even small things cannot be accomplished. Wrong food gives wrong bodies and minds."

I looked around at the rapt faces of the women who surrounded me by the outside windows. In contrast to their plumper sisters sitting inside the hall in modish nylon saris or the equally rotund and well-dressed female guards, the women outside were plain and poor looking. Their thin, worn faces shone with pleasure as they stood beside us, craning their necks for a better view of the saint. As he continued, Sai Baba's words came faster and faster and his voice became more and more excited. Often he failed to pause long enough to allow the translator time to finish the last sentence.

"Wrong food gives wrong bodies and minds!" he shouted. "Of the eighty-four *lakhs* of varieties of animals, man alone cooks his food. Taking natural food promotes longevity. Cooking food destroys the life force in the food, making man subject to several diseases!

Moreover, if you eat too much, you will have to spend two to three hours digesting. Even more important, it could have been given to someone who needs it more."

I gazed through the window at the obese silk sari-clad Indian lady just below me and thought of the emaciated beggars crouched outside the gate. Seated at the front of the hall were several younger sari-clad Western looking women in their twenties and thirties. Later I was to meet many of them.

After more than an hour, Baba's harangue ended. There was a murmur of satisfaction from the crowd. In a high pleasant tenor, Baba once again began singing *bhajans*. The audience joined in uncertainly at first, then strongly, with much feeling of joy. Then it was over and everyone filed out. The crowd outside rushed once again to watch the holy man emerge from the auditorium and enter the waiting Mercedes. Om pulled me along at top speed as we rushed down the road back to the ashram, where we sat on the grass among hundreds of other women and men who lined the streets around Baba's mansion.

"Sometimes Baba gets out of the car and walks back through the people. That's called *darshan*," she whispered excitedly.

"Hush, shh," hissed a plump woman covered in a filmy pink chiffon sari. She was policing the area in front of us to keep the crowd from spilling into the street.

"Sit properly!" she said to me sharply. I looked down hastily and saw that my trousers had hiked up exposing skin two or three inches above my ankles. I tried to cover these bits of naked flesh as best I could. Then I attempted, unsuccessfully, to press my reluctant knees into the required lotus position. Another well-nourished lady guard pointed furiously to my shoulders, which were insufficiently covered by a narrow silk scarf I had moved there from my head. Bare arms were apparently no less a disgrace here than in Islamic territory. Anxious to obey what rules I could, I pulled the scarf over as much skin as it would cover while they continued to cluck crossly and wag their fingers at me disapprovingly.

A hush fell over the crowd as the tan Mercedes reappeared, stopped, and Sai Baba emerged. Smiling, he walked slowly down the center of the road between the segregated rows of worshipful faces. A forest of hands went up bearing small white notes for the holy man. He stopped here and there and took them, then handed them to an attendant who walked behind him. Once or twice he stopped and spoke to someone seated close to the edge of the curb. Many women and a few men prostrated themselves wherever there was space to do so. Others presented flowers. As he walked past us, he neither stopped nor looked at me. I felt vaguely disappointed. Hadn't he called me to this place? Didn't he even know I was here? Reaching the gate and the high wall around his enclave, Sai Baba entered and disappeared.

After retrieving my sandals, Om, as always barefoot, walked with me in the rapidly darkening twilight across the road to a ramshackle tea house. We ordered a spartan dinner of rice and dahl, the only food available. After dinner we walked into the village where Om took me to a small house where the woman rented a room to visitors.

The room was bare except for a single light bulb hanging from the ceiling. Around it, mosquitoes swarmed expectantly. Om sent the landlady's small son to the shop for mosquito repellant candles. Om went "home," which she told me was in a cow barn half a mile distant.

I spread my foil space blanket over the air mattress on the floor and placed three candles on each side of the bed. The scene looked rather like a wake waiting for the body. I spent the night sweltering under the foil blanket, swatting mosquitoes around my face and neck and reading the worshipful Sai Baba book by one of his American acolytes.

When the first gray of dawn appeared through the spotty glass of the tiny window in my cell of a room, I rose stiffly and smothered the smoking, ineffectual mosquito coils. Tiptoeing through the other room where women and children still lay prostrate under their mosquito nets, I stepped out into the cool fresh morning and went to the well to wash. In the distance I heard the sound of singing. I remembered reading in the Sai Baba book that during the summer months members of the ashram walked through the streets of Whitefield at dawn, singing *bhajans* before gathering in front of the gates for *darshan* - viewing - of the sainted Baba. When I reached the main road, two platoons of members of the ashram came down the road from the village singing *bhajans*.

In the forward group were men and boys dressed in white cotton shirts and trousers. Behind them came women and girls like a flock of bright birds in saris of white, blue, yellow or pink. The joyous singing floated over the still sleeping village. From the stalls lining the road, opposite the ashram, a few shopkeepers emerged rubbing sleep from their eyes. The singers turned, marched through the pink and blue gateway of the ashram, and crossed to an open area where a large crowd had already gathered at the wall surrounding Sai Baba's private grounds.

The crowd stood there quietly for almost half an hour. Impatient with the *avatar's* apparent indifference to the waiting multitude, I was about to leave and search for coffee. Suddenly, a door opened at the back of the second floor balcony. The stout little man with the curly black Afro appeared, still wearing his long orange silk costume. He looked sleepy - as though he had just gotten up.

"Probably awakened by the bhajans," I thought with satisfaction. *"Serves him right for ordering these people out to serenade the town at 4 a.m."*

As he stood there, the crowd, men and women, meticulously segregated as always, pressed closer. Several of the women, with ecstatic adoring faces, prostrated themselves on the damp ground. Others bore small candle-lit shrines held high above their heads so Sai Baba could see them. He gazed down from his balcony, smiling ever so faintly. As the crowd gazed reverently back, Sai Baba just stood there for a full twenty minutes without uttering a word.

Then he turned and went into his mansion. The large crowd immediately began buzzing with excited conversation. How happy and thrilled they seemed as they dispersed over the area outside the grounds his palatial house. I tried unsuccessfully to catch a glimpse through the gate of the elephant kept in his private gardens. Then I headed for the tea stalls across the road. Crossing the ashram compound, I passed long queues of men and women in separate lines waiting for coffee or tea. Unfortunately, it being only a little after 5:00 a.m., no village tea shops had yet opened.

I made good use of my time, however, by purchasing a brilliant red cotton sari from a drowsy shopkeeper who had risen for *darshan*. No longer would my bare arms be the subject of complaint by the formidable ladies of the ashram. The kindly storekeeper stored my packsack and offered me a cup of his own tea, which I drank gratefully.

Wrapping the scarlet cloth around me, I started up the road toward the ashram canteen. Unfortunately, it was still closed. I sat down on the floor of the empty veranda, determined, following the uplifting discussions of the day before, to prove the supremacy of mind over body by meditating before breakfast. I might have been successful if it hadn't been for the importunate interruptions by the ashram's omnipresent ladies. They were an aggressive, obtrusive lot who seemed to delight in pressing their rigid rules of dress and conduct on me and, according to Om, on all Westerners.

On the previous day at the darshan that followed Sai Baba's lecture, they complained loudly to Om that she should make me wear a sari, sit in a proper position and above all to cover my upper arms. So today, seated in as full a lotus as my knees would manage, arms concealed under the new scarlet sari, and with the edge of my blue cotton trousers covering my ankles, I was unprepared for the scolding that soon recalled me from the earliest red-blue colors of meditation (an effect, I think, of sun through eyelids).

A harsh voice spoke loudly in unknown but unmistakable words of command. I opened my eyes. A heavy-set young woman stood glowering over me, twig broom in one hand and pointing with the other for me to move. I bowed my head devoutly, indicating that I was in the midst of morning meditation. But it was no go. I moved down to where she had finished sweeping. Once again I folded my legs uncomfortably under me and closed my eyes. In a few minutes I heard the woman's determined breathing above me again. Emptying my mind of all rancor, I tried to concentrate on my own breathing until I felt the stiff twigs of the broom digging into my thigh. Rage suddenly broke through the thin veneer of my newly acquired serenity and I glowered at the woman furiously.

"Is there no place in this entire ashram where one can meditate quietly?" I asked, seething inside.

"This is not the place for meditation," she said angrily and stalked off.

I gave up meditating and watched the plump, self-satisfied ashram ladies stride past the wakening beggars who limped slowly over to take up their daily stations beside the road. My own stomach was already aching with hunger after the spartan meal of the night before. I wondered how it would feel to eat nothing at all, as they often did.

At last, the door of the canteen opened. I rushed in.

At this very moment, Om appeared behind me. Her joyous "good morning" entirely restored my good humor. Inside the canteen, long tables were piled with excellent south Indian fare: spicy saffron rice laced with bits of carrot, savory cakes of crisp dough fried in ghee, and oceans of pre-sugared tea.

"No wonder these ladies are on the chubby side," I said to Om, "but why are they so cross? It shakes my faith in ashrams and the mellowing powers of meditation to be surrounded by such cranky women!"

Om smiled beatifically as she bit into a crisp round flat pastry. We were seated on the floor of the canteen where small bamboo mats were set in rows for place mats. Behind each one, men in white trousers and sari-clad women sat cross-legged on slightly larger woven mats eating with their fingers. A great virtue of the sari is that it hides the legs no matter what activity the owner is engaged in, from morning toileting to evening prayers. Om and I were early and easily found places. However, I was unable to achieve the lotus posture, so I tucked my legs under me and covered them with the red scarf.

"Madam, please sit properly," admonished a girl of around twenty.

"Westerners are unable to sit cross-legged," explained Om to the exasperated girl. "They're built differently." I smiled timidly, shaking my head with regret. Apparently satisfied by my mixture of obsequiousness and physical inadequacy, the girl left.

"How did you like the morning *darshan*?" Om asked.

"The actors were colorful, but the plot is a little thin," I replied. "I'm not sure how people get such a high out of *darshans* - just staring at Sai Baba."

"But we do," replied Om. "At least 500 people gather there to gaze at him every morning"

I told Om about the problems I had with the hostile women disciples who harassed me while I tried to sit and meditate on the steps that morning. "How can an ashram devoted to love of one's fellow man, compassion and renunciation of worldliness develop these unpleasant women disciples? Surely Sai Baba doesn't care how I sit!"

Om laughed with pleasure. She also found these women dreadful with their constant carping, admonishing and directing. Being a liberated being, however, she suffered neither the frustration nor the anger that their constant bossiness fired up in me. Could I do the same? And if everyone obeyed the rules of the powerful, who would look after the weak and the poor?

"Baba always says that those who stay closest to him in the ashram need him most," she replied in a voice quite devoid of annoyance, "and that they have the furthest to go toward real understanding. I just don't pay any attention to these harpies - that way whatever they do ceases to bother me."

I couldn't help smiling at the wonderful mixture of Eastern philosophy and American candor. For the rest of my stay I tried to adopt her cheerful equanimity, albeit with much less success.

After breakfast we walked back to the ashram and entered the gate guarding the grounds. "Better carry your sandals," cautioned Om as I dutifully started to place them in one of the long rows of footwear lined up in the women's section. "Some people help themselves to anything from the West." I stuffed them into my day pack and trotted along barefoot behind Om toward the covered pavilion. Hundreds of men and women were seated in neat segregated rows under the roof. More spilled out over the grounds for blocks around.

There was a rumor that Sai Baba would have another *darshan* this morning. During the summer, *darshan* (the silent audiences), *satsungs* (during which there is singing), and the miraculous materializations are replaced by his daily lecture guiding the progress of students enrolled in the school. Coming from all over India, Sai Baba's summer school students were a chosen few among the many students who apply. The curriculum was largely devoted to the study of religion and ethics. Well-known teachers were drawn from all over India and from abroad. Board and room were free to students. A small number were westerners.

We sat on the ground in the shade of the women's section and waited for something to happen. In addition to hundreds of well-fed ladies seated cross-legged around us, the few westerners, slender, long-haired and sari-clad, sat in groups. One girl, a statuesque blond in a brilliant, blue silk sari, sitting in front of me was writing an air letter in German. Om greeted a couple of attractive young American women across the lawn and explained to me that they were yoga teachers from Southern California. Another American, a rather short, stout, angry-looking man, was busily *darshaning* himself - parading up and down in front of the crowd, stopping from time to time in various Tai Chi postures.

"How come there aren't any beggars, *saddhus*, or cripples in here?" I asked. "There are plenty of them sitting outside along the road."

Om agreed that the ashram was not a perfect world. She explained, as disciples in other ashrams had done for me before, that each person must find his own liberation in his own way. I asked what she thought would become of the world if everyone took her particular route to self-realization.

"I've given up Kantian categorical imperatives," replied Om. "Quite clearly my life is not for everyone. Very few elect to follow this course."

"Shh, shh," hissed a plump member of the female gestapo. The large gold ring in her nose twitched with indignation.

"Why?" I asked her softly, sweetly. "There is no one here yet but us *sunnyasis*!" Muttering in disgust, she sailed off looking for other knuckles to rap, her filmy blue draperies billowing after her.

"Baba says there are two main ways to self-liberation," Om continued when this ogress was out of earshot. "One is devotion and meditation - that is mine. The other is to stay in the world and do worthwhile things for others. Baba does both. He has established not only this summer school but the regular college you saw across from the canteen, and other colleges all over India. Every Sunday the ashram members go to villages to help clean up, build schools, and do other things that are needed. In this summer school, students from all over India are learning the ideas of compassion, humanitarianism, and non-attachment to material things."

Suddenly, a hush fell across the crowd as the gates of Baba's enclave opened. The guards standing outside snapped to attention as Sai Baba emerged in his long orange dress followed by several distinguished-looking men, natty in pressed western gray flannel suits, snow-white shirts and dark ties. Two rows of students rose now and stood quietly as a guard of honor while Baba walked along the wide street from his walled enclave toward several thousand people sitting on the ground in rows around the pavilion.

He walked slowly between the rows, gazing to each side at the reverent crowd. Hands bearing notes shot upward like the heads of baby birds waiting to be fed. From time to time, he stopped, said a few words to someone, and reached for one or two of the folded notes from the forest of extended hands.

Now the need for the male and female gestapo became evident. By keeping everyone seated quietly, they prevented this adoring multitude from engulfing the little man. As he came closer I was surprised to note that his smooth round face had a rather dissipated look - an appearance heightened by bright orange-red lips the exact color of his gown. Now his step accelerated a little impatiently. He passed the handfuls of notes to a solemn attendant behind him. Entering the covered pavilion, he hurried to a raised dais and sat down on a throne-like red velvet armchair overlooking the acre of upturned faces.

"Is he wearing lipstick?" I whispered to Om.

"Stained from betel!" she whispered back. For once, not a soul shushed us. I don't think they even heard. It was unthinkable that anyone would be speaking at this ecstatic moment in which the incarnation of God was showing himself and walking among his people.

Picking up the single perfect white rose that lay on the arm of the chair, Sai Baba gazed out over the crowd without expression. For ten minutes he just sat there, not uttering a word. The silent multitude gazed back, their eyes shining.

Behind me a woman of around fifty wept softly. Fathers held their sons high over their heads so they could see the sainted man. Then, abruptly, Baba's mild gaze altered. His shrewd eyes narrowed. Hurriedly, he descended the few stairs from the dais without looking at the crowd and strode briskly toward the street, where his curtained Mercedes was waiting. An attendant, dressed in dark suit, white shirt and a tie opened the rear door. Baba stepped into the car, followed by one of the dignified gentlemen. Another well-dressed attendant slipped into the seat beside the driver. Bodyguards? Boy-friends?

The crowd jumped to its feet like one giant organism and flowed toward the car for a last glimpse before the Mercedes sped off past the beggars lining the road.

Four or five hundred summer students were streaming to the college on foot. The rest of the community dispersed. I was disappointed that *darshan* had not included a miraculous materialization, not even a few handfuls of *vibutti* (sacred ash). Om and I wandered over toward the ashram bookstore.

The contents of the bookshop were pure Sai Baba: adulatory biographies, colored photographs, and even a comic book recording the story of his childhood. I left, only to find that separate lines, again one of men and one of women, still stood patiently in the hot sun in front of the long low building where tea and coffee would be dispensed.

"Sai Baba is very particular about segregating sexes in the ashram. Even married couples are forbidden to walk or talk together within the grounds," explained Om. "Several weeks before you came, a pair of Baba's gestapo ladies pulled away a poor old woman who was leading her blind husband across the grounds, insisting that she must not touch him."

Exhausted from a night of swatting mosquitoes and without sleep, I bid Om a temporary farewell and caught a ride into town with some westerners who took me to their Bangalore hotel, improbably named the Shilton. I checked in enthusiastically, delighted to exchange my mosquito-surrounded pad on the ground in the village hut for a room with not only a large bed and mattress but a bathroom. Soon renewed by a nap and shower, at five o'clock, I joined my new friends for a ride back to the ashram in the taxi they hired daily. During the half hour ride from the Shilton to the ashram they regaled me with their own Sai Baba stories.

"An electric shock ran through my body when Baba looked at me the first time," reported Joan, a green-eyed brunette former rehabilitation counselor from Cleveland, Ohio. "I was on a continuous psychic high for six months when I went back home after my first visit. Then I began to get depressed. I had to come back here to recapture the feeling. I have to be near him. Now I can no longer live in America."

Another member of our taxi group was Betsy, who was a psychiatric nurse in a large private hospital near Wilmington, Delaware five years ago. She started meeting with consciousness-expanding groups during a visit to California and stayed on to experiment with Rolfing, Gestalt, EST, and the rest. When her husband was cured by a "psychic surgeon" of cancer that had been pronounced incurable by university experts, she went to work for one of the leaders. Soon afterward she began to feel her own hands "pulled like a magnet" toward certain people's bodies. She had the ability to cure their pain by "laying on hands." Giving up her regular nursing duties, Betsy was now a full-time psychic healer in California. A charming girl, she gave me her card: Reverend Elizabeth Schmidt, R.N. I wondered about the Reverend. Later I discovered that such titles can be bought from certain sites on the Internet.

There were at least a dozen other Americans visiting Sai Baba with similar stories. Mostly well educated and all white middle class, they bore none of the hallmarks of the dispossessed or downtrodden who line the roads by the ashram.

One evening after *darshan*, when a taxi strike had grounded our usual cab, we rode back to the Shilton with Irving, a fifty-old Jewish bartender from the Bronx who had rented a car. He told us his story.

"I only came here to deliver a message for my son," he confessed in some embarrassment. "This Sai Baba did such wonderful things for my son's life, I never could repay him. I couldn't understand how or why until I met the man. I came here ten days ago planning only to stay a few days. Now I don't know when I'll go home. He does something to you, this man, and he doesn't even ask for money!"

Baffled, Irving shook his head. His son, a physician in New York, was heavily into drugs before winding up in this ashram nearly ten years ago. "Sai Baba got him clean," Irving explained. "Now my son is too busy with his practice to come back, so he sent me and his office partner instead."

The office partner had apparently overdone it a little. After meditating for three days and nights without food or sleep, he went berserk when the guards refused to admit him to a special audience with Baba.

"Imagine, they had to tie him up and take him to the psychiatric ward of the hospital in Bangalore!" Irving confided. "Today the doctors there sent him back to New York."

The next day, the taxi strike having ended without a settlement, I rode out to the ashram for the last time. Our taxi was full of the Shilton's motley international set. Drawn together by the hotel's modest prices and tolerant management, in our cab were a kindergarten teacher of *hatha yoga* from Laguna Beach, a lady sociology professor from Singapore, a young English journalist, and a mechanic from Utrecht. As we rode through the dismal countryside between Bangalore and Whitefield, I gazed at the windowless tombs of concrete factories belching dark smoke. Papers, trash, and plastic bags littered the roadside. Gone, almost without a trace, were the picturesque (and poverty-stricken) huts and villages. Gone, too, were the graceful women who used to gather to fill water jugs at the wells, and linger to gossip before striding home across green fields. Now, men and women alike disappeared into the factories and would not emerge again until evening. In the evening, I glimpsed them climbing off a crowded bus in Whitefield and watched them trudge, tired and dispirited, through the mean village streets to their huts. Not even children were to be seen along the tractor-scarred roadside. Progress, industrialization, and for some, schools, had made the difference.

We arrived in time for morning *darshan* and the usual rush of devotees trooping after Baba's Mercedes. Afterward, Om and I strolled across the street for tea in one of the shabby little cafes.

"This town seems an unlikely place for a reincarnate god to choose to appear," I commented, swatting flies with one hand and rubbing Cutter's mosquito repellant on my ankles with the other. "Don't you ever get tired of just chasing after Baba all day? It doesn't seem too liberating!"

Om's green eyes were deep pools of serenity.

"You learn to live like a moving piece of string," she explained. "As long as it keeps moving along, not getting tied down, nothing can cling to it. I never know when I get up what that day will bring. I just sort of flow with it, seeing what will happen."

That afternoon was my last at Brindavan. Baba gave a long harangue on morality. It began to rain softly, and the lady gestapo tried to make us take shelter across the road instead of watching through the window. A tall beautiful blond girl with a large gold ring in her nose stood reverently in front of me, and never took her eyes from Baba during the long sermon.

"Baba has told her to go back home to her husband and child," whispered Om. "But she won't go, so he won't let her have a seat inside."

"Hush, hush," hissed the harpies, pushing us back from the outside wall. After the lecture, I decided to skip evening *darshan*. I was disappointed that Sai Baba had not sensed my presence and summoned me for an audience, but accepted this philosophically.

"Maybe you're not ready," said Om.

I was sure she was right. As I climbed into our taxi for the return ride to Bangalore, I caught my last glimpse of her racing toward the corner where the road from the ashram turned into the main road. She would be in the front line when the Mercedes passed.

It is twenty years since my visit to Om and Sai Baba. The shabby huts and fields of Bangalore now abut on the capital of India's computer revolution. Many long-distance phone calls in the U.S. from Los Angeles to New York or Seattle to Chicago, etc., are now connected through Bangalore. Labor, even highly educated labor is cheaper there. And Sai Baba, as far as I know, is still officiating in his ashram. About Om, I do not know, for as a sannyasi, she has no phone or e-mail and is too detached to write.

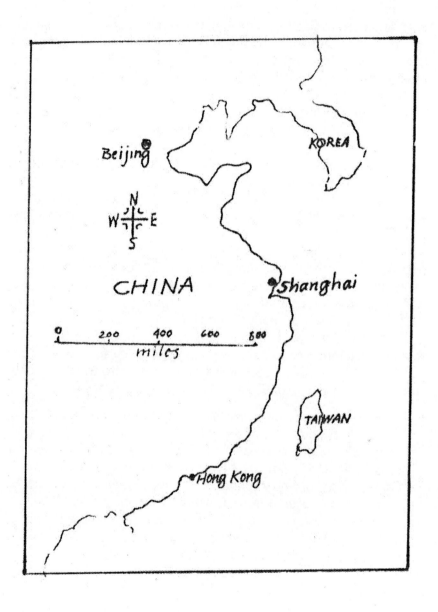

Chapter VII

MAN'S FATE MAN'S HOPE

Life is short, art long, opportunity fleeting, experience treacherous, judgement difficult.

-Hippocrates, circa. 400 BC

China, 1982
Part I Man's Fate
Shanghai

"My brother-in-law committed suicide," said Wang. "He killed himself because the cultural revolution broke his heart."

I met Wang in the late afternoon on my first full day in Shanghai. I was standing on the sidewalk that separates the Whangpo River from the Bund, the broad avenue and promenade where I was filming a junk sailing down the dirty gray water of the river. As I stood there, camera whirring, a few curious pedestrians stopped to watch. Soon there were a dozen, then twenty, forty, or even fifty people crowded around me. I turned to face them, my back to the wall that separated the sidewalk from the river. Mostly young, they stared and stared while I vainly tried to remember how to say, "Hello, I'm an American," a phrase I had laboriously practiced from my phrase book and then instantly forgotten.

Suddenly a young man with heavy spectacles resting on high cheekbones was pushed forward by the friendly mob as their spokesman. This was Wang. In more than fair English he asked me the usual questions - "Where are you from?" "How long are you staying?" "Are you on a tour?"

Scarcely waiting for a reply, Wang began to talk so steadily, compulsively, and passionately that at first I thought perhaps he was mad.

Why was I there? Because China was there. I had been invited to give lectures in Japan for the past week. I had received an invitation to visit Shanghai from a Chinese scientist I had known years before when we both worked at the National Institutes of Health in Washington D.C. Now I was here. After visiting scientific institutes in Shanghai from early morning to late afternoon, My hosts left me off at my hotel. Happy to be on my own for the first time since I arrived, I had picked up my old movie camera from my hotel room before setting out to explore the city. Arriving at the Bund, the broad avenue that flanks the dirty gray water of the Whang Po river, I was filming a junk sailing down the dirty gray water.

This all started around five in the evening, only minutes after I emerged from the sheltered back seat of the dark blue sedan in which I, as a visiting scientist, had been driven around all day in a series of visits to medical and scientific institutes.

I had arrived in Shanghai the evening before by air from Hong Kong. The baggage for all 150 passengers on the plane was dumped by pushcarts in a heap on the floor of the exit area. After a long scramble for my bag and a perfunctory inquiry by customs, I entered the small bare lobby. This was Shanghai, the largest city in China? I was immediately surrounded by half a dozen eager young men in khaki crying, "Taxi."

I was surprised as I had read that taxis were a state-owned enterprise in China. Prices were fixed and tipping was not allowed. Like everyone else in those days, taxi drivers received a fixed salary from the state. *Must be some tipping on the side,* I thought.

Suddenly my smiling host, Dr. X., sent by the Institute of Sciences, emerged from the foggy dusk outside. He greeted me warmly and collected my bag. Then he handed me into the curtained back seat of the embarrassingly long (for a poor and socialist country!) blue Chinese-made limousine.

We sped through dark rainy streets to a guest-house in the suburbs. We slowly ascended in an ancient lift. On the sixth floor, I was shown by the manager my comfortable large room. The room overlooked a lighted square where bicycles, the only vehicles on the streets, still crowded the main thoroughfares despite the late hour. Overstuffed furniture of dark blue velvet, a color TV, hand crocheted antimacassars, covered cups of hot tea and pleasant conversation with Dr. X. were a hospitable introduction to his country.

Early the next morning he escorted me to visits in laboratories, libraries and institutes. Although my research dealt with causes and treatment of epilepsy and schizophrenia, my hosts were more interested in demonstrating their own work. They also discussed treatment of a variety of illnesses with the herbal combinations later to become so popular in the U.S.

Each visit was preceded by a brief introductory talk by a senior person about their research. These briefings were held in a large room furnished with a multitude of chairs and couches surrounding a long table, obviously designed for much larger delegations. Although equipment in the laboratories was limited and often antiquated, all was in good repair and the work in progress was pursued with great diligence and devotion. In every laboratory the investigators and administrators were at pains to point out that all scientific work had been greatly set back by the "cultural revolution and the Gang of Four." Seven or eight years of scientific investigation were lost when the scientists were exiled to the countryside or worse. A second generation of scientists, who under normal circumstances would now have just been entering their most productive years, was never trained and was thus lost as well.

Now, some of the exiled scientists had returned. "But there are no scientists here under age forty," Dr. X. explained sadly. "Many are in their seventies."

Both the training of students and the work of the institute suffered severely during the cultural revolution. There were few graduates during this period and they were poorly trained in their specialities. Although scientific institutes and schools stayed open, scientists were required to limit their investigations to acupuncture and other traditional non-Western practices. Most of the staff, including my host, had been sent to the countryside as laborers. Distinguished professors were imprisoned or placed under house arrest. For many of these scholarly people, being locked out of their laboratories and libraries was a punishment equal to prison.

Now, the situation was much changed. Scientists lived relatively well. Most had apartments of two, three or even more rooms for themselves and their families. Although there was no private automobile ownership, government cars and drivers were available to senior staff of teaching and scientific institutes. In answer to my query, they told me there was little abuse of this system for private or pleasure jaunts. This was in contrast to the situation in many parts of South Asia where official vehicles are regularly preempted by the "big fish" for their private use and that of their wives and families. The Chinese sharply limited vehicular use, not only because of the high cost of petrol, but because they also appeared to have stronger resistance - at least thus far - to the diversion of public funds and property to private use - a curse of most Third World development efforts.

Still, the great discrepancy between the relative comfort of party and government officials compared with the sardine-type accommodations of "little fish" was disquieting in this socialist society.

Back on the Bund, my new acquaintance, Wang, described his living quarters.

"Our entire family of five people live in one room. We share the toilet and kitchen with three other families. Crowded or no, we struggle to stay in Shanghai. The worst fate we can imagine is to be sent to the countryside."

I gazed at the crowded, noisy city and thought of the picturesque photographs I had seen of the tranquil Chinese countryside. Wang soon dispelled these idyllic reveries. He explained that the hard labor of the communes and the intellectual and cultural deprivation of rural areas held no romance or promise of bucolic bliss for him or any other Chinese. This intensely urban young man and his friends had little interest in working for socialist achievement in rural areas.

"The scientists you are visiting will never talk to you the way I do," Wang continued. "They are interested only in protecting their positions, their laboratories and their chances to travel to foreign countries. They will not tell you what they suffered during the cultural revolution, how many killed themselves out of sadness and despair!"

We had been talking while we walked along the Bund. We reached a gate outside a small park at the end of the long promenade.

"We must pay three cents for entry and then we can continue talking safely inside," Wang explained, fishing the coins from his pocket. Adamantly, he refused to allow me to pay for either ticket. The gatekeeper, a dour old man, motioned for me to throw the bright green plastic token Wang handed me into a tin box at the left of the entry gate. Then we passed through the gate and into a charming little park.

Inside, as we walked along the graveled path between neatly pruned shrubs, Wang told me the story of his brother-in-law.

"The work of the countryside was terribly hard, heavy labor," he explained, gripping his hands tightly around the handle of an imaginary pick and stopping to swing it laboriously back over his shoulder. "My brother, a factory worker in the city and a teacher, was not used to such labor. He was exhausted by it. But that was not the worst. They hung a huge wooden sign around his neck - big, like this." He stretched his arms straight out to both sides. "It was so heavy he could not stand up straight to raise the pick he was supposed to be using without the rope cutting into his neck. But the worst was what it said: *"I am a worthless reactionary"* in big letters, of course, in Chinese. Little children spit on him. People laughed and cursed him." Wang stopped walking and faced me. His eyes flashed with anger.

"But why?" - my brother-in-law kept asking - "Why have they done this to me? I was a follower of Chairman Mao since I was a little boy in school. I supported the revolution and the Communist Party always. Our plant exceeded its production schedule and received many awards and compliments from the government."

Wang sighed. "My brother-in-law was my best friend - my school mate - a poet, a sensitive man. It broke his heart. He could not eat or sleep. His wife, my sister, was a teacher. They had three little children. Forced to live in the countryside, they were very, very poor. Never had they seen such hard work, such poverty. Finally my brother-in-law gave up. He hung himself."

Wang stopped talking now and was silent for several minutes. "His parents were broken-hearted. Without a son, no one to care for them in old age, without a son, no use to go on living. They also committed suicide, also by hanging. My sister went to pieces. She cried all day and all night. Someone had to stay with her every minute, for she also wished only to die. I tried to persuade her to live. She had three lovely children. The youngest was only a baby, three months old. My older brother took them to care for as my sister could do nothing."

Wang paused and motioned to me that we should sit down on a wooden bench at a confluence of little pathways. Then he continued. "She lived. Now she is even happy. Her children are grown. One is in the university. The second is still in school. She is a poet, like her husband."

"And the baby?" I asked, "What happened to the three-month-old child?"

"Ah," he sighed. "We don't know. He was given away - a contract was signed when my sister was so despondent."

For a few minutes we sat in silence. Then Wang changed the subject. "Things are much better now," he acknowledged. "But I finally got fed up with it. For eleven years I taught in the high schools. Then I quit."

"But how did you avoid being sent out of Shanghai?" I asked. "You told me earlier that no one dares quit his job here, no matter how much he hates it, as there are no others and he would be sent from the city."

"This is true if you apply for new work, but I am self-employed - private English lessons I give in my house," he said, "for we have massive unemployment here." He grinned. "Only we don't call it unemployment, we call it 'waiting for job.'"

I was to hear this phrase many times. Officially there was no unemployment in the People's Republic. Actually, no one knew how many young middle-school graduates remained for months or even years without finding work.

We got up and walked slowly toward an open space where two old women performed the graceful movements of Tai Chi. A small man dressed in baggy gray cotton pants and shirt slowly raised his arms in repeated parries of Chinese boxing, a sort of shadow boxing in slow motion. He glanced over at us for a moment and then unself-consciously resumed his graceful thrusts into the murky air.

"I started my own work," Wang continued. "I gave English lessons and asked the government for nothing. This way I can work and talk as I please."

Others were not so fortunate. Wang is a university graduate, an essential but not certain key to liberation from toil in field or factory. Only four percent of Chinese middle-school graduates could go on to university. Selection was entirely on the basis of marks obtained in previous grades and on character.

"Now, unlike the situation during the Cultural Revolution," Wang explained, "selection for university has less to do with attitude toward the ruling party and more to do with perserverence, drive, and perhaps public service. Ninety-percent of Chinese youth are not lucky enough to qualify for university. They are assigned to jobs by their unit directors."

China was divided into units for every district and for every other enterprise of more than a few dozen persons. In rural areas, the collective or commune was one's unit. Directors of these units were theoretically chosen by those over whose lives they had jurisdiction. But the selection was limited to those nominated by the Party to the post. Needless to say, Party leaders chose loyal supporters. Thus, the system perpetuated itself - little fish profiting from big fish, big fish supposed to be loyal to smaller fry who thereby gain power over their fellow workers. The unit directors assigned all jobs for their particular unit. This included jobs for students graduating from high school who are not selected for university. There was little choice. A person was likely to remain in the shoe factory or farm group brigade where he or she was assigned for a long time, usually forever.

Knowing this gave me an intense sense of sorrow throughout my stay in China. The ubiquitous groups of blue or gray coated and trousered men and women sweeping walks, scrubbing toilets, pushing carts of discarded planks or loading cornstalks by hand into horse-drawn carts under a burning sun troubled me greatly. Aldous Huxley's term "proles" from "Brave New World" came to my mind. This feeling will always be attached to my first impression of China. My heart went out to these fellow humans who, through no fault of their own except failure to achieve high marks in school, were consigned to a life of endless toil and little joy.

But perhaps that was better than the where and to whom accident of birth that determines most of our lives.

In China, quitting your assigned job to seek a better one was not an option. The state was the only employer. The unit to which you belonged decided where and at what you worked. For life! Except for rare bits of intervening chance, one might stay on the same unloved job for a lifetime. But at least they all had a job. The old dilemna for those of us enamored of equality, even of socialism, was stark. Someone had to use the pick and shovel. Who should it be?

"We are slaves," remarked Wang matter-of-factly. "We eat, we sleep, we work; we cannot stop or we die."

I thought about the difference between these conditions and those of the working class, especially the unskilled and non-white workers of the U.S. They, too, scrub, clean, carry and shove. They, too, work without passion or joy and long for the end of each thankless day of menial physical toil. They, too make me acutely uncomfortable as they appear at dusk, mops, pails and brooms in hand, cleaning my office and laboratory as I leave the hospital each evening. They earned $4.00 an hour, the minimum wage, while I earned ten times more, and my colleagues in private practice of medicine earned ten times that. A whole army of such underpaid drudges exists in every society. Why then lament the fate of the blue-jacketed drones in China who at least have the security of free medical care, shelter, and enough to eat? Perhaps it is the inexorability of their fate, the loss of alternatives and the lack of freedom to speak out or try to change their destinies. Truly, they are consigned forever to move like sleepwalkers in a world of unexplored possibilities. Are most of us any different?

Ironically, sadly, obligate labor sets the working class of Communist countries apart from their brethren elsewhere, so many of whom search unsuccessfully for work. Ironic, too, that the labor theory of value turned into slavery for the very folk for whom the revolution was made. Although told that they are the "owners of the means of production," these workers could not choose the place or direction of their labor. They could not leave their jobs or go to other parts of the country or other lands to seek their fortune. Even the poorest of the poor in India, where destitution is a way of life for millions, could pick up their few rags and pots and seek other possibilities. But in China, in 1982, there were usually no other possibilities for the very poor. It was an ultimate question. Whose fate was worse - those who can move but not eat regularly, or the socialized proles of China who can eat and may even have all the necessities but cannot move or speak freely?

In the park with Wang, I watched an old man with mahogany colored skin stretched taut over high cheekbones pirouette slowly before us on one sandaled foot in the fluid, slow postures of Tai Chi. His hands were hard and callused. His feet were bare. Behind him stood his bicycle. It was attached to a small cart holding the long-handled broom of a street sweeper.

I turned to smile at a round faced doll of a tot who was staring at my strange face wonderingly as she clutched her mother's hand tightly. I could almost feel the preciousness of the one child allowed each couple. Serene little creatures, their hands were held on each side by a devoted parent. There were so few children about, I noticed every one. There was also a total absence of dogs - banned in the city to prevent rabies. Even cats were scarce, as were birds and bugs. The latter I did not regret, having been thoroughly bitten by both mosquitoes and bedbugs before I left India - a land where the press is free and both people and vermin are free to move where they like.

A small crowd was gathering to gaze at me. Wang suggested we move on. Leaving the park we crossed the Bund between the steady flow of bicycles interrupted by occasional trucks and buses. Not one private car passed. There was a rare dark blue official government limousine, usually with a single Chinese in the rear seat.

"We are disillusioned now," Wang continued as we strolled down Nanking Street past the Peace Hotel. A knot of foreigners stood outside. The foreign women suddenly seemed garish and vulgar in their bright colored slacks stretched across great plump behinds. Their painted faces and frizzled orange or platinum hair were an unpleasant shock compared to the unendingly sober garb of the slender black-haired Chinese.

Wang continued his monologue. "There is so little for us to look forward to. Before the Cultural Revolution, we all somehow had faith in the future. We thought we were sacrificing our comforts for something really worth while. Then we found out the Gang of Four was misleading the people, so we lost our faith in the government. There is so little for the average man or woman to look for each day - to just work and return home, without change, for years."

He shook his head but grinned cheerfully. "Where would you like to go? Shopping?"

"Anywhere," I agreed. "You lead the way!"

"The average Chinese worker out of middle school earned around thirty-five yuan a month for the first eight years on his job," he continued. "Then he receives a raise of 7-10 percent, which is added to as his years of service increase. A street sweeper like the one you saw in the park may have twenty-five years of service and could easily make more than a new teacher or doctor."

Although the yuan was worth only $1.25, very low rents - approximately 5 percent of one's salary - and subsidized rice and bread brought these essentials to everyone. Medical care and education were free.

We reached the entrance to the First Department Store, the largest in Shanghai. The windows were full of radios, TVs, fans, serviceable clothing and shoes. The interior was crowded. Plain glass cases of pocket knives, bath brushes, scissors, and household goods attracted many onlookers but few buyers.

"I am lucky," continued Wang. "I make plenty of money -around 200 yuan a month."

This was a large salary in China, available only to top and long experienced scientists and perhaps party officials. I could see why he preferred private enterprise.

"My girlfriend works in a shoe factory - she was sent there right after high school. She only makes forty yuan a month. When we marry we will be given a single small room with shared bath and kitchen to set up housekeeping."

I asked Wang about his girlfriend and what sort of girl he liked best.

"The main thing is she must not care too much for wearing fancy clothes," he replied.

I laughed. Three days earlier when I asked the same question of the university educated young son of my host in south India, his answer was, "She must be slim."

The crowds of lovely young Chinese girls we passed on the streets of Shanghai were certainly not wearing fancy clothes, and slim they were. Some wore the baggy blue jackets and trousers I was expecting - but most were dressed in neat, pressed black or tan cotton slacks and simple white or pastel long sleeved shirts of western cut. Their shining black hair was often modishly cut and waved. But many still wore a long single braid that hung down their backs to below the waist. None wore jeans. Neither did the boys - quite a change from India and Japan, where well-faded blue jeans were an important status symbol among the middle class. Neither did Chinese girls and women bear any visible evidence of facial cosmetics. The only exception I saw was a child of around five with a brilliant red lipsticked mouth, waiting at the curb, holding tightly to her mother's hand.

Not only did Chinese girls dress simply, they were also conformists. During the entire evening I did not spot even one in a skirt or dress, although Wang explained that dresses were common enough only the week before and throughout the hot summer. With the first rainy day of autumn, just twenty four hours before I came, every woman in town had apparently switched to trousers. This says a great deal about how this enormous society holds together under a repressive government.

Even rain gear was uniform and drab. During the steady drizzle that fell throughout my first day in Shanghai, the thousands of cyclists all wore hooded parkas of thin gray plastic - a most impractical choice as they were almost invisible against the gray pavement, leaden sky, and dull gray concrete buildings.

We stopped before a counter of small nailbrushes - sturdy wooden ones with natural bristles. In the absence of much else convenient to carry, I bought one. While we waited for change, we continued our conversation about choosing mates. "What kind of boys or men do girls want?" I asked.

"A girl won't like a fellow who drinks or won't work," he replied firmly. "Those are the most important." Money, looks, personality and intelligence were not mentioned.

Back out on the street, hordes of people walked shoulder to shoulder without shoving or pushing. Our progress was slow. The sidewalk was jammed with pedestrians walking three or four abreast in each direction and spilling over the curb into the street. Most were just walking and talking. A few were window shopping in front of displays of very ordinary clothing, bolts of drab cloth, shoes, plastic pots and pans, groceries and other necessities. There were occasional tea shops. Book stores, bars and restaurants were scarce.

Farther down Nanking Street, described in my guidebook as "the most modern street in China," we reached the Second Department Store. Wang suggested we go in and look around. It was getting on toward seven o'clock and we had been talking steadily for two hours.

"I have students waiting for me at my house," he suddenly remembered. "But if you would like me to, I will cancel my classes tonight so I may talk with you."

I was delighted to have his company. While I inspected very cheap cotton tapestries of tigers and temples near the public coin phone, he rang up his home and rapidly dismissed his class.

The Second Department Store, like the First, was strictly utilitarian. The floor was cement. Very ordinary utilitarian goods were arranged in old-fashioned glass cases. Pictures, clothes, linens, clocks, lamps and sweaters were on the first floor. The typical padded cotton jackets worn by all Chinese caught my eye. With Wang's help I asked a salesgirl if I might try one on. The flustered and surprised sales girl helped me unbutton one and soon the floor manager and half a dozen other sales persons gathered to assist. I was unprepared for the tremendous attraction I was soon to become. I took off the first jacket, the sleeves of which hung below my knees, and asked for a smaller size.

Soon I was surrounded by a crowd of at least fifty or sixty young men and women, who swarmed around the counter on both sides and blocked the aisle behind me. A friendly group, they smiled, whispered, stared and hung on every word between me and the floor manager. They watched carefully as I switched to a maroon plaid jacket with embroidered button loops and sighed with satisfaction when I returned to the padded blue which Wang assured me was the preferred dress of the people in cold weather. A bulky padded jacket was the last thing I needed to cram into my luggage. No day of my journey had been cooler than eighty degrees Fahrenheit. However, I found it impossible after gathering this large audience to walk away without making a purchase - they were so palpably anxious to see me pleased. So I bought a puffy blue padded jacket for the equivalent of $20, half a month's salary in China - less than half an hour's work for me.

When I fished in my wallet for money to purchase the jacket, an American dime fell out on the counter. Rather than put it back I held it out to a wide-eyed youngster of ten or so who stood staring steadily at me as I discussed the transaction with Wang, the sales-person, and the cordial floor manager. The little boy stepped back quickly, hands behind his back, sudden fear in his face. Holding the coin out on the flat of my palm, I tried to give it to anyone.

"American coin - present!" I invited clumsily. No one moved. I put it down on the counter and pointed to it invitingly. Still not a soul responded. In India only two days before, it was hard to leave a store, board a bus or hail a taxi without being set upon by beggars, especially child beggars or emaciated mothers holding an infant in their arms. Poor Indian mothers, with no work or other means of support, were free to beg, or move even to borrow a baby to assist her begging. Would the Chinese mother have traded bread for this kind of freedom? Wang thought not, but wasn't sure.

My hosts were horrified in the hospital the next morning when I announced that my document case containing passport, travelers checks, airline tickets, and a modest amount of American cash had disappeared. My last recollection was placing it on the counter at the travel desk at the Peace Hotel. Pride and honesty were strong points in China. One of the doctors phoned the hotel at once. He was astonished to find my wallet had not been seen. Faces drawn in consternation, my hosts had to conclude it had been stolen.

In the afternoon I went to the large Shanghai Bank across the street from the Peace Hotel to replace my lost travelers checks. When I arrived for this transaction, most of the bank staff was lined up doing *Tai Chi* exercises at one end of the enormous marble corridor across the entire length of the bank. Teapots and flowers adorned their temporarily abandoned desks - hundreds of them, placed cheek by jowl in two rows behind the counters. With some difficulty arising from lack of experience in dealing with careless Americans, the young clerk found instructions and a packet of checks stored away in the top drawer of an antiquated filing cabinet. After nearly two hours of negotiations and reading and re-reading of instructions, he managed to replace my lost checks.

The next day I took a taxi to the government airline office in order to replace my lost airplane ticket. Then I got lost myself. I made the mistake of embarking in a taxi alone with only the travel office address written for me in Chinese by the desk clerk at my guest house. It turned out to be the wrong address, a bicycle tire shop. The taxi had departed. The proprietor of the repair shop and his family laboriously tried to give me directions in sign language how to reach the new office by foot. Inevitably, I lost my way. Hundreds of bicycles passed me. I hailed one or two to ask directions but no one understood English. There were no cars and few pedestrians. I was about to turn back to where I had started when I spotted a young scholarly looking man wearing glasses and carrying a brief-case. He was leaving a building on the opposite side of the street. Dodging bicycles, I crossed the broad boulevard and ran to catch up with him.

"Excuse me, but I am lost," I apologized as he stopped politely. In perfect English he asked me where I was trying to go. When I told him, he said he was going to the same place and kindly offered to accompany me. We exchanged brief introductions. A man of around forty, my new acquaintance was working for the government

"I am really an engineer," he explained. "Before the cultural revolution I was a teacher and designed computers. I won many prizes for my work. Now I work for the government, but not in my profession. The government has me meeting and taking care of visiting business men from all over the world. Most of them are from Japan. I am on my way to the government travel bureau to arrange for their airline reservations."

"That seems rather a low-grade operation for a man of your qualifications," I sympathized. "Do you like this work?"

"I meet many interesting people," he replied. "But no, of course I would prefer to follow my profession. At present, however, that will not be possible."

I could detect no hint of bitterness in his voice. It was taken for granted that since the government is the only employer, to change jobs, and especially professions, was impossible.

"Unfortunately, I am good at what I do," he went on rather sadly. "Here one does what one is told."

He seemed unusually interested in my research. His wife was also a doctor who had wanted a research career but had been sent to a rural clinic.

"At least it is now much better than during the Cultural Revolution," he continued. "Then, like most educated people, we both were sent to hard work in the fields on different collective farms. There was no electricity, there were no books, no journals, and no chance to study. When it was dark we went to bed. We had to leave our children, only five and seven years old, alone in Shanghai."

He held out his arm to hold me back at a busy corner before we crossed the street by weaving between bicycles.

"Who looked after them?" I asked when we reached the other side.

"Neighbors mostly, and they looked after each other. The little girl - she was seven - bought food, mostly ices and sweets I think, and fed herself and the boy. Then every three or four months one of us could get into town to help them," he continued matter of factly.

It was a story I was to hear many times from doctors, teachers, and intellectuals.

"Now, of course, things are much better. Still, I would like to return to my studies and research some day." He smiled at me wistfully and held out his hand. "Here we are at the agency. It has been good for me to talk with you."

We went inside, he to the back of the counter with his sheaf of tickets for the Japanese. I walked to the front to arrange for a new ticket for myself. I still think of him and his hopes and interests, nursemaiding Japanese businessmen. My lost airline ticket did not seem very important. Besides, unlike the computer engineer, I found it the next day. My hosts were perfectly right. My checks and passport case had not been stolen. When I went to the travel desk in the hotel two days later the young woman behind the counter greeted me enthusiastically.

"Why haven't you come sooner?" she cried. "We have been saving your passport and all of your documents for you."

"But how - what happened?" I stammered. "We phoned - they said they were not here." I paused in embarrassment. "I thought they must have been stolen!"

"Please look to see that everything is present," she replied politely, handing me the black pocket case that I have traveled the world with for thirty years and still do. "You left it on the counter and when you didn't come back at the end of the day we were very surprised. We put it away, thinking you would surely return."

I thanked her effusively. She was as happy as I was. No reward was expected and I sensed it would be an insult even to offer one.

After the noisy chaos of the crowded thoroughfares of the great cities of India, Shanghai seemed neat, tidy, and disciplined. Streets were clean, hotels and hospitals spotless. Libraries were well kept and catalogs functional. Compared to the large cities of the U.S., both Shanghai and later in my journey, Beijing, also seemed safe. Although people were very poor and many streets had no lights, there were no muggings, purse snatchings or murders. Rape was almost unknown. So was drug abuse. My scientific colleagues, male and female, assured me that one could walk anywhere in Shanghai safely, even at night.

Although the mental hospitals were as big as ours, only five percent of patients were diagnosed with depression, compared to half of ours in the U.S. Even more remarkable, only one percent were diagnosed with senile dementia. In a hospital that admitted 4,000 patients a year, only sixty-four alcoholics had been admitted in the past twenty-one years. Ten of these were foreigners.

"How do you do it?" I asked, slightly incredulous.

"Our discharged patients are taken care of by at least three people - a family member, a neighbor and a barefoot doctor," explained Dr. Z., chief of one of Shanghai's largest mental hospitals.

"Old people are kept at home. Depressed people are taken care of in outpatient clinics or district centers. Over 75 percent of all the patients in the Shanghai psychiatric hospital suffer from that world-wide scourge, schizophrenia."

"That was also true in the U.S. 50 years ago. But with modern drugs and the astronomical cost of hospitalization, probably fewer than 20% carry that diagnosis in state hospitals today. There were other important differences from the U.S. psychiatry scene. Depression, alcoholism, and abandoned elderlies with dementia make up more than half of the U.S. chronic mental hospital population. Equal or larger numbers are abandoned and live on the street. No one was abandoned in China. Nearly everyone had a family. Everyone was followed up through their work units and by hospitals or clinics in their communes or factories.

My visit was before China began to modernize and westernize. Everyone had a job then. Not now.

There was no psychoanalysis in China. Instead, the mentally ill were given group and family education. In the groups, patients discussed their symptoms and were taught what was known about their illness and its treatment. The hospital used no social workers, no psychologists, no halfway houses.

"When people recover they go back to their homes and families," explained the chief psychiatrist.

The patients on the wards appeared well cared for. All were dressed in clean blue Mao suits just like the people outside. When we entered the ward they all stood and applauded politely. Then those engaged in occupational therapy returned to their work. The men put pins in neat rows in boxes; women painted the faces of dolls for local toy factories.

Their apparent concentration, or was it discipline, were very different from similar patients in Japan. In the mental hospital in Tokyo, the schizophrenic patients swarmed all over me, staring, touching, and asking a myriad questions in a most friendly way.

Unlike Tokyo, where I was ignored on the streets and shops, in Shanghai, I attracted a small crowd of curious citizens wherever I went. In the mental hospital, everyone behaved with quiet restraint and no-one approached me.

"I'm a bit surprised at these patients," I explained to my guide in Shanghai, Dr. W. "They seem so quiet, so docile. In Tanzania, in the huge mental hospital in Dar es Salaam a year ago, I was assaulted by a patient for no apparent reason while I was sitting observing group therapy. I also was hit over the head by a patient in the mental hospital where I work in Washington D.C. Why the difference?" Dr. W only smiled.

In Japan, I received a partial explanation. "Discipline and culture may have something to do with that," laughed my colleague in Tokyo when I quizzed him about these differences several weeks later. "But don't be too sure that this reversal is just schizophrenia. I think those Japanese patients you saw here may have had frontal lobotomies!"

On my last day in Shanghai, I asked the friendly English speaking desk clerk in my guest house if he could find me an unofficial guide to show me the sights of the city. He offered to guide me himself. The most interesting part of our tour was his own story, which he later told me at lunch.

In the morning, we went to the Yu Gardens, where the local populace, armed with cheap box cameras, swarmed like ants on a hill over every path, graceful bridge and pavilion. After a walk around the exotic grounds, all but hidden by the mass of Chinese visitors, we settled down over rice and tea upstairs in a small restaurant that overlooked an incredibly crowded narrow street of take-out food shops. Hordes of people eating Chinese snacks out of paper containers spilled over into the street from the sidewalk. It was well past noon and our restaurant was nearly empty. When we had finished an excellent meal, I asked my guide how he got into hotel clerking.

"I worked in a machine factory just outside of Shanghai for thirteen years before I had a chance to leave," he explained. "I was always interested in languages but I was sent by my district to the factory when I finished high school."

Like the first friend I met in Shanghai, the travel office functionary, the hotel clerk, who was now my guide, taught himself to speak and understand English from taping foreign broadcasts.

"I knew someday that to speak English would be important," he explained. "When China started taking tourists in, I went to the chief of my district and told him I could speak English. He knew the government needed such people and helped me get a job in the guest house. I have been there two years now. Next year I will go to Chicago. My uncle owns a chain of seven restaurants there."

We were the only ones left in the large dining room and I signaled to the waiter standing at the kitchen door to bring a check, for I was sure the waiter wanted to close. Not at all. Instead, he sat down with us and joined the conversation despite the fact that adjoining tables were piled with remnants of food, fish bones, and dirty plates left by previous diners. The waiter also had a cousin in the United States and hoped to join him.

"But I will go to University first, for education in the U.S.," he explained through Huang, the hotel clerk. "I will not work in a restaurant."

"And you?" I asked, turning to Huang. "Will you visit or stay?"

"Ah, that depends," he laughed. "Maybe my uncle will need help in his business."

I paid the small check - off the tourist circuit two could eat very well for less than a dollar. We went down the stairs into the packed streets. The pleasant fragrance of charcoal and garlic wafted through the stale and smoky air. Thousands of well-fed, plainly dressed Shanghaiese were out for Sunday promenades. A rare child peeped out between two parents, holding tight to hands on either side. Every child was precious, for the penalty for having more than one was high. Families with only one child were given better housing, free nursery school, kindergarten and a monthly subsidy until the child was sixteen years old. All schooling was free, including university for the lucky four percent who successfully competed for entry. Medical care was also entirely free. If a second child was born, however, the child subsidy, equal to ten percent of the monthly income, had to be paid back.

"I also wished to go to university," explained Huang, as we walked past a small shop where dozens of people crowded in the doorway to buy deep-fried spiced vegetable patties wrapped in dough. "But since so few middle school graduates can go to university, I could not. It is all decided by grades on examination. Before liberation, English was taught in high school, but after liberation only Chinese. Now students are again being taught in English to promote international exchange. Some also study Japanese, French, or German."

Although he was thirty-five years old, Huang was not married. "I am too young," he laughed.

We entered our waiting taxi and drove toward the edge of the city. Huang wanted to show me the botanical gardens, considered a must among Shanghai's few tourist attractions. When we reached the outlying farms that ring the city, I asked him to have the driver stop so I could take a picture of workers trudging toward us from across the field in front of a cluster of low wooden houses. Surprised at my interest in anything so banal, he nevertheless obliged me.

"But those are only peasant houses with no facilities," he apologized when we stopped. Pointing to a high-rise, Moscow style apartment complex he explained, "Over there are the new workers' flats we can visit."

The farm workers came up to us curiously. They were a jolly lot. After asking their permission, seemed pleased to be part of my amateur cinema. When the guide explained that I was an American, all three grinned with pleasure.

"They like Americans very much," explained Huang. "They are happy you have come here. They want to know what you think of China."

With my guide as interpreter, we exchanged the usual facts and queries of ordinary people who are strangers. They wanted to know the cost of shoes, TVs, and how much American farmers made every month. I wanted to know whether their lives felt constrained and deprived of freedom, but didn't know how to ask politely.

"What do you want most?" I inquired after we had completed the inevitable exchanges concerning the number, age and sex of each of our children.

"Of course, everything is much better now," replied the oldest farmer obliquely, his small eyes twinkling.

"Better than what?" I inquired guilelessly. I got what I deserved in reply.

"Better than the cultural revolution and the Gang of Four!" Perhaps my question had no other meaning. Perhaps taking off the pinching shoe sufficed.

On my last morning in Shanghai, I rose early. Once again armed with my small movie camera, I took a taxi from the guest house to the People's Park to film the *Tai Chi* always in progress there. Although it was not yet 7:30 on a gray and gloomy Sunday morning, hundreds of Chinese men and women garbed in their usual blue cotton clothes were engaged in various traditional exercises. Groups of thirty or forty young men and women performed the graceful postures of *Tai Chi* while facing a leader who called the signals against an atonal "ping poing" background of taped music. Older men and women with calm, concentrated faces were much more expert than the young undertaking similar exertions.

In a corner of the clearing, a young man sat alone with closed eyes, in the posture of meditation. In front of a low wooden building, dozens of elderly men and women sat on long benches. One very tall graying man, distinguished in appearance despite the ubiquitous baggy blue cotton trousers, watched me keenly as I stood about uneasily, camera in hand. I felt it was an intrusion to start filming without someone's permission.

Hesitantly, I approached the tall man and asked if he spoke English. To my delight, his face broke into a marvelous grin of pure pleasure. Educated in an English school in Shanghai "before liberation," for thirty years he had been chief accountant in an American importing company. Twice he had visited San Francisco. After "liberation" he was told to leave his city job and sent to work in a rural commune. Now he was seventy-five years old and retired.

"But you scarcely look fifty!" I exclaimed.

"We Chinese age more slowly than you do," he replied gallantly.

I asked him how his life now compared to when we imperialists were here. Smiling in appreciation, he replied with some reticence.

"Of course, we earned much more then." He paused and smiled wistfully before asking, "How are things in San Francisco?

Part II Man's Hope

I explained to my Shanghai host and the girls behind the travel desk at the Peace Hotel that I wanted to go to the capital by train instead of air so I could see a little of the country. They made a reservation for me for the on the Peking (now, Beijing!) Express. Two days later, armed with my Berlitz English-Chinese conversation guide, I boarded the train at around 5 p.m. for the nineteen hour trip to the capital. All was order and precision. The spacious train depot was nearly empty. There was no crush of customers, no rush for seats, no vendors, beggars, noise or confusion. Reservations were posted on the outside of each gleaming green, clean car of the train. A smiling young conductress in gray uniform and matching visored cap ushered me into my compartment. On the upholstered seat opposite mine, a Chinese businessman and his son sat talking and puffing animatedly on cigarettes. Inwardly groaning, I smiled brightly, pretending I enjoyed the combination of cigarette smoke, loud talk in a language foreign to me and sharing a tiny sleeping compartment for nineteen hours with two strange men.

Fortunately, I learned about these integrated sleeping arrangements years before in the Soviet Union. On a train somewhere between Moscow and Leningrad, I had shrieked at a man who entered my compartment in the middle of the night and began to undress. The poor fellow dashed out, terrified, and spent the rest of the journey standing in the corridor. Only on my arrival in the capital in the morning did I discover that train compartments are co-ed in the Soviet Union, as they are in most if not all of Asia.

The men nodded and smiled at me courteously. We all gave up quickly on an exchange of pleasantries when they discovered I didn't know a word of Chinese. Similarly, they knew no English. Neither, as it turned out, did anyone else on the train.

The little compartment was furnished in a homey fashion. In front of lace fringed white curtains at the window was a small table covered with a fresh white cloth on which were placed a potted plant, a lamp with fluted pink shade and two flowered china teacups with matching covers. The cushioned seats were fitted with tan cotton slipcovers. Red and white pillows were embroidered with tiny flowers. A large lace cloth was draped over the back of each seat. A black cotton sheet and fiber mat completed the sleeping arrangements. A yellow Chinese rug decorated with somewhat soiled blue and white geese covered most of the floor.

As the time for departure drew near, the younger of the two men rose, spoke rapidly and fondly to the older one, hugged him briefly and departed. I fanned away some of the cigarette fumes with my train ticket. My companion, obviously concerned, spoke in his rapid staccato tongue with gestures that signified his regret to have caused me any discomfort. In the nineteen hours that followed he did not light another cigarette in the compartment but disappeared every half hour or so to smoke in the corridor or the lavatory.

And such lavatories! They put all the train loos I have experienced from Cape Cormoran at the tip of India to Switzerland's Orient Express to shame. Odorless, with faucets that worked, toilets that were clean, and dry tile floors, they were a joy to enter - not only early in the journey, but even at the end. The only problem was distinguishing the male facility from the female. I couldn't read the signs. I silently thanked the gods for the Chinese symbols in my Berlitz pocket dictionary.

Soon after departure of the young man - who I later discovered was my fellow-passenger's son, we were underway on the dot of five. While we were still traveling through the jungle of apartments on the outskirts of Shanghai, a smiling conductress in gray trouser and jacket uniform appeared at the doorway of our compartment to take tickets. She was soon followed by another with pencil and tablet in her hand. She handed me a worn menu, mercifully printed in both Chinese and English. Although I didn't recognize any of my favorite dishes from the Chinese restaurants back home, I pointed to shrimp and noodles and beer. After much discussion of possibilities, my compartment companion placed his order.

Half an hour later, he signaled by energetic and unmistakable gestures that the bell ringing in the corridor was our summons to the dining car. I followed him through several train cars past groups of Chinese who also were traveling in first-class compartments. In the dining room, I was ushered to a small single table adorned with a vase with a plastic flower, a soiled white tablecloth, salt and pepper and several bottles of dark condiments. Once again, I was rendered deaf and mute. No one in the dining car, neither waiters nor customers, spoke a word of English. From the menu, I pointed to the picture of shrimp and pantomined drinking a bottle of beer. A plate of greasy noodles and shrimp soon arrived as did a bottle of excellent although warm Chinese beer. When I started to use the chopsticks in my usual clumsy fashion, the waiter rushed to bring me a fork and spoon.

Gazing out the window, I watched a seemingly endless landscape of two- and three-story, block-sized flats interspersed with tile-roofed peasant houses of mud brick. When we left the urban area, figures of indeterminate gender dressed in bulky blue suits and wide straw hats stooped over fields of vegetables that circle the great city.

By the time I finished the last noodle we had passed into flat green countryside laced with muddy rivers and canals. Miles of green paddy or vegetables in long straight rows grew up to the walls of small white houses. Dusk, then darkness fell, but still there were people in the fields - weeding, carrying, and hoeing as the train sped into the black night. Lights appeared in dingy one-room flats in bigger towns. The isolated glow of oil lamps marked cottages in small hamlets. Tall brick factories spewing black smoke from their chimneys rose in the middle of the green fields of collective farms.

After polishing off the last of the large bottle of warm beer, I tottered back to my compartment where the Chinese businessman, his trousers hung neatly at the end of his seat, was snoring peacefully under his sheet. I prepared my own bed by unrolling the fiber mat and spreading the sheet over it. I looked out the window. A vast lake surrounded by trees and cozy cottages were my last impressions of the Chinese countryside before rocking off to sleep on the rough roadbed.

When I awoke a few hours later, the sky was still starless. Pale light from a moon I could not see from the window bathed the countryside. My roommate snored gently. Outside, flat paddy fields traced by short canals sped by. We crossed a giant river - the Yangtze? Factories belched smoke into the night. Again I fell asleep. At dawn, I woke to a vista of high mountains rising over arid empty terraced foothills. My companion appeared at the door of the compartment, freshly washed and carrying his toothbrush. Discreetly, he stepped back out as I pulled myself together, rolled up the sleeping mat, searched out toilet articles and departed to the still spotless Ladies Room. At last, I had learned to recognize the inscrutable letters marked on the door.

When I returned to our compartment, my roommate was smiling and ready for conversation. We pantomined a little and then I got out the Berlitz. When I pointed to the English phrases he could read the Chinese next to it and vice versa. In this way we exchanged "Good morning," "Where are your from?" What do you do?" and "How many children do you have?" I had two; he had five - a surprise for me in one child China. But I could not pursue this topic with the limited vocabulary of the phrase book.

Now we were passing a country town where crowds of cyclists and pedestrians waited at the barrier to cross the tracks. The train halted with a great squeal of brakes and everyone dashed out to buy fish.

I stood on the platform gazing across at the town. Thick black smoke rose from factory chimneys. Wagons heaped high with bags of wheat, cement, hemp, piles of brick, fruit or potatoes were pulled through cobbled streets behind teams of horses. Pushcarts, bicycles, and throngs of pedestrians in baggy work clothes filled the streets. There were no cars. Trucks were rare.

During the brief halt at the station, half a dozen people clutching cloth bags dismounted from our train. An equal number of similarly burdened country folk got on. The train lurched forward again and sped on to the north. Almost immediately, the bell sounded for breakfast. I staggered to the dining room, the train rocking like a small boat on a rough sea. At the other tables people were eating dried green stuff accompanied by noodles and watery soup. The waitress pointed to boiled eggs and toast on the English menu. I agreed enthusiastically.

Outside the window, miles of cornfields and fruit orchards passed by. In great contrast to India, in all the long journey I saw only two defecators squatting by the roadbed. No one was drawing water from the canals. There were no grazing animals in sight - only draft beasts - horses or oxen. In the ten hours before we reached Peking I saw only one tractor.

After breakfast, I returned to the compartment, where my roommate sat reading the newspaper. Once again the train squealed to a stop in a country town. My fellow passengers swarmed from their compartments and descended to small stands on the platform selling ham hocks. The platform was spotlessly clean. The hawkers wore white cotton lab coats and close fitting caps. When I aimed my camera at two very pretty girls, they ducked down and hid behind their stands.

When we started off again, nearly everyone was munching on the ham hocks, including my roommate, although we had left the dining room less than half an hour before. Now we passed fields of sunflowers. There were no dogs, no lonely farmhouses, and no cemeteries. Later I learned that because of rabies, dogs were generally outlawed. The lonely farmhouses of the American great plains were here replaced by communes. And there are no cemeteries. Cremation is a civic right paid for by the state. If one elects to be buried, it would be at his own expense.

As we neared the great capital, I was delighted to see white Peking ducks swimming in the canals and gullies by the tracks. Horse-drawn wagons appeared in the roads, but no cows and no cars. A truckload of picks and shovels passed. Then another truck, full of laborers in blue suits and straw hats, no doubt belonging to the picks and shovels. On the outskirts of Peking, wheelbarrows and small wagons pulled by bicycles were the principal traffic. Laborers in the fields cut cornstalks by hand and loaded them on huge horse-drawn carts. As we entered the city I spotted my first flock of sheep. They were trotting along the side of the wide paved boulevard, clearly on their way to market.

In Peking, I was met by three members of the Peking University staff, all speaking very passable English. Apologetically, they explained that because my visit was so unexpected they had been unable to arrange for a hotel. Would I be willing to stay in a hostel at the University?

Willing? I was delighted! We drove out to the lovely grounds of the University. I left off my suitcase in the spotless, spartan foreign student dormitory. For the next three days I toured the usual sights of Beijing and gave a seminar to medical students about causes and treatment of epilepsy. Best of all, I talked and talked and listened and listened with my hosts and new acquaintances at the University. My special friend and guide was twenty-eight-year old Xing, a university psychologist.

Xing was a splendid companion, well informed about China. However, for a faculty member, he seemed surprisingly ignorant about the West. All of his higher education had taken place during the Cultural Revolution. It is hard to say who was more curious about whom. I was surprised at his good fortune in living quarters - three comfortable rooms for only six people, plus a W.C., kitchen, and shared bath. All six members of his household worked, but still there was not enough money for books, tape recorders, or other "luxuries." Xing's salary after eight years on the faculty at the university was forty-nine yuan a month - about forty-five U.S. dollars.

Xing found the freedom of Americans mind-boggling. To choose our own work, to leave it, to move, to elect our own careers, to go to university, to marry or to not marry or "live in sin" and to have children - as many as we wanted. Conformity was deeply rooted in his character. If my American informants at the university were correct, this was true for most Chinese. Shame for not conforming to others' behaviors and expectations was the rule. The Chinese were "ashamed" to have us visitors from the West stay in their own dormitories at the university or to eat in their dining halls.

"Our food is too poor for you," explained Xing when I urged him to take me to his dining hall since he could not dine in mine.

"Try me and see," I replied.

Visibly shocked, he shook his head. "I could not," he insisted. "I could not."

On my last day in China we visited the Great Wall. The area was crawling with tourists, mostly Chinese, plus a sprinkling of Westerners and Japanese. The latter were easily distinguished from their oriental hosts by their protruding cameras and brightly colored T-shirts embossed with slogans such as "Try me" in English.

On our return trip to town from the Wall, our car passed dozens of large horse drawn carts filled with blue coated laborers, hay, or both. On the roadside the men and women of the People's Republic piled great loads of fodder or vegetables into waiting wagons. Others rested under the shade of large trees that lined the highway and protected them from the broiling sun. I found the sight of these endlessly laboring, still terribly poor people, deeply moving.

It was not as though I was in culture shock at the sight of so much poverty. It was not too long before that my camera was knocked out of my hands in Egypt - for filming "backward areas" like the famous alleys of the Khan el Khalili bazaar in Cairo. I was also threatened in Pakistan and Afghanistan for filming streets or fields where women were walking or working. Here, the Gang of Four was the national scapegoat. All the Chinese I met blamed their current plight - little money, crowded living quarters, few amenities, shortages of many foods and consumer goods on the Gang. There was a general sense of a revolution betrayed. Just as South African apartheid once served many black African leaders by diverting their people's attention from pressing problems of food, water, health and employment, the Gang of Four was the safety valve for the frustrations of a generation of disappointed, hard working Chinese.

The younger generation was particularly disillusioned. They knew the Cultural Revolution cheated them of a proper education. They were even more shocked and disillusioned to discover after what they were so long told about us, how well we actually live in the West. Nearly every university teacher I met had a spouse, son, or daughter studying in the United States. As in India and Pakistan, the affluence of the Japanese posed particular puzzlement and envy.

I had an uneasy sense of official inequality at being housed in the special foreigners guest house and taking my meals in the foreigners dining room at Peking University. This segregation gave foreigners a standard of living far above that attainable by a majority of ordinary Chinese. Because of money, this was true not only for Westerners but also for the ubiquitous and prosperous Japanese travelers all over Asia. The contrived, formalized inequality in China conveyed by the special currency for foreigners was especially painful to me in this land supposedly dedicated to socialism and equality. It was a subject my hosts carefully avoided.

A week later, back in Shanghai, I was again dining with a Chinese colleague from the University. Sitting at a window table on the top floor restaurant of the Peace Hotel, we overlooked the opaque gray swirl of the Hwang Po river. A barge loaded with mysterious straw-wrapped bales of something chugged slowly past. Blue-coated workers hauled at heavy ropes coiled on the deck. On the far bank, others, similarly clad, bent under heavy crates being passed to shore by a human chain.

I looked about the lavishly decorated dining room. Except for my companion, all the diners were foreigners. Only special currency, obtained by exchanging dollars, Japanese yen or other hard money, was accepted here. The Chinese currency for foreigners was of similar denomination but different in appearance than the worn bills I received in change from ordinary stores and restaurants patronized by the Chinese. A wall sign in the dining room announced that only this special currency was acceptable in the restaurant. Similar signs were posted outside the so-called Friendship Stores where paintings, carvings and other tourist articles were sold. Even the taxis usually insisted on foreigners special currency, although if one had no other money, they would reluctantly accept local yuan. This dual monetary system served to reserve luxury items and facilities for foreigners and also prevented a black market in money. The custom is apparently accepted without malice by the locals, but always made me ashamed.

"I was a Communist as a student myself," I confided to the neuroscientist who was my special guide in Beijing. Unmoved, he used his chopsticks deftly to fill my plate from the serving platter of shrimp, green pea pods and other delicacies in a savory sauce.

"But I have almost decided the major flaw in the system here was not anticipated by Marx, Lenin, certainly by their followers," I continued. My companion listened politely, not missing a bite.

"As brain and behavior specialists, the questions are especially interesting for us," I persisted. "Rewarding each individual according to his needs rather than his deeds may be incompatible with productivity because of human character. Perhaps the very wiring of our brains demands incentives and rewards for work. How else can you explain why all of the Communist countries have failed so dismally in achieving high productivity and standards of living?"

Still no reply.

"Beautiful as the idea of working for the good of all surely is, the basic venality and narcissism of the human brain seems to require personal rewards for labor," I continued, somewhat daunted by his silence. "Do you think that greed in man's character has been abolished in the Chinese?" I paused and waited for an answer.

Finally, Dr. X. replied carefully. "The fact that some individuals can work and work well under this system proves that all can if they are properly educated. I will tell you a true story. Then perhaps you will understand why most Chinese people support the revolution and the government."

"There is no simple answer to your question," he explained. "You must distinguish between the choices of workers and intellectuals. This is a workers' state. They are in charge now, and they have put food and shelter first. But do not condemn this. To understand it you must understand much, much more than you have seen in Shanghai and Beijing. To know the real China, peasant China, village China, would take you many years. Then only you might begin to understand why the workers' state is so much protected - so much better than what they had."

I poured more tea and hoped he would continue.

"Take my uncle for example," he began, pushing his chair back from the table. His eyes suddenly seemed to leave the present as though he was seeing events of many, many years before, even before the revolution, the war and Liberation.

"I grew up in a very small village," he continued quietly. "In English you would call it Central Bridge. My father was the doctor of traditional Chinese medicine there. Our family was large and well-to-do, but almost everyone else in the village was very poor. One day - it was during the war - a poor man came into a little store in the village to buy rice. He was very old. His clothes were ragged and his body so thin he was like a bundle of dry sticks. He held a liter jug in both hands." Dr. Chu paused and held up his hands before him, fingers curled around an imaginary container. His eyes were deep wells of distant sorrow.

"The old man held up the container like this," Chu went on, "and asked for his rice. One week before it was one yuan - then two yuan - now the price was ten yuan for a liter. That's like ten dollars!"

He paused and shook his head sadly. "The man could not pay. His hands shook. His face was so gaunt, so hopeless. His hands trembled, but he did not speak or beg. Tears came into his eyes. In the eyes of a man! I was only a child then. I had never seen such a thing before. Someone offered the man two pieces of bread, but he would not take them."

"I must have rice," he said. "I have my father, my wife, and my children at home. It is they who are starving."

"His whole body shook as he walked from that place. A few minutes later there was a great shout outside. I ran out to look. The man had jumped from the bridge into the river to drown himself."

For a long time Dr. Chu was silent. Hesitantly, I finally interrupted his reverie. "And then? What happened to his family?" I asked.

Dr. Chu slowly placed the china cover over his empty teacup. "And then," he continued sadly, "the villagers fished him out. They saved him. They carried him home to his hut and his family. Later that night his family brought this man to our house for our father to help. The fellow had many rags wrapped around his throat. They were soaked with dark blood. His face was pale ivory - almost white - and his eyes were staring. My father unwrapped the rags. The blood spurted out in little red jets from a jagged wound that extended halfway around his neck. The fellow had slit his throat rather than watch his family starve to death."

He paused a long time now, and I did not interrupt again.

"That could never happen now," he said slowly. "China may have big problems. We are very, very poor, but not so bad as that. Nowadays, his wife would have had a job. When she became too old she could live in a hostel. Her children might even go to a university."

Saddened by his story, I spoke slowly. "Yes, the dilemma is clear, but what is the answer?"

"Given a choice, a poor man will choose bread, not freedom - for how and where would he go? What would he say, write, or preach if given the opportunity? He will choose shelter and work above freedom to speak or to read freely what others can also write freely."

"But why does this choice between food and freedom have to be made at all?" I asked. "There is nothing in the *Communist Manifesto* or the writings of Marx and Engels that predicted ownership by the people required loss of freedom of speech and action."

Dr. Chu did not reply.

I have thought about the story of his uncle's fate for many years. In a sense, this story served to disillusion me forever with the opportunities offered by socialism and communism. It was not foreseen by the vanguard of those movements that an economic system based on common ownership of the means of production would prove such an abysmal failure. For this was the real and unexpected catastrophe of the Communist experiment - one that led directly to locking people into jobs behind high walls of barbed wire to prevent escape. This was true not only for China, but for Poland, Czechoslovakia, Romania, Bulgaria, East Germany and the USSR itself.

Moreover, the system was not productive enough economically or satisfying enough for everyone's needs and greeds. Gross national product and output per man hour, the twin determinants of prosperity in our time, failed under the Soviet Union to approach those of the western democracies or Japan. Sacrifice of individual liberties brought economic security and sufficient bread and shelter - if one waited in queues and lived four or five to a room. But the explosion of economic growth and increase in the standard of living enjoyed by nearly all segments of society in the affluent West would not happen until China began to relax the socialist system.

The ruling elite there still want to maintain power and dare not allow too much change. The fate of the Chinese seemed especially heartbreaking because they work so hard, and not only remained abysmally poor but are helpless to change their fate.

My companion pushed his chair back and lit a cigarette. "I have an old auntie who was born deaf," he began. "She cannot speak either. When she was young she married a poor man, a salesman for a food company. This was during the war with the Japanese. One day the village where he was selling his wares was surrounded by Japanese soldiers. They took all his goods and beat him. He was left with nothing and was ashamed to tell his employer what had happened. He went to his home and told his wife he had lost everything. They had to leave their home for another town. He could not find work anywhere. They had no money for food and nowhere to live. They slept at night on the stone floor of an old temple in the village. Their food came from rummaging in garbage cans. Because of the bad food, my uncle got very sick and died. Then my aunt thought she must die too. But she had to go on living because of their three children. She begged, swept the streets, and gathered roots in the forest for food. They survived. Now her life is much better. She lives in a hostel and receives a small pension given by the government. Two of her children go to university and the third is in high school. She is very happy."

"Our country is run by the workers. It is they who have decided what is most important - food or freedom. Intellectuals who have never been hungry might make a different decision."

At the next table, sat four young Japanese, all fashionably dressed and festooned with expensive cameras. They enthusiastically consumed the Western lunch of steak and french fries washed down with Chivas Regal. Dr. X. looked over at them quietly, ignoring their loud shouts for the waiter.

"Lenin thought that if he had a single generation to educate properly in socialism, man's greed for possessions and self-aggrandizement could be overcome," I said gravely. "But even here, where you have had a whole generation born since the revolution, I sense that your young people have still the same thirst for travel and for a better material life for themselves as do ours in the West. Can it be that our brains are wired for ourselves, not others?"

Dr. X. did not reply. For the first time I fully appreciated why the Communists must keep the gates between their world and ours closed. As long as the success of societies dedicated to individual gain and personal freedom are concealed and distorted by local propaganda, the system here could serve as Man's Hope. Communism is perhaps the most idealistic and magnificent conception of a way of life since that urged on a narcissistic world by Jesus Christ. But the system didn't work. It didn't produce enough.

Back to Japan.

Two weeks later, I carried my blue padded Chinese jacket in my rucksack to the top of Mt. Fuji in Japan. Too warm to wear now, it evoked the whole of the Chinese dilemma for me. Clumsy, not too expensive, made for hard work and to replace nonexistent central heating, it was also a declaration against fashion and conspicuous consumption. Uniform dress, no longer necessary in China, was at that time and place a declaration of equality. Equalizing salaries so that the unpleasant work of a garbage collector was paid as well as a top executive in business was fair. But it was a dismal failure economically.

"Bad planning," commented a wise old professor in Kyoto who tried to cheer me up as I excused myself from a lavish cocktail extravaganza on the night of my arrival in Japan from China.

I was still stunned by the steady stream of headlights from three lanes of bumper-to-bumper Toyotas, Mazdas, Datsuns, and Hondas on the superhighway between Osaka and Kyoto. Stunned by the scene at the airport where hundreds of well-dressed Japanese tourists returned to their homeland with bulging plastic bags of Scotch whiskey and American cigarettes.

"People won't work without incentive," he went on sententiously. "Besides, the Chinese have no history for democracy as we do!" (sic!) "Also their smartest people always migrated out of the country." He nodded sagely and signaled a tuxedoed waiter to bring over a plate of delicate canapes.

I was suffering from reverse culture shock. In intensely modern Japan, with its vast air-conditioned malls, shop windows stuffed with elegant consumer goods, and its well-dressed citizens, the entire population seemed to be busy every minute. There was no leaning on shovels, there were no idle farmers resting by the roadside, no leisurely horse-drawn carts.

"Work is the centerpiece of Japanese life," pronounced the professor.

In my hotel room next morning I switched on the color TV during breakfast of fresh orange juice, ham, eggs, flaky croissants and American-style coffee. I twisted the dial past a Japanese dubbed *Sesame Street*, a trained chimp, a visit to the zoo and a station featuring a continuous printout of stock quotations in Japanese and English. At the last flick of the dial I was treated to a visit by a dog and his mistress to a New York veterinarian who obtained a urine specimen from the dog by catheter. Had we reached the culmination of Man's Hope?

Epilogue

Things have changed in China since this visit twenty years ago. Collective security for all has been replaced by the capitalist's dog eat dog struggle for security and wealth similar to the U.S. Can a compromise be found to decrease the gap between entrepreneur, farmer and proletarian? Or will it continue to grow until the hungry hordes from the Third World rebel and insist that they should live decently too?

1983   AIDS virus identified by Montagnier in Paris three years after the disease was identified for the first time at the National Institutes of Health in the U.S.

U.S. troops invade Grenada, a small Caribbean island.

Militant Islamic group Hezbollah ("Party of God") founded in Lebanon: seeks overthrow of Israel.

Diplomatic relations between U.S. and Vatican reestablished after ll7 years.

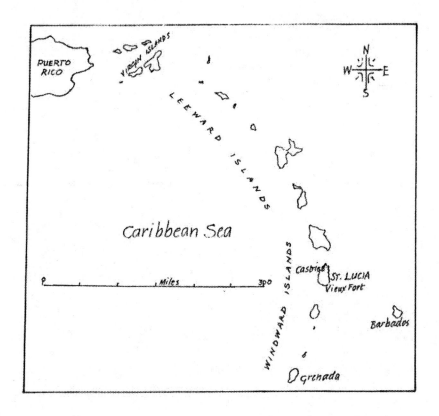

You can't separate peace from freedom because no one can be at peace unless he has his freedom.

(Malcolm X Speaks)

Chapter VIII

PARADISE FOUND

A 238- square mile speck in the southeastern Caribbean, St. Lucia, the largest of the Windward Islands, is forty-two miles long, twelve miles wide and has a 150-mile coastline of steep mountainous cliffs separated by stunning white beaches. After more than a dozen changes of government following repeated armed conflicts between Britain and France between the 16th and 19th centuries, St. Lucia became a British colony in 1814 and became an independent country in the British Commonwealth in 1979. Still influenced by the numerous periods of occupation by French armies and planters, a French patois is widely spoken by the population. In 1772, the population was around 15,000, most of whom were slaves. Two hundred years later the population is over 150,000, ninety percent of whom are descendants of Africans imported in the 17th century to work as slaves on the sugar plantations of the whites.

"You want to make a baby for me?"

"Get lost!" I answered, not looking around. I was lying on my belly gazing at the horizon on the warm sandy beach near Castries, capital of St. Lucia.

Beyond was the world.

In the distance, three tiny white ships converged toward the sloping hills of Martinique, silhouetted against sky and water. Soon tourists would be spilling from their big cruise vessels into the markets, shops and bars of that French-speaking island. Every Wednesday, the big white Cunard tourist boats also came here, to Castries. When they docked across the street from the harbor, which was also the island's worst slum, impoverished men of the neighborhood came out on the street to stare impassively.

Strung with expensive cameras and large handbags, Canadians, Americans, English, German and French tourists descended the gang-plank chattering with excitement.

Powerfully built blacks, heavily muscled arms folded, watched through eyes hidden behind mirrored sunglasses.

Middle-aged white women wobbled down to the sidewalk wearing too-high heels and too-short shorts.

The steady throb of a steel band pounded from the dark bar across the street. Vertical ribbons of red, white, and blue plastic hung in the doorway. White power and black power. Tension. Sometimes you could cut it with a knife.

In 1982 and '83, I worked as a volunteer doctor in the mental hospitals of St. Lucia and neighboring St. Vincent. Most of my patients were very poor and very ill. Even before their illness, few had regular work or income. But half the population of the island had no job or worked only sporadically.

As in most of the Windward and Leeward Islands, the population of St. Lucia is 99% black. They are descendants of African slaves, whose forebears were captured and sold, often by their own tribal chiefs, to generations of venal traders - Arabs, Egyptians, Europeans and Americans. For the British and French who settled these lands, like the Americans in the southern U.S., black slave labor was once the basis of their comfortable, sometimes opulent lifestyle.

Slavery was nothing new for Africans, even in Africa. Black and brown Africans from more aggressive tribes made slaves of neighbors they conquered. As in North America, the vestiges, the scars, remain. Despite decades of independence, St. Lucia was still a two-class society.

Discovered by Columbus in 1502, St. Lucia was named after the saint on whose day it was first sighted. Most of the English who first settled the island in 1605 were killed by fierce native Carib Indian inhabitants. The island was then fought over and changed hands between the British and the French fourteen times in the first half of the 17th century, finally becoming a British crown colony in 1814.

The culture that evolved in the Caribbean islands is a curious amalgam of past and present. Remnants of the African heritage appear in the unique language, art, music, easy sociability, violence and sexual liberty. Now these backgrounds are melded with western materialism, French patois, English language, law and class consciousness. The islands are still permeated by racism.

Initially from whites, racism has been a two-way street since the Black Power movements of the '60s.

In 1503, only eleven years after the first voyage of Columbus, Portuguese merchants sent the first shipment of slaves from Africa to the Americas. In North America, the future United States, the sturdy Africans proved far more useful and viable than the indigenous Indians and Amerindians who died by the thousands of disease and melancholy when forced to work as slaves by the white invaders.

Before slavery was abolished in St. Lucia in 1834, the population was less than 20,000. Two-thirds were African slaves. The whites settled on large plantations or owned businesses in the few towns. Most of the black population lived in mud or clay huts thatched with palm leaves. They subsisted on a diet of coconut, yams, breadfruit, mangoes, plantain, cassava, banana and fish.

Now, "economic development" has fostered a host of new desires: cars, imported food, alcohol, indoor plumbing, TV, trips abroad. A growing population and continued low productivity of most of the African population increasingly polarize the society into haves and have-nots - as in the rest of the world.

Today these startlingly lovely islands belong to the descendants of the African slaves who survived both transport and labor under the rule of whites. Many East Indians live here too. First imported as indentured servants, now they are generally successful in both commerce and the professions.

Brilliant green foliage clothes steep hillsides of St. Lucia that rise abruptly from the sea. Between rugged mountains lie deep valleys rich with crops - bananas, plantains, breadfruit, mango, almonds, cashew and coconut. Red, pink, purple, blue and yellow flowering vines bloom in the hills and valleys. Bougainvilla and hibiscus in all shades of pink and red, fuchsia, oleander, white and yellow trumpet vines, frangipangi, canna, jasmine and wild poinsetta are everywhere. Palm fringed white sand beaches are concealed between mountains whose steep green slopes fall straight into a shimmering emerald sea.

But most people living in this paradise were poor. Housed in the shanties of the towns on the hills behind the beaches, most St. Lucians lived in tiny one room shanties scarcely noticed by the pale visitors from the north. Whisked by air-conditioned vans from their international flights to hotels beside the stunning beaches, they met only the St. Lucians who cleaned their rooms and served their excellent meals. If those visitors could or would walk up to the settlements behind the shore, they would find increasingly demoralized human beings in shacks, struggling for subsistence in this rich and flowering landscape. Beyond poverty, and surely partly because of it, mugging, purse snatching and household theft were the major hazards of life in this paradise.

The general hospitals in St. Lucia were reasonably if simply equipped. In contrast, Golden Hope, the mental hospital where I worked, was comprised of several dark, dungeon-like buildings where amenities were few and plumbing was rudimentary. Laboratories, x-ray and other modern equipment were non-existent. More than a hundred patients were looked after by two dozen aides and four nurses divided between three shifts.

Until I arrived, there was one part-time doctor who visited the mental hospital once or twice during the week to see new patients. Violent or runaway patients were locked in barred cells without furniture or mats to sleep on. A bucket emptied once a day served as a toilet. Even outside these isolation cells on the crowded wards, clothing and furnishings were in short supply.

Who were these patients and why were they here? It was my job to find out and prescribe treatment. Anxiety, violence, drug abuse, alcoholism and schizophrenia were the principal diagnoses. In surprising contrast to psychiatry in North America and Europe, there was little depression, guilt or loneliness among my patients in St. Lucia. Suicide and suicide threats were almost unknown among native islanders, but at least two Caucasian psychiatrists who worked here some years before my visit killed themselves during their tours of duty.

After a few weeks I stopped looking for the scars or slash marks on patients' wrists so common in North American mental hospitals. Neither did I see a single case of *anorexia nervosa*, a disorder of voluntary semi-starvation that is all too common, especially in girls, in the wealthy lands of North America and Europe.

These West Indian patients preferred sex, alcohol, marijuana or hallucinogenic brews made from the leaves and flowers of local vines and shrubs. Anger was turned outward, not inward. They smashed up furniture, dwellings, girlfriends and relatives, not themselves.

Religion, until very recently the first line of defense against anxiety for most peoples of the world, was still a major influence in St. Lucia. In contrast to other immigrants to the New World, education and the economic security of land or business ownership were forbidden to the blacks who were slaves in the Americas. Instead, or perhaps partly in response to the wall of prejudice, they turned to religion with a zeal and passion that continues today. And perhaps to other things as well.

Especially music. Fortunately for the islanders and for us, the enormous talent and zest for music and dance of these unwilling immigrants were not destroyed by slavery. In the late 1960s, the black population of St. Lucia, Jamaica and the other islands discovered Reggae and the music of Bob Marley. Rastafarianism was born.

"We sick and tired of your easy kissin' game
or to die and go to heaven in Jesus name
We know and understand
Almighty God is a livin' man!"

Rejecting the long awaited redemption through Jesus Christ promised by Christian churches, Rastafarians placed their faith in a new Messiah - the first "I" of "I and I" that begins most Rasta sentences. Rastafari was a radical rejection of accommodation and integration with a white society that repeatedly demonstrated implacable resistance to black equality. Rastafari was an end of trying to be white. Rastas rejected a society that has steadily rejected or patronized blacks. They turned their backs on the traditions and expectations of their own parents. Trying to fill the void caused by their exclusion from the establishment ("Babylon"), they "reasoned together" (talked about Africa), and through "insight" (that Africa is the answer and Haile Selassie, dead or alive, would engineer their return). Smoking plenty of "herb" (marijuana) helped to narrow consciousness against intrusions by ugly reality.

The black power struggles of the '60s were not the first attempts to awaken black pride as a counter to the anguish and anger that resulted from continued discrimination of blacks by whites. One of the earliest black consciousness movements was led by Marcus Garvey, a Jamaican who concluded that the only hope for equality for American and West Indian Africans was to return to their ancestral homes in Africa.

"If Europe is for Europeans, then Africa is for the black peoples of the world!" Garvey proclaimed. He promised an imminent millennium when ships would carry all the descendants of the displaced slaves back to their homeland. Although he did not succeed in his plan to repatriate blacks in Africa, Garvey planted a seed that was destined to grow into a new, proud and vigorous movement, *Rastafaria*.

Rastafaria promoted Africanism, the centrality of Africa. Rejecting the old hopeless black yearning for acceptance by whites, Rastafaria was rootsmanship - back to beginnings and belonging. Rastafaria and Africanism were powerful counters to the self-hatred of people whose skin pigment barred them from equal status in the United States and even in these islands.

Rastafaria is a direct successor to Garvey's celebration of Africa and blackness, but went several steps beyond Garvey. Taking their name from Ras Tafari Makkonon, the crown prince of Ethiopia who became Haile Selassie I, emperor of Ethiopia in 1930, Rastafarians believed that this black king, crowned in Africa, was a signal of the day of deliverance. Fifty years later, by embracing Rastafari, blacks gave up on the white race and turned to personal resurrection of their own self-worth.

This new negritude meant rebellion against all that was white. This included life style, beliefs, manners, dress, behavior, hair straighteners, skin bleaches and Christianity, the white man's religion.

But the attack on Christianity was too much for most West Indians and Rastafaria remained restricted to a small rebellious group who met rejection with rejection. Like the black power movement that followed in the U.S., Rastafari changed the attitude of blacks toward whites. Pride in blackness and contempt for whiteness were substituted for the old self-hatred of being black.

Unlike the Jews and Christians, who bow before a God of terrible and demanding power, Rastafarians proclaim their *oneness* with God and challenge the conventional dualism between God and man. Their use of "I and I" and "I and God" expresses the unity of the black messiah with the black man. Rastafarians insist that integration of blacks and whites is impossible. Insecurity is abolished with the declaration, "Africa is best, and I am African. Ergo, I must be best."

"Hey, give me your sunglasses!" commanded a handsome young black on the beach rudely one Sunday morning. I walked on. Nothing happened.

Rejecting the long awaited redemption through Jesus Christ promised by the Christian churches, Rastas believe in smoking "herb" (*ganja*, weed, marijuana) daily. Rastafari was a radical rejection of accommodation and integration with a white society that rejected them. Rastafari was an end of trying to be white.

Rastafarianism still lives in a minority of blacks in the Caribbean and more than a few in the U.S. But Christianity, the white man's religion, is far more important. In these islands, as elsewhere, the first line of defense against anxiety seems to be the church, any church, temple or mosque. Next, in the affluent West, are alcohol and psychiatrists.

More than 150 years have passed since the last slave was freed in St. Lucia. Although a small black elite has penetrated the white socioeconomic hierarchy, white generally still meant rich and black poor. Why?

"West Indians are lazy."

"No one wants to work more than absolutely necessary to buy food and a bit of rum."

"We still have the slave mentality. We have to be told what to do and then we do as little as possible."

"Government is corrupt - no one gives a damn except for himself."

"Most of the foreign aid you Americans keep sending just goes in the pockets of the politicians and their cronies."

These are only a few of the comments I collected during my two 3 month tours of hospital work in the islands, and in my search for the why and why not of development here.

Why have the economies of Japan and Germany, ruined by World War II, taken off after only a tiny push. But here, in the so-called third world, the rich get richer and the poor, poorer. Was it something about the gorgeous and forgiving weather that held the islanders back? This human factor may be the single most important and least addressed question facing the hordes of foreign advisers and professional do-gooders, who, like myself, came to the islands, especially during the cold northern winter, to seek ways to "improve" *their* lives.

Housed in graceful villas or fine hotels, their gardens resplendent with flowering plants and trees, can they, can I, understand the problem or find the answer?

Instead of piling up material goods, religion, music, sex, dancing and emigration were the principal ways St. Lucians, whose ancestors were slaves, dealt with their situation. When these failed, violence, alcohol and drugs took over. But in surprising contrast to my experience in the hospitals of North America and Europe, there was little depression, guilt or loneliness among my patients. But there was violence, less lethal, but scary all the same.

Hiking alone in the forests or walking alone on the roads after sunset was declared madness by my colleagues both white and black. It was not easy for me to accept such restrictions on my freedom. Detesting racism, I thought I was colorblind. In St. Lucia, the unchangeable color of my skin marked me as the enemy. Almost unconsciously, I looked for white faces on the street. On the beach, I sat within hailing distance of other whites. I avoided meeting the eyes of strangers on the street.

Although nothing dangerous ever happened to me, the threat of violence led me into an unpleasant identification of white skins with safety.

Bitterly, angrily and finally sheepishly, I found myself increasingly race-conscious. After a few weeks I reached a compromise between caution and my insatiable desire to know and to belong. I rode the public mini-buses, although (as in Johannesburg in the '70s and '80's) I never saw another white doing so. Sometimes, especially on Sundays when the vans that serve as buses were rare or non-existent, I hitched rides in cars and trucks. Their drivers were always black, for no white ever stopped for me even though there were plenty of them. My benefactors were unfailingly friendly, courteous and gracious. My white friends scolded and urged me to rent a car.

"You'll lose the respect of this community if you hitch-hike and ride the vans (buses)," scolded a long-standing white resident of the island at dinner one night. "A white person, especially a doctor without a car is unthinkable here," he continued, implying that I was letting "our side" down.

Although I felt uneasy on deserted roads and beaches, among the schizophrenics, manics, drug addicts and occasional mad murderers in the hospital, I felt safe. Both patients and staff gave me trust and friendship equal to any I have ever known. Finally, I stopped being apprehensive and fell in love with the islands.

Chapter IX

PARADISE LOST

One sun-drenched Sunday morning during my tour of duty as psychiatrist at the mental hospital in St. Lucia, I set out on my bicycle to explore the island. First, I stopped at the hospital to look in on any new patients or problems. Somewhat to my surprise, for it was already nine in the morning, the only person on duty on the male ward was an aide who was fast asleep on a cot in the small staff room. When I walked through the corridor between the isolation cells, I saw a new patient who stood, stark naked, surrounded by the entire contents of the mattress he had destroyed during the night. In the nurse's quarters, I woke the aide, Mr. Baron.

"What's with the new patient?" I asked.

Mr. Baron jumped up and followed me to the patient's cell. He read from the admission note, "Yesterday this young man suddenly became quite mad. For no reason he stayed up night and day, singing, dancing and saying he was God."

I looked at the treatment chart. Despite staggering doses of tranquilizers the day before, the young man was still on his feet, talking steadily.

"What is he saying? I can't understand him." I turned to the aide.

"Just nonsense - partly in local language," Mr. Baron replied. We discussed possible diagnoses. The aide suggested he looked like he had a reaction to a popular local hallucinogenic plant.

I recommended a sedative.

Ten minutes after the injection, the patient was snoring loudly. There seemed to be no other problems. I wished the aide good morning. He went back to his cot. I set off on my bicycle through the town, heading for the beaches at the north end of the island.

In contrast to the colorful crowds that thronged the town during the week, the center of town seemed deserted on Sunday morning. Now, on the market steps at the far side of town, a large crowd had gathered. An excited man wearing the red heart-shaped insignia of the PLP (People's Labor Party) was haranguing them in passionately shouted patois. His speech was amplified to deafening volume through loudspeakers on top of a VW van in the middle of the crowd.

It was only a few weeks before the national elections. Every day loudspeakers on vans all over the island blasted angry protests at the failure of the political system, despite black rule, to ease the lot of the mostly poor islanders. All candidates promised retribution and justice to the dispossessed.

As in Africa, independence failed to bring St. Lucians the prosperity they so eagerly anticipated. Although most St. Lucians were poor, the political leaders of these ex-colonies now lived almost as lavishly as their colonial masters had. But for most of the population, poverty was a way of life. I was there not only to volunteer some medical service, but also to try to find out, why?

Most black islanders, rich or poor, considered family and friends, not their country, their first obligation. To put the good of the nation ahead of family was unthinkable. This led to much favoritism in politics. Can this be why democracy has failed to bring prosperity to most people in these lush tropical islands or in their ancestral home, Africa?

Or is it because they are victims of the Malthusian nightmare? Unbridled population growth and its consequences were largely ignored in the '80's, especially by left wing political leaders. The many and popular churches were also pronatalist. They were not alone.

"You tryin' to cause race suicide wid your dirty little pills?" shouted an irate stevedore where I had stopped at a bar on a stunning beach at the north end of the island. I explained my job as a doctor on the island. The man glared at me. He was too angry with family planning protagonists to listen to my standard spiel predicting the dire future of countries with high birth rates and low productivity.

"Our only population problem is too few of us and too many of you!" agreed a visiting bureaucrat from Uganda who sat down with us. "In Africa, we need people, we need their labor for development. Sometimes we think you're really out to sabotage us with those poisons for our women."

Even in America, land of the diaphragm and the pill, many highly educated blacks maintained that increasing black population growth fuels black political power.

Pronatalism was also favored by men who much appreciated the free and easy conjugal relationships on the island. Only half in jest, many islanders attributed the tremendous popularity of a Caribbean holiday among white women to the liberal sexual habits and abundant potent willing males.

One morning before rounds on the wards, I was complaining to the nurses about the constant sexual overtures I encountered when I ventured alone onto the beach or into a restaurant. Two of them laughed. The others looked angry.

"Let's face it, most of your women come down here for sex," explained the head nurse. "Everyone knows white women come down here because they think our men better for sex." Another nurse agreed unhappily. "Unfortunately, our men also like white women for prestige!"

"But they like black women too!" I objected rather testily, "especially you young ones!"

More than three-quarters of all births on the island were to unwed girls and women. There were no government welfare programs to provide for these mothers or their children. Instead, the new mother's mother often took on support of the children. It was a duty directly related to the hedonism of males and sexual permissiveness of females in this society

"Any West Indian man who has only one woman, even if she's his wife, is considered a sissy," remarked Ronald, a male nurse.

"Girls prefer men with several girl friends - it gives them more prestige," added William, another staff nurse.

Sister (nurse) Yolande disagreed. "There is just nothing we can do about it," she retorted sadly. "Even if you're married, your husband won't stay home at night and he's gone every weekend."

Several other nurses shrugged and nodded agreement, "It's our culture," Nurse Margaret explained.

Children are often left behind by mothers who "walk away" to search for work in the city, other islands or in the U.K. This practice shook my belief that only severe mental illness could loosen the bond between a mother and her child, a link so basic, so organic, seemingly "hard-wired" into our brains.

There were other signs that all was not well in paradise. Homosexuality was one of them.

"There's a saying in Barbados," explained a local doctor, deadpan, "that if you drop a nickel in Jamestown, better to kick it all the way to Bridgetown than bend over to pick it up!"

"Of course, homosexuality is not considered abnormal in enlightened North America," I replied, rather unnecessarily.

"But it has always been considered abnormal here, and everywhere else, as you well know!" he asserted. "This is something altogether new for us!"

I have thought long and hard about this.

Sex serves functions beyond pleasure and procreation. For men, sexual power and political power often go hand in hand. In a very different culture, Pakistan, I was told by a physician who was also a friend, that many government officials, including his uncle, a prominent member of the former government, were forcibly and repeatedly sodomized by soldiers who were sent to remove them from office following a coup. Pecking order among male prisoners in the crowded jails of Washington D.C., and I suppose many other places, was reportedly determined by who raped whom.

Given the sexual and economic irresponsibility of most West Indian men, the female of the species had little confidence in her mate. He in turn was equally suspicious of her, not trusting her to have any more control than he did.

This was hard on western - type business. Lack of internal discipline and reliance on external authority for control led many employers to despair. They tried to create incentives, tensions, all to promote greater efforts.

But were they succeeding in promoting the material desires and greed that would tempt their workers to work harder and longer? Strikes for higher wages, wanton burning of cane fields or cotton gins has discouraged further development. And for us in the U.S., their rich neighbor to the north? Our slums are like jungles. Homicide, booze and drugs are endemic. Huge sums that would feed, house, properly educate and provide medical care to the poor are spent on armaments.

According to sociologists who studied the culture of the Caribbean islands, in the '60s and '70s, nearly three-quarters of all children there were raised by their grandmothers or other female relatives. This curious state of affairs (to most North American whites) resulted from the attitude of West Indian men. Sex with the widest possible number of sexual partners was their way of life. Most men accepted only minimal responsibility for the results.

Some mothers even accused their daughters of being "mules" if they were not pregnant before they were twenty. I was surprised to find that regular indulgence in premarital sex and serial mating, commonplace in the U.S. only in the last thirty years, had been the norm in the Caribbean islands for generations.

With the onslaught of the HIV/AIDS epidemic in the '80s and '90s, that was now changing. But not fast enough. HIV/AIDS now takes a terrific toll on islanders. In 2001, one in fifty Caribbean women between 15 and 49 were HIV positive, twice the rate in older women but still well behind the almost 35 percent of young women who are infected in southern Africa. In the absence of effective treatment, one-third of their babies were also HIV positive.

Male-male competition for fertile women was basic to sexual promiscuity here, according to anthropologists who have studied these islands.

"Making babies prove a man is strong," explained a St. Lucia doctor to me.

"My boyfriend won't use a condom, and if I take the pill, he'll beat me," insisted a nineteen-year old unmarried mother of two who had come to our clinic for a checkup six weeks after birth of her last baby.

"It's true, her boyfriend will mash her if she takes the pill," confirmed the student nurse assisting me in the clinic. "Even if he don't want a baby, her boy friend be afraid girl will play around if she use pill!"

Other traditions, doubtless rooted in evolutionary laws of survival, caused use of contraceptives to be frowned on.

"Having a child adds to a girl's prestige by proving her fertility," explained my colleague, Dr. M, who had practiced medicine in St. Lucia for thirty years. "It also frees her from childhood status. She may have an early pregnancy at age 14 or 15 with her steady boyfriend. Then generally he moves on to another girl. Her second and third conceptions with others will follow."

"And marriage?" I asked.

"If it takes place at all, it usually comes quite late -maybe after birth of three to five children by two or three fathers."

I gulped and remembered the writings of Michael Horowitz, an anthropologist who wrote about Caribbean culture in the 1950s. He found that all the women under 25 in a Martinique village had at least one child, but only 5 percent were married. None of the men that age were married. Even by age 39, only 4 percent of the women and 33 percent of men had wed. By age 54, the numbers had risen to 80 percent of women and 51 percent of men.

Horowitz pointed out that in preindustrial agrarian or hunting societies, the enhanced status of girls following conception and delivery of a child, especially by a prestigious male, made sense from an evolutionary standpoint. Impregnation of mothers by physically and sexually dominant men assured greater survival of strong and well protected progeny. Unfortunately, these qualities no longer seem the best guarantees of success in the modern struggle for survival.

One morning in the hospital, premarital sex and marriage were selected by my patients as the topics for the group therapy we held weekly on the combined male and female wards. I asked one of the nursing aides to run the session, as patients were more relaxed with them than with "the white lady doctor from the mainland."

The aide who took on the task was an intensely religious young man. He proposed that the group discuss marriage - should it occur before having children? The subject was a great success. Provocative opinions were soon expressed on all sides. With difficulty, I tried to keep the enthusiastic young leader from turning the group session into a sermon by him on Christian morality and the sins of adultery.

Suddenly, a tall young paranoid schizophrenic man who had been silent for the entire first half hour, strode to the center of the circle and began shouting angrily.

"We were turned into studs by you white folks!" he yelled angrily, shaking his fist in my direction. "We was no better than good breeding stock! Now you blame us and say we act like animals." Everyone cheered.

On another group therapy day we were gathered in the usual circle for our session. To warm up the group, I suggested we play a word game of similarities - a great favorite. A boy of 19 whose thoughts wandered ceaselessly between real and unreal worlds suddenly rose.

"What is the difference between a wagon and a monkey?" he asked quietly, his eyes bewildered and wondering.

"A monkey climbs, but a wagon has wheels," interjected Salina, a girl so ill she stood motionless and mute for hours in the day-room. Now she rose from her chair and walked to the center of the circle, where she stood staring vacantly. Suddenly she lifted her arms and cradled them before her as though she held an infant.

Slowly, gently, she began to rock them back and forth across her small breasts. In a high-pitched stilted voice she began to sing, "Rockabye baby, on the treetop...."

Everyone, even the manic patients, suddenly became silent, transfixed by her longing. When she finished, there was a minute of stunned silence. George, a retarded boy, who steadfastly refused to wear trousers or covering of any kind over his dangling genitals, stood and applauded enthusiastically. Everyone in the circle joined.

Suddenly, Salina smiled through her mask of catatonic stillness. Then she walked stiffly back to her seat and resumed her empty gaze into another world.

My colleague, Dr. M., explained. "In the past, girls and women everywhere on reaching sexual maturity had a strong drive for motherhood. It was satisfied only by giving birth and raising children."

That resonated for me. I put off bearing children for 6 years after my marriage in order to finish my medical internship. Then, desire for a child overwhelmed me during my service on the newborn ward of the Boston City Hospital. Within a year, my first child was born.

When men esteem and desire women for childbearing and other opportunities for fulfillment are few, there is little reason to postpone pregnancy. Three of the nurses' aides on our wards were visibly very pregnant during my first tour of duty at Golden Hope. None were married. There was no embarrassment or shame. Their eyes glowed with the same happiness that shines in expectant mothers' eyes everywhere. Awaiting the birth of the first child is a crowning experience in a woman's life.

But in our urbanized, industrialized society, many old traditions have broken down. Young children no longer followed their mothers to her fields. Mother worked in town, if at all. Instead of growing food for herself and her family, food had to be purchased. Mothers needed cash to survive. If there was enough money, older children went to school. If mother worked, younger kids were left with Granny or to the uncertain care of siblings and neighbors.

Wealth is our key to safety and power, I thought to myself – *impossible to mold these people to our way of life without giving them ever greater dreams and desires for stuff, for cars, better houses, long vacations, the whole enchilada.* The most aggressive, most intelligent, most energetic, best connected ones will get it, keep it and want more. They will become more and more like us and the devil take the poor. Perhaps it has always been that way, everywhere.

Two major behavior styles have emerged in St. Lucia, a nation where 99 percent of the population is black and 90 percent are poor. It is a society where the many are servants to the few vastly richer white emigrés and tourists. There was also a small black elite who, by industry, luck or guile, successfully pursued and obtained villas overlooking the sea like the affluent whites. Their aspirations were similar to the whites. They had maids, Mercedes, video recorders and players. They sent their children to study abroad and took their holidays in New York, Paris or Disneyland.

Then there were the poor, who, as Abraham Lincoln famously remarked, "God must have loved best because he made so many of them."

They were the ragged barefoot people who swept the streets of Castries early every morning with brooms of local straw. Their men marched along the pot-holed roads armed with machetes for a day's cutting cane in the fields. Their women were not the ones in the airport waiting for the round-trip flight to Martinique for lunch and shopping.

Their women were carrying great bunches of bananas or plastic buckets of water on their heads and babies on their backs. They washed their clothes in local streams where they were often infected with the water born parasite bilharzia. They scrubbed the bathrooms and cooked in kitchens of the better-off, whether white or black. Their thin, dusty-legged children lounged at the roadside, idle, or playing with a few stones. There was not enough money at home to buy the books and uniforms required for school. Their diet was cassava, plantain and bananas boiled green. They read and wrote with difficulty or not at all.

"You're rich and we have to depend on you," commented Dr. Zani. "If you don't give us aid we are very angry. If we vote with Russia, you give us even more for fear we won't like you best." He laughed uproariously.

Someone's portable radio poured out a triumphant Reggae beat:

"Sidney Rootsman, he just scampin' all night long"

After an all-night party at a local American's, I went home as dawn was breaking. The air was soft as a lover's caress. On the hillside a wiry old man in striped shirt and battered brown fedora led a rope of four goats across the damp grass. His dry stick-lean legs, brown as roasted coffee, protruded from torn knickers. His feet were bare and hard. To the west the sea was deep cobalt, silent, waiting. A hibiscus blossom, broken from the bush by the driveway, lay in its exquisite perfection, red as blood on the path. Behind the mountains to the east the daily miracle began with a faint pink blush over low gray clouds. A glow of red and orange slowly spread like a huge canopy across the horizon. A shining yellow border gradually illuminated the edge of waiting clouds. Behind me, above the sea, all the small scudding white fluffs of cotton cloud on the horizon suddenly turned a delicate pink. To the east, the brilliant yellow border widened above the hills. The sky warmed with new golden light. Slowly, ever so majestically, the sun made its daily *corvée*. I resisted falling on my knees.

Epilogue 2004

The Caribbean islands were rich ground for both power hungry politicians and for those romantic and idealistic souls who still yearned for fulfillment of the great promises of Rousseau, Marx and Engels. Since my tours of duty in the Windward Islands in the '80s, the AIDS epidemic has infected the Caribbean islands and Africa with a vengeance. Frightened, men are looking to monogamy, condoms and young teenage girls with new interest. Does AIDS mean good-bye to that easy-going life style that made music and sex the centerpiece of life in the Caribbean and much of non-Islamic Africa?

1985   20,000 in Ethiopian relief camp die of starvation. A million more are at risk.

Fatal accident in Kisumi: Man and Woman Buried Alive in Collapse of Latrine.

Nairobi: Donkey runs mad in Voy. Five boys mutilated in traditional circumcision.

Lebanon: Irreconcilable conflict between Sunnis and Shia Muslims in Beirut threatens Christian Maronite president Amin Gemayel.

Rock Hudson, American film star dies of AIDS

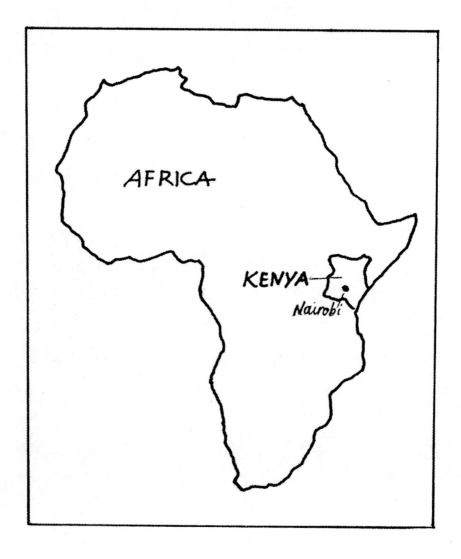

Chapter X

UHURU! (FREEDOM!)

I was reading the headlines of the daily paper in the comfortable sitting room of the posh Nairobi Club while waiting for my hosts. The club was white and British. Although I was not a member, since I am a *mzungu* (white), no one asked for my credentials when I entered. A wide stairway led up to a large sitting room, warm with sunlight and full of deep easy chairs and racks of the latest British magazines and newspapers.

In the adjacent library were well-thumbed books about almost everything. When the ornate old grandfather clock chimed softly once, I got up and went down to the vast dining room. At least fifty tables set with starched white tablecloths and gleaming silver held a centerpiece of fresh roses. Black waiters in tuxedos padded about deferentially, taking orders, pouring wine from bottles chilled in silver ice buckets, wheeling carts of French pastries to the crowd of white diners.

My two hosts, both African doctors, were waiting for me in the lobby. We walked through the bar where sparkling glasses lined the counter into the dining room. Although my companions were the only Africans in the dining room, the pink- or tan-skinned whites scarcely looked up as we entered the crowded room. Before we left, a second group of handsome Kenyans, business types in immaculate monogrammed shirts and beautifully tailored suits, sat down at a table at the far end of the enormous room. *At last, an end to segregation,* I, a newcomer to Kenya, mis-thought with satisfaction.

Outside in the parking lot, two white Mercedes, belonging to my colleagues and watched over by zealous drivers, gleamed posh and hot in the equatorial sun.

Kenya's new elite was young, black, rich and elegant. Following the example of their white predecessors and counterparts, they lived in large suburban houses surrounded by high walls. German shepherds or uniformed guards protected them and their possessions from the barefoot and ragged poorer citizens of the city. In at least one suburban enclave, guards patrolled the grounds armed with bows and arrows.

Well-off African businessmen, lawyers, doctors, politicians and well heeled whites frequented the few top restaurants and filled the lobbies and bars of the clubs and first-class international hotels. They examined the batiks and safari shirts in the ubiquitous upscale tourist shops and piloted their Benzes, Volvos, Rovers and Audis through the maelstrom of traffic-choked boulevards and roundabouts of this crowded city.

Drinks, followed by a lunch of creamed chicken, French rolls and butter, tossed salad, and pale green ice cream were served by the ultra-polite black waiters. Refusing post-prandial brandy, I went off with Dr. R. to visit a rural health center.

Leaving the city, we passed women of all ages who trudged barefoot along the roadside. Many were bent double under huge bundles of firewood, barrels of water or giant piles of grass for animals.

"Where are all the men?" I asked Dr. R. "Don't they do some of the hauling here?" This was my first trip to Kenya.

"Kikuyu women," he explained, "like most rural women in Kenya, are expected to take care of the household. They must collect the wood and water, grow the food for their children and husband, look after them, pay the children's school fees and produce a child every year or two, Men may be at work in the city or resting in their villages."

"Or strolling down the road," I said indignantly, "Like those chaps over there, carrying absolutely nothing except a walking stick! And they have shoes or sandals! But the women walking behind them with loads on their heads and babies on their backs are barefoot!"

My companion laughed. "But it has never been men's job to carry loads, gather fodder or hoe and till and weed on the *shamba* (farm). In old times, men hunted and fought in wars. When they were in the village they drank beer or talked together in the men's meeting area," he continued.

"Now, thanks to the long occupation by you whites, there is no more hunting allowed. Our people have lost thousands of acres of fertile land where their cattle and goats used to graze and multiply before the colonials came. Only a few men have taken on the hoeing, cultivating, and harvesting of crops. Those are traditionally the work of women in Africa."

"So what do men do all day now that there is no more fighting and hunting?"

"Men build the houses, put on the roofs. But bringing in machines has gradually changed men's aversion to working the soil since they are the only ones who can drive tractors and trucks."

I shook my head. "No wonder the young women look so old!"

"Now, many men leave to work in the city. They come back once or twice a year to make a baby."

"And when they come back do they help working the land and taking care of the children?"

The doctor laughed. "Not much. But the strange thing is that it is not the hardworking country wife who complains," he continued. "Depression, divorce, anger, suicide, we see much more of that in what you call liberated women - educated women, professional women in the city. They are torn from the supports of village and family life. Although they live in good houses in town, their husbands are seldom home. Most of these women are the first generation of the family to be educated and leave their roots in rural areas. But they are unhappy!"

"Why?"

"Because they are expected to accept the same responsibilities for home and child care as their country sisters. They are also expected to earn a living for themselves and the children by finding work in town. Unlike the rural women you feel so sorry for, these city women are cut off from their village support systems of family, neighbors, and in-laws. Many are terribly lonely - something previously unknown in African society."

"And is that why they come to us in the hospital and clinic with all sorts of body complaints - most of which turn out to be anxiety, depression or both?" I asked.

"Right on!" Dr. R. replied. "Depression didn't exist before all this change in African life style - at least according to the old-timers here."

We had reached the health center in the village of V. My host, Dr. R., a government doctor for this center, greeted the nurses who came out to welcome us. Inside, he checked the supply cupboards and inspected the record book listing patients' names, diagnoses, and treatments. Looking over his shoulder, I saw that more than half of the nearly l00 patients seen that day were seeking treatment for infections, diarrhea, cough, rash.

"Any problems?" Dr. R. asked the nurses

"No problems," replied one of the nurses, smiling broadly as the doctor patted her very low on her back. And that was the end of our visit.

Several days later, sitting with the nurses after morning clinic at the Nairobi mental hospital, I checked out Dr. R.'s ideas with them.

"Yes, it is lonely for us," acknowledged Sister Maude, head nurse. "I leave for work before my children go to school so I cook their breakfast and leave it out for them before I go. When I get home in the afternoon I cook, wash clothes, clean house, and fix dinner. Sometimes my husband comes home, so I must always have his dinner ready. Most of the time he doesn't. Or he just comes in, eats, and leaves without speaking to us at all. Hours later, he comes home drunk. Or, he comes home very late, watches me warm his food and then says he isn't hungry. Then he expects me to be ready for him in bed. I'm not the only one that lives this way - most of us do. If we refuse them or don't have a baby every year or two, they'll take a second wife."

Another nurse agreed. "I work, rush home to take care of the house and children, shop for food, pay the school fees, feed the kids, and then stay home every night alone."

"And they expect us to continue bearing children as long as we can," explained Melinda, the handsome young ward clerk whose black hair gleamed in tight corn-rows. "At least four or five, two of whom must be sons. If we don't, they take a second wife. In fact, we'll help him find one so we can be sure it is someone compatible for us, since they'll be living in our house."

"Do you like that?" I asked naively. "I mean, doesn't it bother you if your husband brings home another wife?"

"Of course it bothers us, but what can we do?" she asked patiently. "We're helpless."

"Then why not divorce these men?" I asked. "You're not getting much out of this deal that I can see."

Rueful laughter from my three companions.

"Because he would keep the children," explained Sister (nurse) Collina quietly. "And another wife might treat them badly."

"The children are legally the husband's," explained Melinda. "That's our culture. Anyhow, a divorced woman couldn't look after the children alone. She could live with another man, but she would never be accepted by his family, so her children would get nothing."

Although men, urban or rural, married or single are free to have sex with as many women as they wish, custom prohibits adultery and promiscuity of married women. The use of contraceptives by women was also frowned on. As Jomo Kenyatta, Kenya's widely venerated first president, wrote:

"The Kikuyu are taught from childhood that to be a man is to be able to love and keep a homestead with as many wives as possible. Boys are brought up to believe in extending their love to several women and to look upon them as companions and members of one big family. Women, on the other hand, are valued for their ability to work and to bear many children. Girls and young women are taught to behave like gentlewomen, not to raise their eyes or voices talking to men in public, not to bathe in the open nor eat in the presence of men other than those her own age or her kinfolk."

"We are really trapped," continued Nurse Collina. "If we leave or divorce them, the father has the right to keep the children. Even if he lets us have them, we must support them alone. If we marry again, the second husband is not likely to want to look after our children."

The following year, I spent a month in Malawi where the story was much the same. Nurse Cynthia, working with me in the hospital clinic, was the best and the brightest in her class. The AIDS epidemic was upon us and I was warning both men and women patients that they must use condoms. (How to get them was another matter, as there were none in the country then, except at exorbitant prices.)

"But the men won't use them anyway," Nurse Cynthia assured me. "At least my husband won't."

"Is he out at night, seeing other women?"

She laughed. "Of course, they all do that."

"Then you are in real danger!" I cautioned. "If he is going with many other women, chances are very good he will get infected with HIV and bring it home to you. If he won't use a condom, tell him to get lost."

"So then what would I do?" she replied. "Another man would be exactly the same."

"But you have four children already. Isn't that enough? The risk is too great for you."

"But I must have more children, otherwise, I will be laughed at by my own people!"

In older times, before the whites came to Africa with their modern diseases, infections and high child mortality kept the number of children down. The population was fairly static. Although a woman might have a dozen births, often only half the children survived. Now, immunization prevents many infectious diseases (especially imported diseases brought by the whites). The population has outgrown the food that was previously grown by traditional methods - generally a hand-made hoe or pointed stick.

Tractors, ploughs and draft animals belong to the wealthy. Africans must import food as well as medicine to care for their rapidly growing populations and their new diseases. First men, and now also women, leave the village to earn cash in the cities. This has disrupted an entire traditional way of life. It also brought new desires that require money. Africans want good health care, schools, houses, fridges, TVs and all the other accoutrements they have learned from the whites to need.

Women of Africa have much to deal with. At puberty, most boys and girls are circumcised. Although this does not interfere with the boy's future sexual pleasure, for the woman the consequences are very different. The custom of female circumcision varies from clitorectomy in Kenya to infibulation - "pharonic" circumcision - excision of clitoris and adjoining soft tissues of girls in Sudan, Somalia and Egypt. This custom is not only extremely painful but often destroys a woman's capacity for enjoyment of sex. The resultant scarring, particularly of the pharonic circumcision, frequently causes severe complications at childbirth.

"Why," I asked a head nurse in Nairobi, "is this done?"

"To keep women from playing around," she replied. "The only exceptions in Kenya are the Masai. They don't circumcise their women. Both men and women enjoy sex from an early age."

In most of central, east and southern Africa, a young woman is married only after her father arranges it and accepts a suitable bride price (*lobola, roora*) from the father of the prospective groom. A young man's family buys him a wife, usually by paying a specified number of cows. In return for this payment, the woman is expected to work for the man and his family for the rest of her days. Although boys are prized above girls, an equal number of both is best of all, since each daughter's bride price will be used by her father to pay for a bride for one of her brothers. A woman who fails to perform her many household duties or have many children may be returned to her parents. Sometimes, if the marriage is unsuccessful, a substitute wife will be provided by her family so they won't have to return the bridewealth of cattle or money.

At the time of marriage, the husband builds each wife her own round thatched hut and clears a plot of land for her to grow food for herself and her children. Each wife must bring her husband a basket of food at least once a day. He eats what he wants and sends the rest back to be shared by the wife and children. He sleeps with whom he wants - most often the youngest and fairest wife. But he is duty bound to be sure each wife gets her "share" of his seed and thus continues to produce children until her fertility ends. At that point, her husband's sexual interest in her terminates.

"How did this obsession with fathering more and more children get started?" I asked my African host as we sat down to dinner one evening in the quiet elegance of the Safari Club. A psychiatrist, wise in the ways and history of his countrymen, Dr. Nandi put down his glass of French wine and leaned across the spotless tablecloth.

"In our country, we say a man with one wife is not yet a man at all," he explained. "He cannot speak beyond saying his name at tribal meetings. With two wives he can announce his name and his tribe, but only after three wives can he take a serious part in the deliberations of his village. Then, each child brings additional prestige - not only to the husband but to each of the wives or mothers. They may compete with each other in the production of sons."

I groaned, muttering something inane about birth control and family planning, population explosions and poverty. My friend exploded with laughter.

"You Americans and family planning," he chortled. "You'll never get anywhere here with our women. It's the men who must be convinced about family planning! A woman who does not conceive in our society is considered abnormal. She herself will look for another wife for her husband."

He excused himself to visit the Men's Rest Room.

My mind went back four years. I was suddenly sitting again in the neat little cabin by the river that belonged to the District Commissioner in Keylong, a village in a long, narrow Himalayan valley in north India. It was a hot summer evening and I was drinking the DC's excellent Scotch mixed with dubious water from the tap. His enormous wife snored softly on a high bed on the other side of the living room.

"Yesterday I thought I'd seen everything,"I commented, as the DC accepted my packet of American cigarettes with great satisfaction. "A man was loading a group of women as if they were pack animals. The women wore large burlap bags on their backs. The men shoveled dirt and manure in the bags for them to carry out and dump on the fields."

"Uh-huh," he smiled. "Yes, this is common here. Women work very hard, but so do the men."

"But what was even more surprising," I continued, "for the first time, I saw women yoked up with the yaks pulling the plow!"

He laughed and reached for a book at his side. Then he read me a passage.

"The ideal wife is one who obeys her husband at all times, who responds quickly to his demands for food and drink, who works hard in the fields and house, and is always deferential to him. If she fails in these duties or takes any important action without consulting him, he can withhold affection. He can refuse to sleep with her, or even, and this is the supreme insult, refuse to accept the food she cooks for him. Refusing to sleep with her means loss of her only route to status, more children."

So women in Africa were not unique in their servitude!

Back in the club dining room, my companion returned from the loo. I told him about the women of north India.

"Women are treated as inferiors in much of India too. Probably it was like that in the U.S. 200 years ago. But in Kenya, one of the most economically advanced countries in sub-Saharan Africa, rural women are treated like slaves and this country has the highest birthrate and population growth on the continent! Perhaps in the world! You can't sustain a population that doubles every twenty years, can you?"

Dr. Nandi knew the figures as well as I did. Around a third of married women were in polygamous marriages. The average number of children per woman was seven or eight. Only after seven children were born and living did the number of women wanting no more children reach 50 percent.

There was more than female prestige and male machismo to explain this pressure for large families. High infant mortality and dependence on children for support in old age were, as in most developing countries, important factors. But thanks to western donors promoting midwife training, abandonment of cow dung as a poultice for healing the tied umbilical cord after birth, promotion of clean water supplies, infant mortality had declined substantially in recent years.

Although the HIV-AIDS catastrophe may lower the numbers, Kenya's population was due to double in 20 years. Women's status and women's health bear the brunt of this endemic pronatalism. The economy suffers as a woman cannot bear and nurse a child every two years and also work in the fields and grow most of the food. The children suffer from being born to increasingly depleted mothers. Then there is not enough food and funds are not sufficient to pay the required school fees. Worst of all, as reported by WHO in 1985, out of 21 mothers in Africa, one will die during pregnancy, childbirth or its complications. Half of those deaths were from botched abortions. As the population grows, men migrate to the cities to seek work where the money is. This leaves only women to grow food for the family.

The men come home from the towns once or twice a year, often bringing a sexually transmitted disease, including HIV-AIDS. His wife or wives, mothers of his children, get pregnant again. Both husband and wives are then infected. In the absence of modern treatment, HIV-AIDS will weaken and kill them and several of their children in 5-10 years.

As basic to African society as the production of many children and the dominance of men over women is the hierarchy of age groups. Elderly men are at the top of this pyramid. They are only one step below the Ancestors. Ancestors are often worshipped as gods. Men with wives, children and circumcised sons rate next, followed by young married men and circumcised youth. Last of all are the women and children.

Circumcision for both boys and girls is traditionally the single greatest event in their childhood, sharply marking the transition to quasi-adult status. Before circumcision, Kenyan boys live in their mother's hut, sleep with her and obey her implicitly. If they fail to obey her, she frequently disciplines them by beatings or food deprivation. But after the boy is circumcised, all is changed. Boys move out of their mother's hut to one for adolescent boys. Affection and tenderness between mother and son abruptly cease. Sex play with circumcised girls may be allowed.

I asked Dr. N. how life had changed in his time.

"Only a generation ago, young men spent much of their time practicing use of their weapons," he replied. "In those times, circumcised boys were trained for war, not domestic tenderness. Among many tribes the sexual act was one of deliberate cruelty. Causing pain was proof of virility as well as a demonstration of a man's domination of women. Sex and power were displayed in our dances and stories"

"And now?" I asked, thinking about the outrageous prison rate for African-Americans back in the U.S. "What about crime? Poverty? Unemployment?"

"Times have changed, but customs take longer. A generation ago, chiefs and elders had absolute authority in the tribe. Such a concentration of power was essential to the survival of the clan and tribe in the jungle."

"But surely it is poorly suited to peaceful coexistence of people in your over-crowded cities?" I objected. "Equal opportunity for women really begins when her fertility is under her own control. That's probably one of the reasons African men resist birth control for their women."

"That and fear of wives having other men's children to look after. In those times, fear kept the African family together," explained my companion as he ordered coffee to cap off our excellent dinner. "Fear and a rigid hierarchy made it clear that the father is head of the family. He maintained his status by keeping his wife pregnant and the children cowed."

The old culture is changing rapidly. East Africa's long standing measurement of prestige by cattle, wives and children is giving way to money and what it can buy. I ask sometimes if they think UHURU still means freedom.

"A child who is easily sent is the one with the biggest shit is one of our proverbs," laughed Dr. Netti, a doctor from our hospital, who had just joined us.

"But is this learning the rules then internalized?" I asked. "Does it become an internal ethic that is independent of food or beatings?"

Dr. Netti laughed. "You must understand our culture. I may seem as northern or western as any of your friends back in America. But my background is completely different. I have internalized different values. So have our women. Each rural village has a meeting place where only men gather to talk, eat and drink together from morning to evening. These habits remain from the days when men were hunters, warriors, protectors of home and village. Wives gathered food and firewood, cooked for them, cleaned their huts, made beer for them."

"Not to mention bearing, feeding and bringing up the children, hoeing, weeding and harvesting the crops!" I exclaimed.

"But *they* didn't object," Dr. R. assured me. "Not until the white men came and destroyed our entire way of life. They took our land. In order to get labor for the mines, they required us to pay hut taxes, cattle taxes and even rent for our own land. This forced men to leave their homes and families to work long hours under dreadful conditions for wages of a few shillings a month. Failure to pay the taxes meant going to jail. Women were left alone on what land they allowed us to use, usually the worst land. Women had to do everything: plow, plant, weed, harvest and grind the maize. They looked after the children and the animals if there were any. Failure to pay the taxes meant losing their bit of land or going to jail. When the whites needed more workers, they just raised the rents and taxes, not the wages."

We sat silently while the waiter brought the bill. The cost of our dinner would feed the average rural Kenya family for a month.

I tried to mount a defense. "The history of the human race is filled with abominable practices that both you and we have now given up. Two hundred years ago my forebears were killing Indians and grabbing their land. Yours were attacking other villages, killing the men, stealing the women and cattle and enslaving the children. That doesn't happen anymore. It was a bad culture. We both gave it up."

"And what about Hiroshima?" asked Dr. Ndeti wryly. "Was that an improvement?"

Epilogue: 2004

Frightened by the AIDS epidemic, African men are looking at their children's school fees, rapidly rising prices, monogamy, condoms and young teenage girls with new interest.

1988 Tigre People's Liberation Front increases struggle for independence against Marxist regime in Ethiopia.

Iran-Iraq war ends with no clear victor.

Communist regime seizes power in Burma and renamed the country Myanmar.

Earthquake in Armenia kills 60,000.

Suspected Lisbon terrorist bomb destroys Pan Am jet over Lockerbie Scotland; 269 killed on board, ll on the ground.

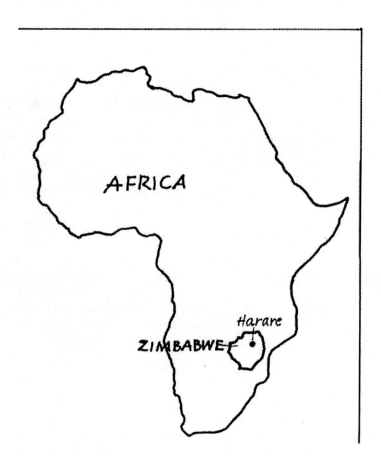

Chapter XI

EIGHT WOMEN OF AFRICA

Witch doctors, abandoned wives, and nurses who are the mainstay of the medical profession in Africa

My doctor says I'm fine, but why do I feel so bad?

I. NGANGA

After a few seconds, my eyes became accustomed to the gloom in the small house. Seated in the middle of the floor on a clean patchwork quilt was a small African woman of around 40 wrapped in a length of bright blue cheap cotton cloth over a faded print gown. Around her close-shaven head was a band of yellow, blue, and white beads woven into a simple geometric pattern. Otherwise, Mrs. M., a well-known *Nganga* ("witch doctor") in Harare, capital of Zimbabwe, was without adornment of any kind. Her dark face was calm and kind. She welcomed us courteously, clapping her hands before her three times in the Shona manner of greeting. We did the same. She motioned to me to be seated in the single wooden chair placed near her. My companion, Dan Mboye, sat on the reed mat on the floor.

I was in Zimbabwe as a visiting professor of psychiatry at the University of Zimbabwe's School of Medicine. Soon after starting my work, I discovered that most of our patients consulted a *Nganga* (traditional healer, "witch doctor") and took various potions prescribed by the Nganga before they came to the psychiatric clinic to see us. I wanted to find out first-hand just what these Ngangas do. I was lucky to have as guide and interpreter Dan Mboya, a Zimbabwean who was assistant curator at the Harare Botanical

Gardens and a long-time student of traditional medicine. During my stay, I rented a car to reach the two hospitals where I was posted. On weekends, Dan took me to the homes or practice sites of a number of traditional healers.

Today we were visiting the home of Mrs. M., a well-known Nganga. A light rain fell steadily as we drove from Harare, capital of Zimbabwe. We left the main highway that passed through tractor plowed, lushly verdant fields owned by white landowners. Then we turned onto a mud road bordered by fields of dry stubbled maize.

As we entered the tribal lands, scrub bush struggled to survive in reddish-gray earth. Groups of barefoot little girls in faded cotton dresses and boys in ragged shorts stared at us from the side of the road. A girl of five or six walked slowly down a dirt path, a large sack of mealie meal balanced easily on her small head. A mongoose dashed across the road and disappeared in the bush on the other side. At the crossroads, knots of men lounged outside the inevitable bottle store. Two young women, each with a baby tied to her back, trudged into a squat cement building painted pale blue and marked "Cheap Butchering."

Following Dan's instructions, I turned up a narrow dirt road. The old car lurched on for several kilometers past fields where women and children were attacking the hard-packed earth with short-handled hoes. The first rains had fallen, marking the time for planting the new crop of maize.

At the end of the track, we stopped at a clump of pole and *dagga* (mud) huts surrounded by fields of corn stubble. Two scrawny chickens pecked in the bare front yard. Around the corner of the farthest hut, a bright-eyed toddler peeked out at us and disappeared, shouting to someone inside.

Dan got out of the car and entered the open doorway of a small house. I sat contentedly enough at the wheel, dreamily watching the parched fields turn reddish brown in the welcome rain. Timelessness - a gift of Africa - lay over me like a soothing robe. Although the Ngangas of Zimbabwe were new to me, this was not my first brush with the traditional healers who were the first line of defense against illness in much of Africa. In Ethiopia, nearly 20 years earlier, I traveled from Addis north toward Gondar to attend the healing rites of a famed doctor-priest who exorcised devils from "mad" men and women by spraying them with jets of water while praying loudly. He also cast spells and hung preventive amulets of herbs and other concoctions around their necks. In

India, I met diviners who "cured madness" by scorching the skin with glowing coals or placing heavy stones on the patient's chest. In Nepal, holy men rushed evil spirits from the sufferer's house in smoking frying pans.

After ten minutes or so, Dan emerged from behind the small house and said that we could soon go in. Although it was just after noon, he had found the famed lady Nganga still in bed. Now she was getting ready to receive us. After another ten minutes, a barefoot young woman in a scanty pink dress signaled from the doorway for us to come in. We climbed out of the car and ran quickly through now heavy rain to a rectangular hut of mud and brick behind the others. Dan removed his shoes at the doorway and I followed suit - my toes squishing in the cold mud in the doorway. Inside, it was dark.

"This is an American doctor working in Harare who has come here to learn about African medicine," said Dan introducing me in Shona, turning to someone I could barely see in the dark gloom. I bowed and clapped my hands 3 times as is the Shona custom. Beckoning me to sit in the straight back wooden chair, the only one in the room. Dan sat with folded knees on a straw mat and explained the purpose of our visit.

I looked around the hut's one room. The Nganga, a small dark woman, a blue scarf wrapped over her shoulders and a pleasant intelligent face was sitting on the floor, her legs folded beneath her. The short iron legs of a nearby bed were propped up on overturned lactogen cans next to my chair. The bed was covered with a worn spread of black shiny material trimmed with a tasseled fringe from which most of the beads had dropped off. On the wall beside the bed, a couple of homemade wire clothes hangers hung from a nail below a shelf containing an assortment of round skin drums. On the opposite side of the room on a large glass-fronted armoire, were a few thick china plates and various jars of dark roots and herbs. Three dusty wooden elephants decorated with bead necklaces stood staring moodily at a heap of blackened tin pots, a homemade paraffin stove, some black cloths and old pottery crocks. In the far corner, a drum four feet high made from skin stretched over a hollowed log stood next to an old-fashioned metal bathtub.

Accustomed to the darkness now, my eyes came back to the Nganga, who was looking at me expectantly as she twisted the handle of a small covered basket in her right hand.

"Now the Nganga is ready to answer your questions," said Dan.

I leaned forward. "Please tell us some of the things you do to help sick people," I began. "I am a doctor, but most of my patients see a Nganga or even several Ngangas before they see me. Probably many never have to see a western doctor because they are cured by the Nganga."

I waited while Dan translated.

The little woman, still twirling the basket on the mat in front of her, began to speak in a strong, low voice.

"I find the cause of sickness and other problems by divining with this basket," she explained. "My spirit brings the spirit of the person into the basket. If that person is suffering because of angered ancestral spirits, the basket becomes heavy to lift. Then we must divine the proper treatment for their condition." She paused and pulled the basket toward her as Dan translated for me.

"Yes, I think I understand." I spoke quietly. "But please, I have a special interest in the cause and treatment of epilepsy. I wonder if you could tell me something about epilepsy, about people who have fits, fall on the ground, lose their senses, and shake all over."

"What is it you want to know?" she asked.

"What is the cause and treatment of this condition?"

"Ngozi" (angry ghosts of the dead), she answered without hesitation, "and in some cases, witchcraft."

"And the treatment?"

"I have medicines I can give you for that," she answered. "Some are to mix into porridge to eat, some are to put on the stove and inhale."

I remembered the stories told to me a week before by community nurses. They treated many patients with epilepsy, young and old, in the rural areas. Often these patients, especially the children, were brought to them with extensive burns of the face and chest. They had been to a Nganga who steamed them under a blanket thrown over their head and body like a tent. Underneath the blanket, they were forced to bend over and breathe scalding vapors of some concoction the Nganga brewed for their cure. Trained in the use of modern western medicine, the nurses gently but firmly discouraged such practices and prescribed appropriate western remedies.

"And does your remedy work?" I asked the nganga.

"Almost always," she replied. "But if it is not successful, we send them to another Nganga who may be better placed to deal with certain kinds of witchcraft. Sometimes a cow or goat must also be sacrificed."

I recalled a 17-year-old girl I had seen days before in the hospital clinic. She had suffered from epilepsy for nine years and had been taken by her parents to many Ngangas, "more than ten," without success. She had to stop school. Her very poor family further impoverished themselves by paying "at least 500 (Zimbabwe) dollars and many cows and goats" to the Ngangas. Last year, after their funds were exhausted, her parents brought her to the free government clinic in the town near her village. There, the western trained nurses gave her tablets containing a small dose of phenobarbital to take once a day. Since she started them, her fits stopped completely.

After a few more questions about causes yielded no new information, I decided to leave the subject of epilepsy and try to discover how and why this lady had become a witch doctor.

"I would like very much to know how you happened to take up this profession and how you were trained to do it," I asked respectfully.

She smiled and was evidently pleased to tell me. For the next five minutes she talked steadily, meanwhile twirling the handle of her magic basket on the floor before her.

"When I was twelve years old, I got very sick," Dan translated. "Then I died and was submerged in a deep pool for two years. From the spirits in the pool I learned everything. When I was reborn, it was with the power to divine the cause of sickness and to treat it. Then I died again, and again I was reborn. Since then I have treated many hundreds of people." She continued in her calm, matter-of-fact fashion, "I would be glad to collect some of these treatments for you if you wish to use them in your work."

I thanked her for this offer of professional courtesy. "Perhaps you can show me how you work with a problem," I began. "Before I left the United States last summer, I had a rather serious medical problem that has not resolved. Can you tell me what is the matter?"

After listening carefully to Dan's translation, she nodded quietly and replied.

"She says if you were to put two dollars in the basket she will diagnose your trouble," said Dan.

"Oh, oh! I left my money outside in the car," I said. "Can I just run out and get it?"

The Nganga nodded, cheerfully patting the woven basket and pulling the blue cloth up over her shoulders. I hurried out the open doorway and slipped on my sandals. They were rain-soaked now, as I had left them on the stoop when we entered. Splashing through pools of reddish-brown rainwater that had collected in the mud road outside, I retrieved my wallet from under the car seat and sloshed back to the hut. A young woman with a huge jerry can containing the day's water supply on her head appeared around the corner and disappeared again down the road. A thin yellow dog raised his head in the doorway of a hut across the clearing. Apparently bored by the sight of just another patient, he dropped down again and closed his eyes.

In the steady drizzle, I had somehow taken a wrong turn in the little compound. I had wandered toward huts belonging to the Nganga's sons' wives. I retraced my steps and found my way back to the Nganga's open doorway. I kicked off my sopping sandals again at the door sill. Before sitting down I extracted a Zimbabwe two-dollar bill (then about U.S. 20 cents) from my wallet and placed it on the empty basket held out by the Nganga. She replaced the lid silently. Eyes cast down, she twirled the basket by its handle several times and belched loudly and repeatedly. Then she delivered the diagnosis.

"You have pains in your muscles and ribs," she said emphatically, "difficulty breathing and general pains." Staring at the basket she continued, "Yes, in your back, stomach and chest especially. You have leg pains."

Actually, my only medical complaint was a stiff and painful left knee ever since I had made an ill-advised effort to learn Tai Chi several years before. But the Nganga was still talking.

"This is pain due to the spirit of your ancestors who are unhappy with you. You did not give them their due on the anniversary of their death."

Also true. I have long ignored the yearly cards sent from my deceased father's congregation requesting donations in order that he be named in the annual memorial services. For me, God died at Auschwitz and Bergenbelsen. I have never prayed to him since.

The small seeress was now giving the prescriptions for what I should do for my bodily pains.

"You must prepare beer and meat for a big dinner to appease your ancestors. You are their child and they want you to live in peace." Dan translated. "Your family and friends will come. First some of the beer and meat must be offered to the ancestors' spirits. You will say, 'Here, grandfather, here is your meat and your beer. Take it and leave us well.' She stopped and smiled. The consultation was over.

Kindly, very concerned, she asked if I had any more questions. *An excellent attitude*, I thought. Most of us in the Western clinics in Africa, and in America for that matter, never take time to let patients talk about their problems. Here in Zimbabwe, with sometimes 200 patients to be seen in three or four hours, how can we? The Ngangas always seem to have plenty of time to listen. This may explain their popularity and their undoubted effectiveness for certain conditions, especially those due to anxiety. Moreover, there is always an answer for a patient or family as to why they are suffering, whether from stomach ache, death of a child, or loss of a husband's interest.

Also, there is something to blame each disaster on and the blame is outside the self, absolving guilt. Better still, there is something to do about it. Brew beer, kill a goat, eat and drink well with friends and family happily joining in. Offer some to the ancestors, who will then protect one from further evils.

But now the Nganga was talking again. She asked Dan whether I would be willing for her to treat my leg pains with incisions to let the bad spirits out.

"Next time," I assured her, "not today. Let me try the beer and dinner first."

She nodded. Still seated on her quilt, she let go of her basket and pressed her hand over the back of her neck and left shoulder in an obvious expression of distress.

"She wants to know whether you have any medicine for her neck pain," Dan translated with some surprise.

The little woman nodded. More than willing to return her therapeutic favors, I left my chair and padded barefoot past the piles of soiled bags and dusty jars of roots to kneel down behind her. Gently, I probed and poked at the offending parts as the three wooden elephants stared at me in the gloom. The Nganga's neck and back muscles were firm and tense under smooth brown skin. She winced slightly as I moved her head from side to side.

"Tension," I proclaimed, after this brief examination. "Probably from sitting for hours each day in this uncomfortable position with no support for your back." I moved one of the large wooden elephants to a supporting position behind her.

"It's so bad at night, I often can't sleep," she complained. "Can't you give me anything for that?"

Oh, oh, I thought. *She wants an injection.* I fumbled in my carryall for a small vial of codeine I carry for emergencies - usually gastrointestinal. I took out two small round pills and handed them to her. Gleaming white against her dark skin, the tiny tablets seemed strangely out of place in this room cluttered with dusty herbs and bottles and with the black "witch doctor" costume swinging overhead.

"These will give you total relief for four or five hours. You should also apply heat for ten minutes several times a day and sit with a backrest to support your back and head when working." I looked around the disordered room and up at the thatched roof overhead. No electricity meant no hot pads. "Would she have a hot water bottle?" I asked Dan.

"No, certainly not," he replied. I was not sure he knew what I meant.

"Then hot towels applied to the back and neck will help. Not too hot, though. She must avoid burning herself." I remembered the scalded face and chest of a child treated for epilepsy over the kettle of boiling herbs in India.

The Nganga was grateful.

"I will cut your legs for you at no charge," she offered generously.

Scarcely a patient who consults our clinic in Harare is free of the small multiple dark scars on head or chest, arms or legs, from previous Nganga treatments.

"I'll wait and see how I am after the beer and meat for my ancestors," I demurred.

She appeared satisfied and replied, "Perhaps we can work together."

I agreed and we exchanged warm handshakes and formal clappings of farewell.

"Do you really have pains all over your body?" asked Dan sympathetically as we walked toward the car. The rain had stopped. Brilliant yellow sunlight flooded the yard between the huts and sparkled in the puddles. An old pickup drew up and half a dozen young men and women, all clutching bottles of beer and cartons of *chibuko* (home-brewed turbid millet beer) jumped out and greeted us boisterously.

"Some of her family," murmured Dan. "I'm afraid they are already quite drunk." It was two o'clock in the afternoon. After raucous greetings on all sides we piled into our car.

"No, I replied to Dan's questions about my diagnosis from the Nganga. I have no pains at all. I thought if she was a real diviner she would tell me about an operation I had just before I left the States last summer. My doctor said I might have cancer. Next month I am to go back for a report. I thought she might give me a preview."

2. ROSI

"Why are so many African women divorced or living apart from their husbands?" I asked Rosi. "It is almost as bad as the U.S."

Rosi was one of my favorite nurses. Small, smart, and cynical, she was one of the most talented community nurses working in our district. With two other nurses and our driver, we were on our way out of Harare in the Land Rover one clear, hot November morning traveling to the monthly clinic in the village of Z, 80 km to the north. Brilliant red-orange flame trees lined the broad streets of the "low density" (high income) suburb of the capital city as we headed out of town. The ride to the rural clinics was always a propitious time and place for gossip and small talk. Today, we were discussing divorce.

"African men are great until you marry them," explained Rosi ruefully.

"Or until a girlfriend has a baby," Sister (nurse) Ruth chimed in. "Then they don't want to know you."

"Take my case," Rosi continued. "I met my husband in London, where we were both students. We had a grand time there - films, parks, museums, dancing. After we got married, we took a small flat. After my little girl was born, he helped me with everything. If I had to work nights, he looked after the child. Evenings we watched TV, we went to the movies, except when he was at school or I was at the hospital. We were always together."

We had left the town by now. The Land Rover sped down the gray asphalt highway that cut between endless brown fields of dry grass and parched bush. Small round huts of pole and *dagga* (mud) with thatched roofs clustered in the corner of great fields of newly plowed commercial farmland owned by whites. Two little girls in soiled cotton dresses trudged barefoot along the roadside, each with her bundle of something balanced on her small head.

"Then we came back to Zimbabwe and everything changed," continued Rosi. "No more coming home at night except for an occasional meal, then it was right out again on 'business.' Business my foot. It was bars and it was girls."

"I know about these stories," I chimed in, trying to be comforting. "I've heard them a hundred times when I used to work in the Caribbean. I also heard them last summer in Kenya from the nurses, from the secretaries, from the psychiatrists, and from my patients there."

I remembered Steven, a male nurse who became one of my best friends during the six months I worked in hospitals in the West Indies.

"A man is not a man if he only has one woman," Steven assured me.

"And a woman?" I asked. "Is she a real woman if she only has one man?"

He laughed in astonishment and replied, "A woman is real when she has a baby!"

I turned back to Rosi. "But I put my husband through school," she explained. "For three years I did night duty at the hospital because I could earn more for him by working nights. Then we get back to Harare and what happens!"

"Don't make her guess," interrupted Ruth, who knew the whole story. "Get on with it, because mine is worse!"

I settled back and smiled at the young woman sitting across from me. She was a health assistant trainee coming along with us to gain experience in community psychiatric nursing.

"You know," I said, only half joking, "the most important lessons you are going to learn today might be right here in this drive to the health center."

"But that's what *roora* is all about," interrupted the driver from the front seat. "When a man pays a woman's family for giving him a wife, he expects the woman to work for him and have his babies."

"Fair enough," retorted Rosi, "but doesn't he owe her something as well? This guy was keeping another girl in another apartment. That's where he was running to every night. Then one fine day, out of the blue, with no warning at all, he told me that he wanted a divorce. Seems like the other girl - she was only 19, and him already 34 - was having a baby. He was afraid of a court case from her parents unless he married her."

We were speeding past empty countryside now. We had left behind the rich brown fields freshly turned by the white farmers' tractors. Now there was only parched stubble over hard gray soil. Women with babies strapped to their backs laboriously chopped at the unyielding ground with hoes and pointed sticks. Little mud shacks opened onto dirt courtyards where small children sat listlessly gazing at the road. Young men idled in front of an open bottle shop painted robin's egg blue. Lean humped cows with long sharp horns sauntered across the highway oblivious to the speeding car.

"I gave him his divorce, what else was I to do? But I wasn't prepared for what happened next. He absolutely cleaned us out. He took everything, even the children's toys and clothes."

"But how could he? Why would he?" I asked in some astonishment.

"To sell them, I suppose," Rosi explained in disgust. "To get money to buy cows for the new *lobola* (money or cow payment to the bride's family in exchange for the wife). Probably seduction fees too - he was really worried about that."

"Couldn't you go to court and get your stuff back?" I asked innocently.

Both nurses, the health assistant, and the driver exploded with laughter.

"The man has all the rights to his wife's property, including their children, if he paid *lobola* for her," explained Sister Marie. "She should be able to get a support award for her children, but the man rarely pays it or if he does, only for a short time."

"Sometimes you can get help from his family, but not in my case," Marie declared. "On our way back, I'll tell you my story."

We reached the health center in the little village of Z. A couple dozen patients, men, women with babies tied to their backs, small heads twisted sideways to keep their faces from being pressed against their mother's body, were waiting outside. Behind them stood three teen-age girls in clean cotton dresses, and a barefoot old woman wrapped in a blue cloth with a pink knitted wool cap on her head. Beside her stood her tall son of nearly 30, recently recovered from a bout of *ganja* (marijuana) psychosis at our hospital in Harare.

The young man greeted me warmly with the special handshake of these parts - first whole hand, then hand gripping thumb, then whole hand again. I turned to his mother and clapped my hands three times, bending my knees slightly as she did.

"Mangwananny amba" (good morning, Mother), I said respectfully, although I was probably older than she was. Then she dropped to her knees on the hard packed ground and held the edge of my skirt to her forehead.

"Tahtendah, doctor" (thank you, doctor), she cried in a broken voice.

Such show of emotion and gratitude was not common - especially back in Harare. I was embarrassed and pulled her quickly to her feet by her thin callused hands. We entered the little wooden building that housed our clinic. The nurses and I sat down around the table while the local health assistant bustled for tea. Then our nurses ran the clinic while I observed, pitching in only if they had a question. There are 200 psychiatric nurses in Zimbabwe and only seven psychiatrists for nearly eight million people. Five of the psychiatrists were located in the two large cities, while 80 percent of the people lived in the rural areas and small towns, where doctors were reluctant to go.

Before independence and liberation from white rule in 1980, psychiatric care was concentrated in two government hospitals - one in Harare, the other in Bulawayo, capital of Matabeleland in the southwest. Now a strong effort was under way to deliver services in all the medical specialties out in the rural areas where the people are. It was the psychiatric nurses - most of whom had trained in mental hospitals in England when Zimbabwe was still Rhodesia - who were the backbone of this rural medical delivery system. They diagnosed, counseled, prescribed treatment, and followed their patients conscientiously. Their competence and effectiveness were impressive. They treated epilepsy, depression, schizophrenia, and anxiety, giving out the correct medicines for each. Only the occasional unusual medical or psychiatric problem and operative surgery were beyond their competence. In general medicine, and especially in obstetrics, the situation is much the same. Either the nurses deliver the goods, or they won't be delivered at all.

After independence established majority and thus black African rule, half the country's doctors, the majority of whom were white, left. Their departure meant that there was only one physician for every 20,000 inhabitants. These were mostly in the cities. Only about 80 students, a majority of whom are now black, graduated each year from the one medical school in the country. A majority of them left for posts with higher pay in other countries. It would be a long time before Zimbabwe and other much less well provided African nations approached the Western ratio of 1:400 or even 1:1000 doctors to population. In the meantime the nurses did a tremendous job.

3. NONA

Rosi, the nurse who was also an abandoned wife, turned to me as Nona, her 17th patient, quietly took a seat across the table from us. She was an attractive woman of around 35 years with the inevitable infant tied in an uncomplaining bundle on her back.

"This lady recently tried to kill herself," Rosi explained, after greeting the woman in Shona. "She drank insecticide and was hospitalized in Harare for nearly two weeks. I'll tell you about her."

First she turned to the woman and asked a few questions in the local language. From the patient came a long and bitter reply - a reply delivered in a tone of such anguish and resignation that translation was hardly needed.

"Nona has six children," explained Rosi. "Two others have died. She was sick all the time but her husband wouldn't let her use family planning. Finally, she came to us. We gave her some birth control pills. When her husband found them, he threw them away and beat her. For a long time afterwards, he didn't come home at night and she suspected he was with some other woman. She consulted the Nganga, who told her that her husband had a second wife. When she accused him, he denied it. She went back to the Nganga for advice. He told her that her husband's second wife was trying to poison her and was a witch. Frightened of what might happen, she took poison herself."

Africa's women are in a bind. In Zimbabwe, as in much of East Africa, men are required to pay *lobola* (*roora*, bridewealth) for each wife. Formerly, a few goats or cattle, lobola now includes a sum of money varying from ten to several hundred dollars. This should increase the value of the wife, but having "bought"her also means the husband and his family expect the new wife to work. They also expect her to bear a large number of children. In the rural areas, her work is to plow, plant and grow food for herself, her husband, and children. She is also required to cook, keep house, fetch water and firewood. The harder she works and the more children she bears, the greater her own and her husband's prestige.

"But if women don't work, how can we have money to buy?", explained one nurse.

The husband takes another wife or two if he can afford it. Often he obtains the money to pay for the new wife or wives from the brideprice given to his parents for his sister. Thus, to have a good supply of both boys and girls makes sense for the family's well-being. Chiefs, Ngangas, and other wealthy men may have five or six wives, for there is no limit in Christian Zimbabwe of four wives as in Islam.

With each wife comes a new batch of children, adding further to the man's status in his community. More wives also provide him with labor, wealth, continuity of his line, and social security for his old age. If a wife is barren, she can be, and generally is, sent back to her parents who must refund the brideprice. To avoid repayment they usually provide another daughter to replace the first. Occasionally the infertile woman may insist it is the man who is at fault. In this case, arrangements may be made for her to have sex with the husband's brother or some other close male relative of proven fertility. A woman who stops bearing children while she is still fertile and before her husband is satisfied that she has had plenty may be replaced by a second wife. If she leaves her husband for any reason, for example, if she objects to the second wife, to his beating, drunkenness, or insufficient money for food, she loses the children. For if the husband has paid the lobola, all the children belong to him."

Nona listened to our conversation, not comprehending, but seemingly comforted by our sympathy.

"There is so little we can do in these cases," Rosi sighed. "Even though our government is trying to make things better for women, most women don't know how to get their rights." She wrote out a prescription for antidepressants for Nona.

I asked if we couldn't also provide her with family planning through Depo-Provera or an IUD (intrauterine device for birth control).

"Our women don't use IUDs much," explained Sister Marie. "Too much PID (pelvic inflammatory disease)."

PID is usually a result of sex transmitted infection and is much more common in promiscuous women or in women married to promiscuous men. As the danger of AIDS suddenly emerged in Africa in the mid-'80s, the normal promiscuity of African men became a lethal habit for both men and the women they had sex with.

"And Depo?" I asked.

Rosi laughed. "You know the story of Depo (Depo-Provera). It was a favorite with our women until the government stopped its use because it was banned in the United States."

Indeed, I knew the story.

"Tell me about it," urged the student nurse. "I don't understand."

"Well," I began, "the American women's movement, after reading about cancer induced in beagle dogs injected with enormous doses of Depo-Provera, raised such a hue and cry that the U.S. Food & Drug Commission took it off the market. This was a shame because Depo had proven extremely safe for thousands of women throughout the world. Now, as a result of good scientific evidence of its safety in the prescribed dose, it is available again. The beauty of Depo is that it only has to be injected every three months for 99 percent protection against pregnancy. Husbands who beat their wives if they use birth control pills don't have to know about Depo. Of course, now with AIDS, condoms would be much better - but most men won't use them."

"Right on," said Rosi," they say it's like taking a bath with your clothes on!"

4. BALLOU'S MOM

A worn-looking woman with dark rings around her eyes and close-cropped black hair came up to us next. Clutching her hand was a terrified small boy with frightful fresh burn scars on his face and neck. Ballou, a boy of eleven (he didn't look more than seven or eight!), was her ninth child. Ballou had been having convulsions since he was five years old. Naturally, the family had consulted a traditional healer. The healer divined the cause of the illness by throwing his special *hakata* (dice made variously of flat bits of carved wood, bones, or the empty shells of a hard nut found in elephant turds). The Nganga then declared that the boy was possessed by evil spirits that must be eradicated. To accomplish this, the child was led to an anthill. The family was instructed to hollow it out. Then the boy was told to defecate in the depression so contrived. The *Ngange* made two small cuts on each side of the child's forehead and dripped blood on top of the excrement in the hollowed-out anthill. Then he covered it all up with dirt. He pronounced the patient cured.

Unfortunately, the treatment did not work. Ballou continued to have epileptic seizures several times a month. He was unable to start school. During the last seizure he fell into the fire. His face and chest were badly burned. I examined Ballou carefully while Sister Anne cleaned and dressed his burns. Then I turned to his mother. With Rosi's help I tried to explain to her that Ballou's illness had nothing to do with evil spirits.

"Some people have even accused her of being a witch because Ballou doesn't get well from the Nganga's treatment," said Rosi.

"These fits come from the brain," I explained lamely. "Sometimes from a scar."

Mother of eleven children, four of whom had died, Ballou's mom was not at all satisfied by my explanation.

"But why did this happen to *him*?" she insisted. "Will the medicine make the scar go away so he doesn't have to take it any more?"

"That's where the Nganga's are ahead of us," I said to the nurses. "They have a reason for everything. We don't know why Ballou has epilepsy. But the Ngangas always give a reason. Even if it's not true, if their treatment is successful, that proves they were right. If not, the nganga will advise them to see a more powerful healer." The nurses nodded. "Although we may never know the cause of Ballou's epilepsy, we do have medicine that will stop seizures in most patients. But Ballou may have to take our western medicine for a long time. Please explain that to him and his mother."

Then I turned to them and speaking very slowly said, "But you must come back next month and every month to see if this treatment is working. He may have to take it for many years, but he must take only one a day and no one else can take his medicine. That would be very dangerous."

I tried to imagine where Ballou's mom would keep phenobarbital tablets in her one-room hut of thatch and mud. "Tie them in this small plastic bag and hang them from the ceiling rafter of your house," I said. "Keep them from other children. They are only for fits." Could she remember to give one every day? Could she find time to come to us every month?

When Ballou heard the translation in Shona his face broke into a broad smile. "Can I go back to school?" he asked.

"Yes, certainly," I assured him.

Then Ballou's mom started to cry. "It's too late for that now," she murmured in despair. "There is no money for school fees and no money for notebooks or pens. Ballou's father has gone away. I need Ballou to help me in the plot."

She rose to go, taking the lad by the hand. I handed Ballou my pen and asked his mother to bring me some mangoes when they were ripe. I paid $5.00 in advance - enough for school fees for a whole semester.

"You shouldn't do that," said Marie after they left. "Now they'll expect that every time."

"You Africans share everything with your families," I replied. "Why shouldn't I have a family too?"

At last we were through. The nurses had seen and treated 22 neuropsychiatric patients in two hours. Ten had epilepsy. Many of these had previously been treated without success for years by local traditional healers. Under the nurses' care, all were now doing well. Two patients were retarded children. One was an adult with a stroke that caused paralysis and speech loss. Four patients had schizophrenia and received their medication injections from the nurses every month. Because they took regular medicine, they were able to stay out of the hospital. The other patients were anxious or depressed women. All of these had devastating social problems of extreme poverty, wandering husbands, large numbers of children, more on the way, and no money for food or school fees.

Why do these patients, and many, perhaps even most people in similar circumstances in Africa consult the Ngangas instead of the western practitioners in the government health stations? Sometimes to save money, but usually the traditional healer costs more than the government health station (when there is one!). The difference is that the traditional healers have an answer to *why* the illness happened to that person. They can answer every question. Western doctors often fail to give any explanation or the causes are too hard to explain. Traditional healers' explanations are based on explaining causes by outside events beyond the patient's control. Their reasons make people pawns of the universe and place them at the mercy of the Ngangas. The same credulity often extends to the policies and prescriptions of their politicians and leaders.

We had another quick cup of tea and piled back into the Land Rover for the two-hour journey back to Harare. It was Sister Marie's turn to tell her story.

5. NURSE MARIE

"I have two children," began Marie, as we sped over smooth asphalt road between miles of empty bush. "And it is a good thing I don't have more. When I went to Canada to study for my nursing degree, my mother looked after them. Then, during the second year of my studies, I received a letter from a lawyer in Harare. It said that my husband was divorcing me for desertion. How could he do such a thing when we had agreed I would go? I had written to him regularly and sent money for the children. But that's the way it was."

Marie turned her head to the window and gazed at the endless flat countryside, brown and parched for want of rain. *Rondavels*, round mud thatched single room huts, one for each wife and a larger one for the husband, formed small clumps dotting the bleak fields. We all sat quietly until we left behind the tribal trust land and entered the white commercial farming area once more. Now, the dry land that had stretched hard and bare behind us was again replaced by rich red, freshly turned earth. Nothing else could be seen as far as the horizon.

It was hard to argue that population and birth control were the number one priorities for development in this big country of only seven or eight million people. Following forced exodus of white farmers, professionals and businessmen, confiscation of their land, the majority of Zimbabwean now live in poverty. Even worse, this year, because of the drought, hunger, famine, and starvation were stark realities. A combination of low prices for food crops and a depression of overseas markets for copper, iron, and other metals pushed the economy to the wall. If the population continued to double every sixteen years, disaster seemed inevitable.

6. NYEMA

Nyema is 47. She was brought to the hospital by her family after drinking insecticide. This is a favorite suicide method in rural areas because of its ready accessibility. Mother of seven (five still alive), Nyema has worked hard all her life, brewing beer as well as taking care of the plot where she raised food for her family. By selling the beer, she was able to pay school fees for her children. She also made enough to build two houses, one for her own family and one rented out. Ten years ago she began to have epileptic seizures. So many seizures occurred that she had to enter the hospital.

While she was there, her husband installed another wife in her house. When she returned home, he said he didn't need her. She became very depressed. She wandered around her village half-naked. In despair she stole some insecticide late one night and drank it. After becoming violently and dangerously ill, she was brought to the mental ward of our hospital. Two years later, she still remains here because she has nowhere to go. A sister and her family have taken one of her houses. Her husband and his new wife are in her house.

Only a few years ago this situation would have been impossible. Traditionally, a man took care of his first wife even if he took a second or third, and he was supposed to treat them all fairly. As more men went to work in the mines or in the cities to earn cash for food, clothing and small luxuries like beer, village culture and discipline broke down. Thus, with "development," even the traditional small protection of women's rights and men's obligations began to disappear.

I thought to myself that the "development" which we are all seeking here has fractured old life styles. Transport of Africans as slaves to America 200 years ago led to breakdown of traditional ways of life not only in my own faraway land but also here in Africa. Nearly half of African-American women have children but no husband at home. African-American men land in jail five or 6 times as often as white men. Ancient ways of life, perhaps hard-wired into the brain, die hard.

7. GWAMBU

Gwambu is 20 years old and not yet married. Her hair was plaited in neat corn-rows. She sat, dressed in a gray hospital gown draped untidily over her thin body. She was mute and unresponsive, eyes staring straight ahead. Brought in, wildly excited, by her family three days earlier, she was so combative that she had to be restrained and put in an isolation room. Now quiet after three days of antipsychotic medicines, she still had not spoken. Her sister told me the story.

"Last year our father took a second wife," she explained. "My mother and the new wife did not get along. The new wife stole her firewood and would not work in the garden. The new wife told our father many bad things about my mother."

She paused and tears ran down her face. I handed her my handkerchief and waited until she could go on.

"Last week my father decided to take my mother's menstrual cloth to the Nganga so that he could injure her by charms applied to her cloths. By mistake our father took Gwambu's cloth instead of our mother's."

I turned to the nurse, who explained to me what this was all about.

"Menstrual cloths are always carefully tied up in a bag after use and no one is allowed to touch them for fear they may be used to bewitch the owner," explained Sister Marie. "Because her cloths were missing, Gwambu was sure they had been taken to bewitch her. She became too afraid to live. She drank insecticide." Fortunately, she became sick and the family brought her here.

In Zimbabwe and elsewhere in Africa, belief in witchcraft and fear of ancestor retribution are kept alive by the *Nanga* (traditional healer). It is his or her business to diagnose and treat all disorders that are believed to arise from these two causes. For most healers this includes nearly all illnesses. The traditional healing sector in Zimbabwe is represented by more than forty thousand indigenous practitioners -diviners, healers, and herbalists. They were consulted for any illness by at least ninety percent of the African population. These practitioners learned their trade from an elder kinsman or were called to their profession during a dream or state of possession. Many reported that they became healers during or after experiencing a personal psychosis - itself considered evidence of spirit possession. A majority had little education and could neither read or write.

Traditional healers in Africa, as in many parts of Asia, diagnose and treat not only mental disorders but nearly all other ailments as well. Diviners also profess to predict future events and fortunes and to discern the cause of death, accidents, or other calamities by entering spirit possession states or throwing traditional hakata (dice of bones or seeds). Herbalists sell charms and dried plants or perform magic ceremonies to protect against misfortunes of all kinds. The traditional healer is the first source of consultation for patients with mental illness and epilepsy. He or she is also visited by most families when Western medicine fails to effect a rapid cure for a variety of illnesses. Even when Western treatment is successful in relieving symptoms, it seldom explains *why* the sickness occurred *to them*. And it is this aspect of cause or misfortune, not the causal bacteria or parasite, that most interests these families.

8. WANTHIRA OF KENYA

Wanthira has eleven children; eight children living and three have died. Her husband lives in Nairobi nearly one hundred miles to the east where he has taken a second wife. Wanthira and her children live in a thatched mud hut. She farms an acre of sloping land in the rolling hills of coffee and tea plantations near Kisii in Kenya. Her oldest child is a boy of 17 who finished grade seven in school. She does not have funds enough to pay the school fees required to go on to secondary school. Five younger children are in school. She pays their fees by growing and selling coffee. Her son cannot find work. Asked for her hopes for her children, she replies, "I hope they will be obedient."

Wanthira works very hard in her garden - the acre where she must raise the family food supply plus something to sell. All the children, from the three-year-old who watches the goats to the oldest boy, help her with growing the coffee, maize and beans. She works hard so that all may have at least a primary school education. She, herself, had no schooling. She hopes that school will allow the children to find work outside the bare subsistence level provided by her plot and goats. Now the children help by carrying water and finding firewood in the depleted bush. They carry the youngest child for her when she is washing, cooking, or cultivating. When all these chores are finished, she works out for others, hoeing and weeding in their fields. At harvest time, she carries the coffee beans to market on her back and sells them for school fees and clothes for her children. Once a year her husband comes home. He does not bring money.

"When he comes I must cook the best food for him. The children get what is left. When he leaves I always hope I won't have another child. But last year when I did not, he took a second wife. Next time he will bring her to stay here for she will have a child to care for."

The husband will then build a hut for this second wife and clear a field for her to cultivate and grow food for herself and her children. When he returns to Nairobi for another year he will undoubtedly find new women to sleep with. Given the infrequency of contraceptive use and the high prestige attached to child-bearing, these new women will also likely become pregnant. If he has enough land, he will take them on as additional wives.

A Kenyan's woman's inferior status begins before her birth. As in much of Asia, it is sons that are most wanted, for only sons can inherit their father's land. The mother owns no land, she only works on it. If she fails in her duties as either a laborer on her husband's land or as a successful producer of children - especially sons, she is returned to her parents.

"But to continue to produce children and let half of them go hungry or without education doesn't work in modern society," I argued with my colleagues from the university at dinner that evening in the faculty guest house. "When half of the kids died there was enough food to go around. You are doctors. You are advising immunization, treatment for diseases, many were previously fatal! No wonder you had no population problem before."

"But look at Switzerland, look at Japan," argued my colleagues. These men, all teachers at the university, were professors of medicine, of psychology, of law, of political science. But they could not accept or believe that too many children were a problem for this huge continent.

"We are much bigger in land and richer in resources than Holland or Japan, but we haven't even half of their population," another insisted.

"And we Africans believe a man is not a man until he fathers children, the more the better," claimed another.

"But for a woman in Africa it is even worse. If she doesn't have children by the time she is twenty, she is not a woman at all, "exclaimed a young teacher of history.

"To join the community of elders in traditional Kikuyu society a man must be married, have sons, and sacrifice a goat or several goats," explained a well-known doctor from the University. "The head of the sacrificed beast is presented to the eldest member of the council of elders, who in turn cuts off the ears and gives them to the women or girls who are present. *This is so they can hear what they are told to do!*"

I could not persuade them that it makes a difference whether development comes first or population explodes before development. Women, especially rural women in Africa, may not know much about politics, psychology, or Japan, but they know when they have had enough. For it is the women in Africa who must feed the children.

Epilogue:

These stories were recorded in the late 1980s when I served as a visiting professor in Zimbabwe and in Kenya. The scourge of HIV-AIDS was just beginning. The few cases of a previously rare skin diseases soon recognized as associated with HIV were a curiousity for us then. Now, nearly one-half of men and a slightly higher percentage of women, especially young women, in Zimbabwe and Zambia are infected with AIDS. Many have died. One-third of their children are also infected and will die. There is no money for treatment except for the few wealthy Africans and the politicians. Opponents to the current government in Zimbabwe have been jailed and beaten. In 2004-5 seizures of land from whites led to sharp fall in food production and starvation. In 2005, 70% of the population lives below poverty level, the poor as well as the well off have been evicted from their homes. HIV-AIDS and poverty have lowered life expectancy to 34 for males; 33 years for women. No one knows where the present chaos will end. So much for independence in what was once the most advanced country in southern Africa.

1989   Last Soviet soldiers occupying Afghanistan leave under pressure of guerilla war supported by U.S., Saudi Arabia and Pakistan.

Sheffield England. 94 English football fans crushed to death at match between Liverpool and Nottingham.

Beijing China. Chinese army massacres more than l000 unarmed protesters demonstrating for democracy in Tiananmen Square.

Berlin wall torn down.

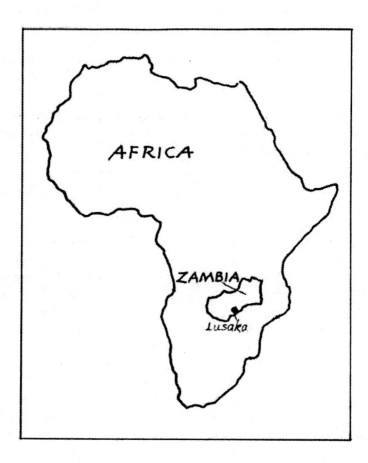

Chapter XII

LIFE AND DEATH IN THE COUNTRY LIFE AND DEATH IN TOWN

"Sometimes I live in the city - Sometimes I live in town Sometimes I have the notion - To jump in the river and drown."

Lead Belly

PART I
At the Mental Hospital

"Who is this lovely young girl" I asked Mona, one of the medical students accompanying me on our morning rounds at the psychiatric hospital in Lusaka, Zambia.

"Her name is Lossi, doctor. She is 17 years old. She killed her husband and has been here almost 2 years. It's a legal case."

Lossi was plump and healthy-looking, with a fine face, prominent cheek bones and black hair cut so short she looked almost bald. "Easier to keep the lice down," explained the nurse. Lossi's skin was smooth, brown and shining clean. Her shapeless, wrinkled gray hospital gown barely covered dark knees above strong legs and wide bare feet.

Her face was expressionless as we approached. After a long pause, she bent her knees slightly in the polite greeting given by Zambian girls and women to a stranger. Then she slowly placed her hand in mine when I reached out to greet her. Together, the three of us walked out of the spartan ward furnished only with two rows of narrow cots, each covered with a single gray cotton blanket.

Outside, it was a splendid day, brilliant with sunshine as most days are in Zambia's Indian summer. Black and white birds the size of crows gazed down from the thorn tree in the yard. I invited Lossi to sit beside me on the edge of the cement veranda. Other patients, all clad in sack-like gray cotton dresses, looked on curiously. Doctor's visits were a break in the endless monotonous days. But what was the white lady doctor doing sitting on the ground?

"Can you find some chairs?" I asked Mr. Phiri, as another medical student joined us. He was a tall dark young man neatly dressed in white coat and gray slacks. The tools of our trade, stethoscope, pencil flashlight, pens and pencils, protruded from various pockets. As he went off to look for chairs, Mona sat down rather gingerly on the cement floor on other side of Lossi and continued her patient's story.

"This patient was sent here by the court for the murder of her husband," Mona read from her case notes. "She was born in the village and had a normal birth and development. There were no serious childhood illnesses. She went through school till grade 7 when she was taken out by her family and married to a man 44 years old whose first wife had died. The marriage was against her wish. The man was too old. He was not clean and drank too much."

Lossi, the patient, listened impassively. Although English is officially Zambia's national language, I was not sure she understood and watched her face for any sign of emotion. There was none. One of the ward sisters (nurses), smart in starched white uniform and cap, wearing a dark cardigan against the morning chill, came up behind Lossi to listen.

"It was a traditional marriage," she interjected, "arranged by the families; lobola was paid to her parents."

"Cows or money?" I asked.

Among many central African tribes, lobola, or marriage price, was traditionally cattle, but now may be money instead or even include both cattle and money. Although the term "buy" is vigorously protested by most Africans, the lobola system repays the girl's family for loss of her work in their home. It also assures that the man can earn or borrow enough to support a wife. Payment seals the marriage and the girl cannot return to her home unless her family repays the same amount to the deserted husband. This, the bride's family were often loath to do as the money or cattle received were greatly prized and were saved to pay for a bride for their own sons.

After the wedding, daughters usually moved to their husband's village. Their labor and their children then belonged to the husband

and his family. Ten cows would be quite a good price for a very desirable wife. However, some poor families could only offer one, or lacking that, a goat or chickens.

"They gave 3 cows for me," Lossi replied softly in English, her head hanging low over her chest.

"Can you tell me in your own words what happened?" I asked her gently.

Lossi did not reply, looking down at her hands, at her fingers locking and unlocking in her lap. After a long pause, I turned to Mona and asked her to continue. She put down the case notes she had been reading and told us what Lossi had told her about the marriage.

"In Lossi's case the marriage was wretchedly unhappy. The husband beat her often and severely. The pressure for her to conceive quickly was intense. Her husband's family taunted her with foul names and blamed her for not becoming pregnant. Her husband demanded nightly and painful sex that hurt her insides so much that she often bled after being with him. She was only thirteen years old you must remember." Mona smiled sadly. "She ran away several times and begged her own family to let her end the marriage and come home. Her father would not listen. Her demands made her father angry with her. The husband had paid her father the lobola. So he always sent her back.

Aching inside myself with Lossi's pain, I tried to keep my face empty, non-judgemental as a good psychiatrist is supposed to do. After all, this was not my culture. I was a visitor here. I remembered a Nigerian sociologist, a woman, who once told a large audience in America of a similar case of an unhappy bride. She repeatedly ran back to her parents and was sent back three or four times to a husband who abused her and whom she hated. Finally, so the story went, her father cut off one leg so she could no longer run away.

Mona continued Lossi's story. "One night she couldn't stand it any longer. She left the bed where her husband had been forcing rough sex on her for the third or fourth time. She ran out into the bush behind the house. He chased after her and began beating her with the handle of an axe. She screamed for help but no one came. When he stopped beating her, he threw down the axe. Then he pulled open his pants and urinated on her."

Mona stopped talking and looked up. Another student, Mr. Phiri, had returned with a rusty folding chair for me. I motioned him to sit down on it and turned back to Mona.

"Please continue."

"Like lightening, without thinking, Lossi snatched the axe from the ground, raised it over her head and struck him an enormous blow across the chest. He made a strangling sort of cry and a queer sucking noise came from a gaping wound that soaked his shirt with blood. Her husband fell to the ground, his legs twitching, his arms flailing, his mouth open and filled with bright blood."

Lossi sat quietly listening, her face empty, without sorrow, without anger, without remorse.

"What did you do then?" I asked gently. There was a long silence before she answered. The young nurse who had been listening to us walked off. It was time to give the other patients their noon medications. Behind her, barefoot and wearing gray shapeless dresses, women and girls were lining up in front of the nurses' office for the tranquillizers that muted their hallucinated voices, calmed their screaming fears.

"I was frightened. I looked around for help." Lossi spoke in such a low voice I could hardly hear her. Then she was silent again. I wondered what thoughts were going on in that well shaped head with its tiny tufts of close cut black hair. I asked the student to continue.

"She looked around for help but it was just barely light, there was no one to be seen," said Mona. "Then she thought of her husband's relatives. What would they do to her? Would she be beaten by them? Would they kill her? She thought she must get rid of the body. She tried to hack a trench in the dirt beside her with the axe, but the ground was hard as stone. The sky was beginning to lighten and a red glow filled the east. Daylight was coming. Her fear grew greater. She gave up slamming the axe against the unyielding earth and turned to the body."

"He was still now. Flies were already buzzing and feeding on the bloody mess across his chest and in the dried pink foam that came from his mouth and nose. The hated face and wide staring eyes gazed straight up at her. Lossi raised the axe high and brought it down across her husband's neck. The head turned, the staring eyes now gazed emptily toward the east, where the rising sun stained the sky bright pink. Twice again she struck the lolling bloody neck as hard as she could. The head rolled free. She picked it up and ran down the hill to the river and threw it away. Then she washed the blood from herself and the axe and walked slowly back to the mud shack that was her home, crawled into bed and went to sleep."

There was a long silence while we sat, all of us, lost in our own thoughts.

"And then?" I finally asked softly. Mona did not answer. She herself was so young, still unmarried and perhaps virginal - she had been a Catholic Sister before entering the medical college. Although deeply religious, she was also a woman. I wondered if she was turning over in her mind the injunctions of her church about marriage vows, divorce and fidelity. As for me, daughter, mother, grandmother - was my anguish listening to this tale part of all women's pain or just because I was a stranger, a foreigner, an American from another culture who would not, could not bear such suffering?

Finally, Lossi spoke. "It was nearly noon when I woke up. My brother-in-law, Joshua's brother, was standing over me. He asked me, "Where is Joshua?" and pulled the rag of blanket off of me. I told him I didn't know. I was barely awake and tried to cover myself with my skirt.

"He shouted at me, 'What are you doing in bed? You should be working - weeding the plot."

Lossi stopped talking and looked away across the patches of green scrub grass at the edge of the veranda, toward the fields of brown and withered maize beyond the hospital compound. Finally she spoke again, her voice so low I had to strain forward to hear her.

"I told him I was sick, that I had fever. He stared at me and I felt ashamed. I wore the same old dress that hardly covered me up, day and night. I knew my face was swollen from the beating the night before. He looked at the unwashed little pile of dishes on the dirt floor, and the few rags of clothing in a box in the corner. I was ashamed of this poor place. He shouted at me to get up and get food for him, but I lay still on the mat.

"I can't get up," I told him. I am not well and I am bleeding. He was angry and spat on the dirt floor of the hut as he walked out."

The story was over. Lossi turned to me for the first time and looked straight into my eyes.

"I am free now."

Part II
At the General Hospital

Gwen stared at the stained walls of the small room in the hospital where she had spent the last three months. Looking down at the meager ridge of her wasted body under the bedsheet it was hard for me to remember that she had once been the plump, jolly, all-knowing head nurse of this very ward.

It all started six months before. For the third time in a month she awakened feeling too exhausted to get up, get the children ready for school and herself ready for work. Her head ached. Her legs burned. She dragged herself from bed and went outside to the shed over the pit latrine. Nauseated, she wondered if she could be pregnant again. What a disaster that would be. Her little Susan, the youngest of four, was not yet 2 and was still nursing twice a day.

She thought bitterly about David, her husband. "I shouldn't have played with him when he refused to use any precaution. Now he is dead."

She turned on the tap at the side of the house and vigorously splashed cool water on her face. Suddenly, without the slightest warning, she lost consciousness and fell to the ground. A few minutes later when she came to herself again, Mwilo, her oldest child, stood over her, looking very frightened.

"Momma, you okay?"

"Are you all right, Gwen?" asked Patricia, her worried next door neighbor standing beside Mwilo. How frightened they looked! Patricia told her when she looked out her doorway that early morning, she saw Gwen thrashing on the ground in what seemed to be an epileptic fit. When it was over and she was lying quiet, Patricia ran inside to call Mwilo, the oldest boy. He was still sleeping beside his brother and sisters on straw mats on the floor of their two-room dwelling.

Mwilo was 12, a student in Form 6 at the Boys Primary school. Rubbing sleep from his eyes, he pulled a pair of trousers over his thin legs and followed Patricia outside to where his mother lay moaning on the ground.

Other neighbors came. Frank Mwewe from across the road, a tall thin man with skin so dark it was almost black. His long narrow face was full of concern. His clothes seemed too loose over his huge frame. Behind him his wife May, heavy like many Zambian women when they are healthy, peered apprehensively. From the other direction came Brenda Lewanagolu, already dressed for work in her crisp white nurses uniform and Mumba Mwape, looking smart in a bright pink and green *chitenge* wrapped around her ample form. More than a dozen children appeared from inside the small houses allotted to nurses. They hung back shyly, peeping out behind the grown-ups' skirts. Gwen raised herself on one elbow, looking bewildered at the crowd. Patricia and Brenda leaned over her and helped her to her feet.

"It must be late," Gwen murmured. "Why am I so sore? Why am I out here? I have to get to work!"

"You've been sick, Gwen," said Brenda comfortingly, "I don't think you can go to work today."

That was only three months ago. Gwen never worked again. Now she was reduced to a silent agonized witness of her own slow and painful death. Two days before she died, she at last spoke the forbidden words.

"It's AIDS, isn't it?" she whispered softly. "That's what happened to David too. But I never wanted to know." David was Gwen's husband. He was a clinical officer (junior doctor) at the hospital and had slowly wasted away 3 months before. Even when he had lost half his weight, his clothes so loose they seemed to cover just bones, he continued to work at the hospital, talk softly with patients, try to ease their suffering.

Gwen was speaking again, her voice so low that we had to lean forward to hear her. "You can tell me now, though, not that it matters. David was always good to me, but I knew he had other girls."

Her friends seated in the creaky hospital chairs around the bed were silent. David really was popular with everyone. Like most men, he did "play" with more than one of the women they knew, especially when Gwen was pregnant, which was often. Before he got sick, he even bragged about it a little.

"Girls like a man who can play well," he used to laugh. But we didn't talk about AIDS, even when we saw him dying a little every day in front of us. It was sort of an unwritten rule, even among hospital staff, that no one talked about what was happening when the disease finally caught up with one of them.

After a long silence, Brenda spoke. "But we do know," she said softly. "All of us nurses who are married know it will come to this. All of our husbands play around. We can do nothing."

"No one spoke about it, but we were all thinking of our families, about our husbands and brothers. We were feeling fear and we were feeling anger," Brenda continued. "If we spoke to our husbands about it, they abused us. If we left them, they would take the children. If we asked them to use condoms, they called us whores."

Gwen could not reply. Her mouth was painful with sores from a yeast infection. Her thin body scarcely raised the sheet from the mattress.

"Help me go quickly," said her eyes. She never spoke again. Although she was not a Catholic, when Nurse Mary put a rosary in her hand she smiled faintly. A week later, she closed her eyes for the last time.

A few months later, one of the nursing sisters and I visited Gwen's four children in one of the compounds. It was a bright clear day. Fluffy white clouds drifted high over the tops of dark green flat-topped thorn trees. The earth was brown and dry - fields of dead and dying maize spoke of the long drought and of the approaching time of hunger. There would be no harvest this year.

Gwen's children lived in the house of their dead father's brother and his new wife. The children were all in the yard of hard packed earth next to the neat brick house. They all were as thin as toothpicks. They stood up from where they had been sitting on some old cement blocks and walked slowly toward us as we climbed out of the pickup.

Sister Mary went immediately to Mwilo. "How are you doing, Mwilo? How's school?"

I winced inwardly at the question. I knew Mwilo, now almost l4, had failed the 7th grade examination by only three points last month. Only those with a grade of 4l0 could continue in school. His grade was 407.

"Are you studying to take the exam again?" asked Nurse Mary.

"Naw, no place to study here," he said. "We all four in one room and the other room has TV going all the time. Makes too much noise."

"But you should try again," I said, trying to sound encouraging. "407 is really a wonderful grade for someone who missed so much school while your mother was ill! I'm sure you'll make it if you try again."

Mwilo kept his head down, scuffed his bare toes in the dust and did not reply.

A handsome full-figured lady of about thirty came out from the back of the house. She wiped her hands on a clean cloth that she tucked into her bright red and green *chitenge* (wrap-around cloth skirt worn by Zambian women).

Sister Mary introduced us. "This is Marguerite, who married David's brother after his wife died last year. Now, as is customary, she is looking after Gwen's four orphaned children."

Marguerite bent her knees slightly and clapped her hands politely in the traditional Zambian greeting. After some preliminary small talk about weather and drought, I brought up Mwilo's school problem.

"It's too bad about Mwilo," she agreed. "He's a smart boy but the rules are strict. There is a sharp cut-off at 7th grade and no one can go on to secondary school without passing the cutoff grade."

"This cutoff business is designed to limit the number who can go on to the available places," Sister Mary explained to me. "There are pitifully few places in secondary school here. There are a million primary school children but facilities for only 25,000 or fewer places available in the secondary school."

The two youngest girls stood staring at us curiously while Sister Mary asked young Mwilo how he was spending his time.

"Doing nothing," he replied, his head still hanging down.

"Don't forget your reading and writing while you are out of school," she urged. There was a long silence while he continued scuffing the dirt with his toes.

"I have no books," he finally replied in a low voice. "How can I read?"

"But there are free libraries in town," Sister Mary exclaimed. "The city library, the British Council Library."

"But how can I go there? It is far and I have no bus fare," he muttered, half angry, half in despair.

"But if you really want to go, you would go! You could hitch a ride - you could even walk!"

"Aw, I got no clothes to go in." He was resigned now.

"But you don't need special clothes to go the library!" I objected.

"Need shoes. Rules. Must have shoes to go into library." Mwilo hunched his shoulders, looked down and was silent. Obviously I, a white lady, a doctor with plenty of clothes, didn't understand how things were for him, what a humiliation it can mean for someone without shoes, without proper clothes.

Feeling his misery at our scrutiny, at our tactless questions, I tried to shift the subject to his brother and sister.

"How about this girl and her brother? Can they go to school?" I asked Marguerite.

"Yes, the boy goes, but we've no money for a uniform for Melba. The rule is that she must have a uniform. If she misses this year they probably won't take her back. She'll be too old."

"Too old at 11?" I objected. "Can't she go without a uniform under the circumstances? I mean, losing both her mother and father?"

"No, the teachers are very strict about uniforms - if they don't have them plus shoes and socks, they send the children home."

"But that's a crazy rule! It must keep lots of poor kids out! Especially now when money and jobs are so scarce, many people can't afford uniforms. Why don't you and your friends complain to the authorities?"

Marguerite looked surprised. *Who was this foreign lady to be challenging rules of the government?* I imagined her thinking. *Rules are rules and not hers to question why.* After a long pause, she answered thoughtfully,

"You see, it's always been this way. In many ways it's a good rule. Uniforms are to make everyone more equal. A poorly dressed child couldn't study or learn if she had to sit in class with well-dressed children from better off homes. She would feel too inferior!"

"But won't she feel even more inferior a few years from now when she can't read or write and it's too late to go back to school!" I was indignant. Her argument was one I had heard many, many times before but could not accept.

"It seems to me that this uniform rule, which is probably left over from when the British ran the country, is keeping too many poor kids out of school!"

Marguerite looked quietly at the children, who stood clustered around her, listening intently to our conversation. Her face seemed to say, "What can we people do? Government makes these rules." Finally she spoke slowly, her voice resigned,

"Yes, it's true. Many children can't go because of no money for uniforms. We used to have free adult education classes for people of any age, but I guess the money for that was shifted by government to other projects. I myself would like to go to such classes. My daddy didn't believe girls needed to go to school, so they took me out at third grade. But the adult classes are finished. Maybe the new government will start them again." Marguerite wiped her hands on her *chitenje* and sighed.

"I doubt it," said Sister Mary grimly. "The new government will have to do something first about the schools for children. More than half are without desks or seats, windows are broken, there are no books. There are not enough places. Children sit on the dirt floor and listen to the teacher read. There is nothing for them to work with."

I thought of schools back home - the bright pictures, the computers, libraries. Even the poorest schools had seats, chalk, books, free lunches.

"Where has all the money gone?" Marguerite wondered aloud. "When I went to school, things were different. Even in third grade, we had what we needed - government gave books and writing paper. We had nice desks and even playgrounds. Now I think there are too many of us, too many children. All our time and money goes for finding food for them."

Marguerite spoke passively, without complaint. She was just stating the facts and accepted there was nothing to be done. The end of white rule had been a mixed blessing.

The smallest child, Susan, dressed in a soiled faded dress that hung below her knees came up beside me and slipped her hand in mine.

"How old is this little one?"

"She is 2 1/2 now, but not doing so well."

"What's the problem?" asked Sister.

"Those boils she had on her legs are coming back - now they are all over on her body too."

I knelt down to examine the child, pulling the ragged dress up to her chin. Over her thin brown back were scattered half a dozen ugly pustules with yellowish hard centers. Similar sores disfigured her plump baby thighs and calves. Three hard lumps clustered just above the crease between her little buttocks.

"HIV," whispered Sister Mary softly. "If the government had money, if the people had money, they could buy AZT and help this little one. But here, only a few rich people have enough money to get the medicine from abroad."

I put my arm around the little girl and asked her if she had three wishes, what she would like. When she didn't answer, Mwilo translated for her. Although English is the official national language,

Nyanja, one of Zambia's 70 or so native languages, was spoken by this family and by most Zambian families at home.

Before the little one could answer, an old red car drew up and honked loudly in the driveway. The large dark skinned man at the wheel signaled to us impatiently to move our pickup out of the way so he could drive in.

"It's Daddy" shouted Mwilo, "Daddy's home!"

Marguerite looked up the dirt driveway apprehensively and asked, "Who's that with him?"

"Its only Jason, his friend," said Mwilo. "They coming for dinner I guess."

"I better get to the cooking then." Marguerite looked at us with regret. "Thank you for coming to visit. Maybe you can help with the school business for Mwilo."

"We'll try," replied Sister Mary, "but you must try too. "Don't let him just waste his time. Try to get him to the library and get him reading his books again. He could easily make secondary school standards with a little extra time studying."

We climbed into the pickup, the children following us quietly, asking for nothing. Mwilo walked toward "daddy," who drove past us without speaking.

"Muli bwino," (good morning), I called out cheerfully. There was no reply.

"Daddy doesn't seem very friendly," I remarked to Sister Mary watching him get out of the car carrying 2 cartons of *chibuko*, the local beer. "And I thought daddy was dead!"

"Yes, their real daddy died almost a year ago, but now uncle is daddy. It's the African way - all a man's brothers are called father by his children, even when he is still alive. And all a child's mother's sisters are mothers. This man's first wife and two of his girl-friends have died. He knows I know he is HIV-positive and he doesn't like to see me."

"I suppose he'll be next, and then Marguerite, this nice new wife? But he must know. She must know too."

"Yes, many of these men who know they have HIV don't accept it, don't talk about it, don't want to know it. Some actually say they don't want to die alone. They want to take as many as they can with them. That's one reason we don't tell them all to get tested. It could do more harm than good."

"But that's incredible! Horrible! Why is that? Some sort of revenge against whoever gave it to them? What about the children?"

"As you must know very well, to face HIV in yourself would be terribly hard," Sister said sternly. "It obviously feels much better to deny. As for the children, one out of every ten in the compounds is an orphan now. But the African family system is so strong - as long as there is family, someone will try to look after them. It's not like the West. No one here could imagine not sharing what he has with family."

Sister Mary backed out of the drive onto the road. A flame tree in full bloom cast its shadow over two children selling plantains by the roadside.

"Of course, as the parents die, there is less and less to go around for those who are left. So many of the children are on the street. Selling things. Peanuts, a few tomatoes, fritters - if there is someone home to make them. For the girls, finally, many sell themselves. Men like the little girls because they think they are less likely to have HIV!"

Little Susan and her sister, barefoot, thin brown legs pumping hard, ran after our pickup as we pulled away from the drive. They stood at the edge of the road and waved goodbye. My eyes filled with sudden tears. I waved back.

Epilogue:

These true stories were recorded in the late 1980s, when I served in successive years as a visiting professor in medical schools in Kenya, Zimbabwe and Zambia. The scourge of HIV-AIDS was just beginning. The few cases of a previously rare skin diseases soon recognized as being associated with HIV were a curiousity for us then. Now, nearly one-half of young men and a slightly higher percentage of young women, in Zimbabwe and Zambia are infected with AIDS. Many have died. One-third of their children are also infected and will die. There is no money for treatment except for the few wealthy Africans and the politicians.

Zimbabwe, then newly independent from Britain, was until 20 years ago, one of the richest countries in Africa. This was thanks to the high income from tobacco and grain crops planted and harvested by blacks on the huge 1000+ acre farms of the whites. Beginning in the 1990s and continuing to the present, President Robert Mugabe, himself educated in white missionary schools and previously a schoolteacher, has encouraged blacks to take the land back from the whites. This has led to growing chaos and poverty as the whites move out and jobless blacks, many claiming to be veterans of the wars against the whites 40 years ago, burn down the barns, tobacco curing sheds and houses of black laborers who work and want to remain on the farms. Government has taken over more than half of previously white owned farms leading to sharp fall in food production and severe food shortages. Income has fallen until over 70% of the population are below the poverty line. Life expectancy has fallen to 32-33 years for men and women, respectively. Yet, Zimbabwe's close neighbors, Zambia and South Africa, do not raise any objections to Mugabe's apparently insane destruction of a previously wealthy country and people.

1990   11 February. Capetown S. Africa: Nelson Mandela, leader of the African National Congress freed after 26 years as a prisoner on Robben Island.

21 March. Namibia wins independence from white rule.

2 August. Iraqi troops overrun oil rich Kuwait; U.S. mobilizes 200,000 troops to get Iraq out.

3 October. East and West Germany unite.

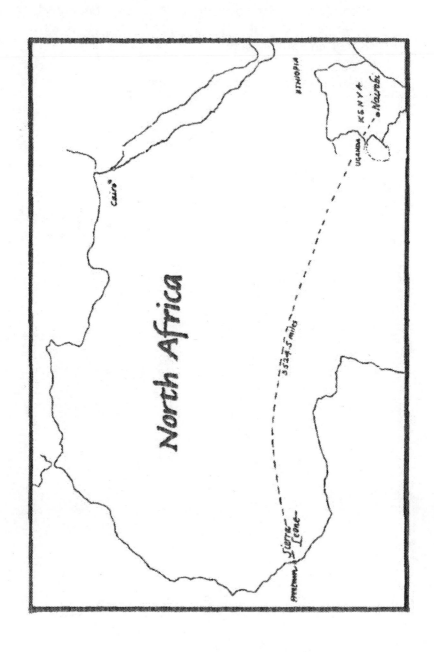

Chapter XIII

PEACE CORPS

La esperanza muere ultima

(Jessie de la Cruz)

Hope Dies Last

(Studs Terkel)

Don looked down at his hands. The palms were deep yellow from two years of subsisting on food fried in palm oil.

"No one even thanked me when I left," he said slowly.

It was late March, l990. Don was sitting next to me on the Kenya Airways flight from Freetown in Sierra Leone across West Africa to Nairobi.

"I liked it and hated it too," he continued. "Sometimes, when I felt as though I was accomplishing something, it was terrific - most of the time I thought I was going nowhere. All in all, it probably balanced out."

A young American Peace Corps volunteer, Don had a scraggly beard and anxious eyes. He looked out the window as our plane climbed swiftly from the tarmac and rose over green acres of ragged coconut trees and banana plantations interrupted by small clearings of golden brown earth and round thatched huts.

"I was supposed to be a science teacher in the girls' high school," he explained. "The village was small and hard to reach by road but we had 300 students and some of them were very good. It's the system that crushes them. Perhaps it crushed me as well."

We were higher now, passing over dense forests, blue waterways, swamp and jungle. The stewardess, tidy in navy blue and scarlet, bent over us solicitously from a cart laden with bottles.

"Beer," said I.

"Beer," said Don.

Presto, she opened a secret door disgorging golden cans that were deliciously cold and dewy to touch. After a long, satisfying pull of great German beer the plane had taken on in Frankfurt, Don continued.

"You see, we were supposed to stick exactly to the biology lessons in the syllabus. I wanted to take my students on field trips so they could actually see where the plants grew, how to find the insects and study their habits. It's fascinating country, alive with life. But the school was supposed to teach only by rote learning. Not so much as a frog was dissected. Even though we had all the tool kits, the glassware, even microscopes, all donated to the school from abroad, not so much as one chemistry experiment was performed!"

"Why not?, What stopped you?"

The plane broke into clouds. The vast rainforest below suddenly disappeared. All around us was white, opaque, without direction or distance.

"The other teachers kept all the equipment locked up," he continued dispiritedly. "They were afraid the students would break something and that it couldn't be replaced. Also, the new equipment meant extra work for them. They had no motivation for that. So the rote learning continued. It crippled the students, even though they were smart, worked hard and memorized all the facts we threw at them. But I simply could not get across concepts like evolution, for example."

We shot out of the tops of the clouds into blue sky and sunshine. If there was earth below, we could not see it.

"My biggest project was helping to get a new school building. When I came, the girls' school was crammed into two old army barracks. The U.S. Embassy pledged $20,000 to build a new school if the community raised some funds - *community participation* was the buzzword, you know."

Mountains of softly solid looking white clouds were below us now. I was sure they would hold me if I could tread them lightly.

"The students worked hard to raise the matching money. They organized two disco parties. With the proceeds they hired laborers to build the school. But no one on the faculty or in the town pitched in to help. The principal refused to pick up nails or other stuff in town when we needed them, even when she was going there in her car. I used to go over and help with the work on weekends, but the other teachers, all locals, ridiculed another teacher who went with me so much for working without extra pay that he never went again!"

Don bent his head and turned to look out the window at the floor of inviting clouds far below. When turned back to look at me, his eyes were full of dashed hopes.

"After the school was built, a visiting high muck-a-muck from the government came to town. The officials took him to see the school. All the people of the village were really proud. They asked the official for a donation. He gave almost $500. Since I was the Peace Corps volunteer who had charge of donations for the school, he gave me the money to take care of. I gave it to the electricians who wired the school and who had never been paid. Then all hell broke loose. Those teachers were furious with me. They wanted me to use the money to throw a party."

Don paused now for the first time. His eyes, pale blue and enormous behind thick rimless glasses, sent mine a message of defeat. Raising the golden beer can, he finished it in three huge gulps.

"I told them we couldn't do that. We had asked for the money to finish the school!"

He gazed out at the sky.

"They told me I had no right to spend the money. When I asked them who would pay the electricians, they wouldn't even listen. It was useless to get them to answer this question - all they could think of was that the money belonged to them and that I was causing them to miss a party. They called me dishonest and threatened to go to the American Embassy and have me arrested or thrown out of the country. I finally walked out of the school last week. My students begged me to stay, but it was too much for me. It took me three days hitch-hiking to get to the capital. Now, here I am, leaving." Dan looked down at his bony knees and the empty floor at his feet.

We plunged down into a bank of gray cloud and the plane rocked violently. When we reached Nairobi, we shook hands goodbye. Don was on his way to Burundi, where he had signed on for another year's service in the Peace Corps.

"Maybe East Africa will be different." Don grinned weakly.

Although I only knew him for a little over three hours, I still think of Don with his yellow hands, broken fingernails and defeated eyes. I hope he is happily dissecting frogs and explaining the wonders of their anatomy and physiology to students in some remote Burundi school.

But can he break the chains of convention and feelings of entitlement that bind the young eyes and close the ears of his students? Can he bring them new answers? Especially, can he encourage new questions from minds trained to obey, memorize, and regurgitate exactly what has been taught? This is a challenge for those of us who love to teach in the schools of the so-called third world. How to make minds trained to obey go beyond the books and the lectures, the newspapers and the politicians, to ask for more information, and to ask "why?"

Treblinka, Bergen-Belsen, Auschwitz, Hiroshima, Nagasaki, Phnom Phen, Viet Nam, the Gulag, Kosovo, Darfur. The mujahadin, the Taliban, the twin towers in New York, the American war in Iraq. The world is really not a very nice place.

ABOUT THE AUTHOR

Janice Stevens is Emeritus Professor of Neurology and Psychiatry at Oregon Health and Sciences University, Portland Oregon. A graduate of Reed College and Boston University School of Medicine, her post graduate training included residencies at Harvard and Yale medical schools and the Hôpital Bel Air in Geneva, Switzerland. She served as a research scientist at the National Institute of Mental Health in Washington D.C. studying neuropathology of schizophrenia. Dr. Stevens is the author of more than 150 scientific papers and book chapters. Outside of her scientific achievements, she has devoted substantial time to volunteer work overseas, including serving as a visiting professor or physician in medical schools, hospitals and clinics in India, Pakistan, Nepal, Zimbabwe, Zambia, and several Caribbean islands. Twelve years ago she started free schools for underprivileged children in Zambia. With support of many donors, these have grown to serve over 8000 students yearly.

Her husband, Carl Stevens, is Professor Emeritus of Economics at Reed College. Her two children are professors on the faculties of Colorado and UCLA schools of medicine.

Printed in the United States
50819LVS00003B/202-210